TELEVISION AND CHILD
DEVELOPMENT

LEA's Communication Series
Jennings Bryant/Dolf Zillmann, General Editors

For a complete list of other titles in LEA's Communication Series, please contact Lawrence Erlbaum Associates, Publishers

TELEVISION AND CHILD DEVELOPMENT

Second Edition

Judith Van Evra, PhD
St. Jerome's College
University of Waterloo

160201

LEA LAWRENCE ERLBAUM ASSOCIATES, PUBLISHERS
1998 Mahwah, New Jersey   London

Lawrence Erlbaum Associates, Inc., Publishers
10 Industrial Avenue
Mahwah, New Jersey 07430

Cover design by Kathryn Houghtaling

Library of Congress Cataloging-in-Publication-Data

Van Evra, Judith Page.
   Television and child development/ Judith Van Evra. – 2nd
   ed.
      p. cm.
   Includes bibliographical references and index.
      ISBN 0-8058-2800-1 (cloth: alk. paper). – ISBN 0-8058-2801-X (pbk.: alk. paper)
         1. Television and children.   2. Child development.   I.
   Title.
HQ784.T4V333   1998
302.23'45'083—dc21   97-14860
                                             CIP

Books published by Lawrence Erlbaum Associates are printed on
acid-free paper, and their bindings are chosen for strength and
durability.

Printed in the United States of America
10   9   8   7   6   5   4   3   2   1

To Katie and Patrick

Contents

III Theoretical Perspectives
and Future Directions

Preface

Research into the relation between children's television viewing and their cognitive, social, and emotional development has continued unabated since the first edition of this book, and the results are significant. Many of the basic parameters remain unchanged, but newer research studies have raised serious and provocative questions about earlier findings and have suggested new avenues and directions for future research. Technology has continued its explosive growth with very significant implications for the media experiences of children and their families.

The purpose of this book is to present as current and complete a summary and synthesis as possible of what is already known about television's role in and impact on children's cognitive and social development, and to discern the complex and significant interplay between other forces in a child's life with the television viewing experience. The book relies on information from communication literature as well as that from child development and other psychological domains and seeks to integrate these diverse sources into a coherent conceptualization of the major variables operating in children's television experience.

This revised edition retains some of the basic organization of the original book, but it includes significant changes both in content areas and in chapter organization. It updates research findings in the major areas and includes changing trends in television content and viewing patterns. It includes new sections on technology and its influence, and offers an entirely new chapter on television's impact on exceptional and high-risk children.

The first section of the book is devoted to a look at cognitive aspects of children's television experience. It includes material on their processing of television information in order to better understand just how information is extracted from television, which material affects them, and how child and content variables interact to influence this process. Knowledge of what children actually *attend* to is basic to our understanding of how much they understand and what they are likely to remember. Consideration of television's effects on children's cognitive development generally, as well as on their reading and academic performance specifically, is included. Comparisons of various media also are discussed.

The second section of the book deals with television's impact on various areas of children's social and emotional development and on their behavior. It includes discussions of television violence, advertising, and stereotypes. Family issues in relation to viewing are also addressed. Because children are in their formative years socially and emotionally, as well as cognitively, it is important to assess television's role in their development. Moreover, it is necessary to study how differences among child and content variables, and the interactions among them, affect children's experience of television and its effect on them, and who is most vulnerable.

The final section of the book reviews specific theoretical perspectives, such as social learning theory from the psychological literature, and cultivation and uses and gratifications theories from the communication literature. Further, it offers an integrative approach, a means by which these two bodies of literature can be bridged in order to better understand and explain television's influence on children and the variations and differences among children in its impact.

The chapter on new technologies has been expanded greatly to include research findings on the many other media uses now available to children besides television as well as those that affect children's use of television—VCRs, cable, computers, the Internet, video games, and virtual reality—as well as a chapter on intervention and critical viewing strategies.

It is hoped that by understanding more about how and to what extent television and other media actually affect children, and what role other variables may play in mediating their impact, we can maximize technology's potential for facilitating and enriching children's cognitive, social, and emotional development, at the same time minimizing any negative influence.

Acknowledgments

Thanks are due to many in the development of this book. First, thanks go to Kathleen O'Malley for her enthusiastic initiation of this revision. Thanks also to all of the other supremely capable and wonderful to work with editors, editorial assistants, promotional and production staff, and others along the way—Linda Bathgate, Sara Scudder, Sharon Levy, and Nicole Bush—and to the series editors, Jennings Bryant and Dolf Zillmann, and series advisor, Alan Rubin. Thanks also to Don Roberts who kept my computer and me on reasonably friendly terms and also helped with the graphics. Finally, special thanks to my husband and all my family whose enthusiasm, patience, and loving support meant everything.

Introduction

Television's significant role in the lives and socialization of children has been thoroughly documented. People worldwide spend more than 3.5 billion hours watching television daily (Kubey & Csikszentmihalyi, 1990), and the average U.S. 19-year-old has spent more time in his or her life viewing television commercials than an employee spends on a full-time job in a year (Dworetzky, 1993). Given a conservative estimate of 2.5 hours of watching television each day over a lifetime, and assuming 8 hours of sleep a night, the average American would spend 7 years out of the appoximately 47 waking years we have by age 70 (Kubey & Csikszentmihalyi, 1990) watching television. This figure is even more striking considering the approximately 5.5 hours a day, or 16 years total that Americans have for leisure time in the same 47-year period. Based on these figures, television viewing would account for almost half of their free time.

Although it is difficult to know just what actually is partially or fully attended to, what is learned, what is remembered, what impressions are gleaned, and what images are formed, such questions are especially important in relation to child viewers because they are still in very active stages of development. Their attitudes, beliefs, and ideas about the world—as well as physical, cognitive, and social skills—are taking form, and they absorb information from everywhere. Because of the considerable number of hours children spend viewing television, however, television becomes a disproportionately large potential informational and attitudinal source.

Concern often has centered on the short- and long-term effects of TV viewing on the development of children of all ages. Much of the early research focused on preschoolers, who are in the most rapid stage of social, cognitive, and emotional development. Programs like *Sesame Street* alerted consumers to the creative learning and entertainment possibilities that exist through the television medium. The wholesome values and educational tools that *Sesame Street* seemed to provide eased the concerns of many parents about television viewing in young children. They allowed and encouraged their children to watch it with almost the same sense of good parenting with which they gave their children vitamins or read them stories.

Others worried about the possibility of becoming too dependent on television to entertain their children or about the effects on young children of passively engaging in this activity in lieu of active and imaginative play with other children. Other questions relating to chil-

dren's television viewing experience also commanded increasing attention. How do children respond to violence that they see enacted daily,
either in the news or in prime-time programming? Which children
choose to watch violent television? What perceptions of adult men and
women are children developing from viewing situation comedies, soaps,
and commercial advertising? Do they understand and how do they
interpret the many sexual innuendos and jokes that play an increasingly
significant part of many shows? How do television portrayals affect their
perception of ethnic minorities or of individuals from other socioeconomic levels? How does television viewing facilitate or interfere with
relationships with parents and siblings or with peers? How much
television is "safe"? When is it "harmful"? Parental concerns, then,
coupled with those of psychologists and educators, generated a considerable amount of research.

The number and complexity of the interactions are great. The viewing
experience of a 4-year-old boy watching a violent show alone is quite
likely different from that of a 10-year-old girl viewing the same program
with her mother. If one adds to that picture variance in their socioeconomic level, family background, and school experience, as well as
differing motivations for viewing and other variables in all of the
possible combinations and permutations, one catches a glimpse of the
magnitude of the problem facing researchers.

Even asking what appears to be a simple question in fact raises very
complex issues. If one hypothesizes, for example, that viewing violence
on television has negative effects, many possible directions and definitions emerge. What is meant by violence on television? Should only
gratuitous violence be included and necessary violence excluded, as, for
instance, that required for self-defense? Should one include or exclude
violence in aid of a good cause or violence on the news? Further, how
should violence be measured? Should there be a clear indicator such as
number of fights per half hour or should one try to assess verbal violence,
the violence of a mood, or violence "in the air" as in a sinister and
foreboding atmosphere?

These questions, of course, are affected by individual variables such
as age. Young children, for example, are more likely to react to fights
that are clear and concrete, whereas more subtle forms of violence might
elude them. The other two parts of the sample hypothesis can be just as
thorny to study. Consider the same hypothesis again: Viewing violence
on television has negative effects. How should *viewing* be defined?
Should it include everything from a quick glance to hours of viewing?
Should it include only the shows that a child chooses to watch, or also
those selected by others? Should it include viewing time that is simultaneously spent on other activities, such as homework, while the television set is on? Finally, how should negative effects be assessed? Should
this include a greater tolerance for violent behavior in others as well as

increased aggressive acts on the part of the viewer? Should subtle and hard-to-measure changes in the viewer such as increased fearfulness and distorted perceptions of the environment be included? Are the effects short- or long-term ones? What is short term, and how long is long term?

The point is clear: definitions and issues vary from researcher to researcher and from study to study, making simple comparisons of results impossible. Thus, frequent statements such as "viewing violence on television has negative effects," in the absence of elaboration and greater specificity regarding definitions and populations involved, are not very meaningful.

Fig. I.1 provides a more graphic representation of the variables involved in this area of study.

If we are to evaluate television's actual impact on development, then it is essential to study not only the types of content children are viewing, and the amount of viewing they do, but also differences in their developmental level and background variables to see how they influence the child's viewing experience and mitigate television's impact.

Much has been blamed on television viewing—obesity, low metabolism, poor family relationships, lower academic achievement, aggressive behavior, insensitivity to others, and weakened attention and concentration, to name a few. It is not difficult to see that when children are viewing television, they are not exercising, playing outdoors with friends, reading, helping with chores, or practicing piano. If they are, these activities are being done peripherally or superficially, with one eye and ear glued to the set. Moreover, even children whose parents have removed the set from their lives are affected by it directly or indirectly, in exclusion from various peer interactions related to television viewing or in the changing behaviors and values of peers and others in society that are brought about, facilitated, or accelerated by television.

The question of the influence of television on the many facets of child development is highly complex, indeed, and the full extent and precise nature of television's impact is still unclear. Dorr (1986) said of the many hours of television that children watch each week, most is not developed with their well-being in mind and "...some of it is decidedly aggressive, sexist, ageist, racist, consumption-oriented, sexy, inane, or moronic. Little of what children watch is truly uplifting, visionary, educational, or informative." (p. 82)

Thus, she noted, there is reason for concern about the role that television plays in children's lives and for efforts to control what is broadcast and what is viewed.

The amount of research into the effects of television programming and advertising on children's development is staggering, and the range of research topics is wide indeed. Many studies have focused on the relation between aggressive behavior and television violence. Others

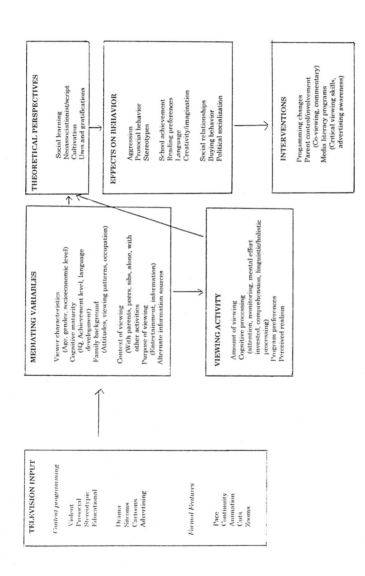

FIG. I.1. Summary chart of variables involved in children's television viewing experience.

have investigated prosocial behavior, such as sharing and cooperation, and other aspects of a child's socialization. Still others have considered the influence of television's stereotypic portrayals on children's gender-role development and occupational choice, as well as on their attitudes toward various age groups and minority populations. Some have focused on the ways in which television viewing enhances or interferes with reading and learning, and on how children process television information. Considerable attention has been paid to which television forms and techniques lead to highest attention and comprehension among children and how these technical differences affect children of varying age, sex, intelligence level, and socioeconomic background. Some writers have focused on the sheer magnitude of television's presence in our lives and have attempted to assess the impact of the act of watching per se, regardless of the content (Cullingsford, 1984; Winn, 1985). They have sought to discover whether children who engage in television viewing differ in important ways from other children, regardless of the specific programs they watch.

Newer research efforts in both communication and developmental psychology have emphasized the complexity of the television experience and the interactions among child, program, technical, familial, experiential, motivational, and contextual variables. It is precisely this complexity that needs to be addressed if we are to understand the nature and extent of television's impact on children and youth. Much developmental research to date has focused on child variables (e.g. age, sex, socioeconomic background, intellectual level) as though television content was much the same. Other psychological research has focused primarily on the television content (e.g., violent, stereotypic, or prosocial) as if the audience was a largely homogeneous group. Still other research, particularly from the communication field, has emphasized technical characteristics and formal features of television itself, as well as programming issues, motivations for viewing television, and the context of viewing. What clearly is essential is a careful look at the interactions among all of these factors and characteristics, and an integration of communication and developmental perspectives. By building a bridge between these two broad perspectives, we can come to a much more thorough and meaningful understanding of children's television viewing and its impact. Failure to build such a bridge between relevant bodies of research or focusing on one at the expense of the other provides us with a seriously incomplete picture of children's viewing experience; it is not unlike clapping with one hand.

For the most part, highly specific problems have been addressed, using very diverse methods, populations, program content, and conceptual models. Not surprisingly, this diversity has yielded fascinating, provocative, and, at times, seemingly contradictory findings, but definitive results and coherent theoretical explanations of the findings are not yet in evidence.

The paucity of clear, unequivocal findings is due in part to methodological problems. The number and complexity of the variables involved and the limitations in the research instruments available to measure those variables have plagued researchers. Some variables are simple to identify and measure. Age and sex can be specified clearly and easily. Intellectual level and socioeconomic background, although somewhat less objective, can be coded according to relatively common standards and practices. However, when faced with the need to measure such variables as violence, gender-role stereotyping, attention, comprehension, attitudes toward television, impact of advertising, or modeled behavior within the family, one encounters many loose definitions, fundamental differences in assumptions, and varying emphases among researchers. It is an even more taxing matter to assess the interaction of such variables as age, sex, intellectual functioning, level of cognitive development, socioeconomic background, and school or employment status in evaluating television's impact, not to mention all of the formal features of television as well as variations in program content and format. Rarely have significant numbers of these dimensions been taken into account in any one study, and yet the interactions between television and the many facets of child development require such efforts.

Finally, the mere inclusion of many variables in specific studies does not guarantee clear, interpretable results. Appropriate research designs and statistical analyses are required to evaluate not only the potency and significance of each of the variables but, more importantly, their complex interactions. In fact, some of the newer research studies that have used more sophisticated and complex methods of investigation and data analysis have yielded evidence that seriously undermines previous findings. It is to a new examination of the data from many corners that we now turn our attention.

I

Cognitive Aspects
of the Television Experience

1

Information Processing of Television

ATTENTION

The question of whether children are passive or active viewers of television fare has important implications for their cognitive processes, including attention, comprehension, and retention. Disagreement continues in the current research literature as well as historically between those who view the television viewer as an essentially passive individual who absorbs information and television content indiscriminately, and those who see the viewer as an active, constructionist individual whose own characteristics and past experience determine what is attended to and retained.

Much research has been guided by a reactive view, one in which the formal features of television control attention and dictate a child's viewing experience (Anderson & Smith, 1984). However, many studies have also noted the significant reciprocity between levels of attention and the comprehension, or anticipated comprehension, of television content.

Comprehensibility of Content

Children's assessment of the comprehensibility of television content affects the levels of attention that they direct to the material (Lorch, Anderson, & Levin, 1979; Pingree, 1986; Ward & Wackman, 1973). Even 2-year-olds direct attention to television because they are strongly motivated to understand it (Hawkins & Daly, 1988), but content beyond their level of comprehension also may lead to reduced attention by children (Wright, St. Peters, & Huston, 1990), as does engaging in other activities while viewing (Comstock & Paik, 1991; Wright et al., 1990).

Monitoring comprehensibility is one of several cognitive activities in viewing, and if a television segment is clearly not understandable by a child, there is little reason for that child to continue attending visually even though much effort has been invested initially (Pingree, 1986). When Hawkins, Kim, and Pingree (1991) studied the visual attention of children aged 3, 5, and 6, the children showed early increased attention to random segments shown them as though they were trying to deal with difficult content, but when language in a segment was incomprehensible, attention at all ages decreased and stayed low, and there was little developmental change in the results.

Older children increase their visual attention and put more effort into incomprehensible or challenging sections than do 5-year-olds (Pingree, 1986), and older children who watch educational and child-informative programs that are appropriate for their level of comprehension and who coview with a parent may learn to attend more closely (Wright et al., 1990).

Thus, attention is guided actively by the child's assessment of the comprehensibility of the content, attempts to comprehend content, situational variables including other viewers, and other activities.

Auditory and Visual Attention

Levels of visual attention and auditory attention vary greatly depending on program content, age of viewer, and the viewing context. Even infants, however, typically are exposed to television for more than an hour a day, and they spend about half of that time looking at the screen. They show more visual attention to sound and picture together than to either one alone (Hollenbeck & Slaby, 1979).

Children also monitor television auditorially while they are engaged in other activities. When they note something of interest—or auditory attributes signal informative content or content changes, and it is comprehensible according to the codes they have developed—they will give it their visual attention as well (Lorch et al., 1979) and then pay full attention. If the content becomes redundant or incomprehensible, they return to their alternate activity. Further support for the importance of the audio component in maintaining attention is the finding that a reduction in the comprehensibility of the audio portion has a strong effect of reducing visual attention (Anderson & Collins, 1988). Even preschoolers can use cues from auditory input while engaging in other activities to tell when visual attention is necessary; and they can spontaneously adjust their visual attention (Pezdek & Hartman, 1983; Pingree, 1986).

The percentage of visual attention tends to increase during preschool, level off during the school years, and decline in adults (Anderson, Lorch, Field, Collins, & Nathan, 1986). Visual attention to television actually likely accounts for only about two thirds of the time spent with the television set, as children may spend considerable time with television doing things other than looking at it (Anderson & Collins, 1988; Anderson, Field, Collins, Lorch, & Nathan, 1985). Thus, "heavy viewers" (i.e., those spending much time with television) are not necessarily heavy viewers in the amount of time spent attending to television (Anderson et al., 1985). In one study (Anderson et al., 1985), for example, a child who spent almost 40 hours a week with television (heaviest viewer) only looked at it for about 3.5 hours (light viewer). Thus, visual attention is a reliable indicator of television viewing, but it may not be a valid one.

However, important interactions operate as well, and even the percentage of visual attention is not a clear determinant of influence or involvement. Children who glance briefly at a television program and then look away to think about what they have seen may actually be using a relatively greater amount of mental effort; or children may use different levels of effort with equivalent levels of visual attention (Pingree, 1986). Moreover, viewers who appear to be attending may actually be daydreaming about something totally different (Lull, 1988a).

It is clear, then, that studies that define attention as visual orientation to a television screen may overlook important auditory perceptual activities that also affect attention and comprehension, and they also may miss other cognitive activity in which a child is engaged. Behaviors other than visual attention also need to be considered in addressing a child's meaningful attention and involvement with television content. Such findings highlight some of the methodological problems that perhaps have resulted in inaccurate conclusions.

Stimulus Characteristics and Developmental Level

Attentional level is not just a matter of whether the stimuli are visual or auditory. Much depends on the nature of the stimulus and its complexity. Many studies have focused on television's formal characteristics and features that attract a child's attention to the television. The importance of the formal features of television (e.g., pace, cuts, sound effects, the presence or absence of dialogue) as distinguished from its content has been well established (Huston, Greer, Wright, Welch, & Ross, 1984; Huston & Wright, 1983).

Formal features can signal what content is to come; they can function as the syntax and grammar of television content (Huston & Wright, 1983). When masculine or feminine content is presented with different forms, the child uses those formal features to assess the interest and comprehensibility of the material, and then makes a decision about whether to continue attending (Huston & Wright, 1983).

Important age differences in attention to such features have emerged, however. Young children are much more attentive to highly perceptually salient features including animation, peculiar voices, lively music, rhyming, auditory changes (Anderson & Levin, 1976), and sound effects (Calvert & Gersh, 1987). Whereas young children rely on salient features to attend, older children's attention is more dependent on learned signals, although older children do attend to salient features when those features are informative (Calvert, Huston, Watkins, & Wright, 1982).

As children become older and more knowledgeable about and experienced with television, the cognitive demands of a program become more important. The issue of salience is more relevant in determining initial attention which is based largely on perception, particularly among young viewers; it becomes less important as children's cognitive skills and viewing experience increase (Wright et al., 1984). Despite a decrease in level of attention, however, older children are able to grasp the television content as accurately as younger ones do (Zuckerman, Ziegler, & Stevenson, 1978). They appear to be using more active and schematic processing of information and attending more strategically depending on what they perceive the processing demands to be (Wright et al., 1984). Thus, they do not require the same focused attention needed by younger children in order to obtain information. These data run counter to the idea that children passively absorb television information, and they suggest that children's cognitive processing abilities and strategies are active and fairly sophisticated (Anderson & Smith, 1984; Pezdek & Hartman, 1983).

Gender Differences in Attention

In one of two studies of gender differences in attention by Alvarez and his colleagues (1988), 5- and 7-year-olds were shown four animated programs with combinations of high and low violence and high and low action. Visual attention was greater in boys than girls, but that did not mean greater comprehension. Boys showed more attention to high violence than low, and their attention did not change across conditions. Girls, on the other hand, attended more to low-action programs than high.

In their other study of children ages 3 to 11 (Alvarez, Huston, Wright, & Kerkman, 1988), boys showed significantly more attention than girls across experiments, and most content and form characteristics did not explain the gender differences. The researchers found weak support for the greater appeal of violence and animation to boys. They concluded that girls focus more on verbal or auditory content, boys on visual content.

Conclusions

Children's expectations, mind-set, activity, and experience serve as determinants of attention. The view that children are active viewers who attend selectively, generate and check hypotheses, and interpret new information in ways that reflect more general efforts to understand the world has led some to espouse a bidirectional approach to the viewing experience (Durkin, 1985). From this perspective, one assumes that although specific television information is transmitted, the way in which it is interpreted, and even perhaps discounted, depends on an individual child's social and cognitive needs, level of development, and experience, and these variables change from one situation to another (Durkin, 1985). These viewers are not passively incorporating content uniformly; rather, they apply their own experience to the content (Anderson & Lorch, 1983).

COMPREHENSION

Age differences in levels of comprehension, both for central learning and for incidental learning, have been reported frequently. Although understanding is clearly related to age and experience with the medium, other variables such as amount of effort invested, reason for viewing, input from others, and socioeconomic level also affect how much and which content a child can grasp and master.

According to Clifford and colleagues (Clifford, Gunter, & McAleer, 1995), children from age 8 to midteens have been largely ignored in most research, which is unfortunate because information-processing skills as well as social and intellectual schemas are developing during this period. The researchers focused on the cognitive impact of programs with informational content to see what information viewers absorbed, how they thought about issues that the programs raised, and whether short-term changes occurred as a result of exposure to those issues. This approach assumes that television effects are mediated by a child's understanding of the content, whether they believe it, and whether it is consistent with what they know.

The basic premise of Clifford et al. (1995) was that what children get out of television depends heavily on what they bring to it, and age and experience are important, although Clifford et al. claimed that even young viewers can distinguish real from fantasy television content. Moreover, according to the researchers, children's cognitive processes and the constructs they use to understand and interpret television programs are different from the ones adults use. They found few gender differences, and prior viewing and amount of viewing had little relation to comprehension, although background knowledge did.

Information Processing of Content

The information-processing problem facing the child viewer, as described by Anderson and Smith (1984), is a very demanding one. The television content is highly varied and open to several levels of analysis, and the content that the child perceives may not be what the producer intended. They also must learn to understand the formal features of television that maintain attention, mark important content, and transmit meaning. Finally, important differences exist in the viewing environment or the context in which television is viewed, including such factors as the choice of other activities, distractions, others watching, general family or cultural attitudes, and other demands (Anderson & Smith, 1984). These contextual factors are discussed more fully in chapter 7.

Important in children's processing is their ability to achieve cognitive continuity and to integrate and make sense of television's dynamic flow of information (Anderson & Smith, 1984). Integration of simultaneous and sequential content elements and attribution of motives or purposes are required to make sense of what is seen (Dorr, 1986), and parental commentary can help young children compensate for their lack of strategic skills in understanding certain aspects of a program (Collins, Sobol, & Westby, 1981).

Because much of the material necessary for full comprehension of television programs is not presented explicitly and requires drawing of inferences, such as causation, motivation, time passage, and others, a distinction must be made between the specific cognitive activities involved in processing television information and the amount of effort applied to those activities (Hawkins & Pingree, 1986). Fowles (1992) noted that children will absorb more than adults per hour of TV because they are always trying to learn about the world, but compared to the number of hours they sit there, they learn a small amount, and at a slower rate as they get older and more discriminating.

Developmental Differences

There are very big and important developmental differences in the understanding of television, according to Young (1990). For example, three-year olds think television characters are real and they don't understand narrative or dramatic structure, and they may not understand sarcasm and irony until late childhood or perhaps early adolescence.

The ways in which age is related to children's comprehension levels are very diverse. Young children's inability to associate events with antecedent and consequent events would presumably affect their overall understanding of a show and contribute to the poor recall seen in young children (Hayes & Kelly, 1984). They do not distinguish clearly between imaginary and real or between commercials and programs (Canadian Association of Broadcasters, 1985), and some programming practices may make the distinction between real and TV life more difficult (Dorr, 1980). This is important, because although preschoolers see more that is informational or educational, they watch more and more comedies, cartoons, and adult entertainment as they get older (Huston, Wright, Rice, Kerkman, & St. Peters, 1990).

In Calvert's (1988) study of children's comprehension of temporal aspects of content, flashbacks were introduced either by a dreamy camera dissolve or with an abrupt shift [visual] and were or were not marked by sound effects [auditory]. Ten-year-olds understood flash-backs better than 6-year-olds, and Calvert concluded that formal fea-tures affect children's understanding of complex temporal concepts that are presented on television.

Hirsch and Kulberg (1987) also found significant differences in accu-racy of temporal judgments as a function of age. Children tended to underestimate longer 45-second segments and overestimate those of 15-second duration. Those who watched less television performed better in estimating the length of television segments. That is, participants, especially preschoolers, performed less accurately in direct proportion to the amount of television that they reportedly watched. This was less the case for older children, whose skills at estimating time lengths were more clearly established. Hirsch and Kulberg concluded that children's age and the amount of television they watch during preschool are significant factors in the development of their ability to make temporal judgments.

Imagine the task facing a very young child who is attempting to comprehend what he or she is watching and compare it with the events that the same child perceives and experiences in real-life interactions.

> They [television personalities] have no substance, they're only human-seeming shadows moving on glass, but they can go anywhere and do anything—one minute a male and female shadow will be in a bar and zap! a second later they're in a bed together. They disappear at regular intervals and in their place come earnest ones talking about suppressing our odors or keeping us regular. Then the first ones are back, acting as if they never left. They dance, they sing, they drive very fast. They seem sure they can make us laugh, cry and watch them, but if we don't, they vanish. ("Celebrating television," 1989, p. 6)

Children are much less capable of organizing and integrating essen-tial plot information spontaneously, and children younger than 7 or 8 years old do not appear to grasp the abstract lessons that are a part of some shows (Christenson & Roberts, 1983). As Rubin (1986a) noted, the behavior of preoperational children is closely related to perception, and judgments are based on perceived appearances and immediacy. Signifi-cant changes occur, however, around age 7 or 8 when conceptual and symbolic skills develop and mediate television content, allowing slightly older children to be less affected by TV portrayals because they can understand the complexities better (Rubin, 1986a).

Young children are unable to discount certain perceptual features and information (e.g., a person's appearance) in favor of conceptual and actual behavioral information and hence are likely to misinterpret important information (Hoffner & Cantor, 1985). Moreover, as much of television programming shows people in social interaction, children's comprehension of television may be influenced by their ability to understand such character depictions (Babrow, O'Keefe, Swanson, Meyers, & Murphy, 1988). Their comprehension of much of television's content, then, depends on their more general interpersonal experience.

Conceptual Changes

Children's comprehension of TV content clearly improves with age, also because they develop the ability to focus on information that is relevant to the plot and ignore information that is not (Kelly & Spear, 1991). Children with good verbal skills are better able to process and remember information that is central in what they see, whereas children with lower verbal ability may need extra help sorting out relevant from incidental information (Jacobvitz, Wood, & Albin, 1991). Children also become increasingly selective in their viewing. Television viewing increases until about age 10 to 12 and then decreases during adolescence (Gunter, McAleer, & Clifford, 1991).

Kelly and Spear (1991) found that children's comprehension and retention of content could be facilitated by placing a viewing aid within the television program itself in the form of short synopses of centrally relevant scenes, to mimic chunking skills that older viewers use. Synopses placed after commercials helped second graders remember central content better than placement before commercials or none at all. In fact, in that condition, their recognition was similar to that of fifth graders, and the various conditions did not affect the comprehension of fifth graders. Kelly and Spear suggested that inclusion of such synopses after commercials could improve young children's comprehension without coviewing with adults.

Comprehension increases only gradually with age, however, and young children may get quite different information from television than older children who can process larger amounts of information more efficiently. Of the 4- to 9-year-olds in one study (Rice, Huston, & Wright, 1986), for example, the older children were more likely to detect a replay, whereas younger children saw them merely as repetitions, suggesting that they are likely to be rather confused about much on television—or at least might misinterpret and distort a good part of what they see.

Not everyone agrees that young children's comprehension is as poor as this, however, and early studies may have underestimated their levels of understanding. Some research suggests that children may comprehend a good deal more than has been thought. Lemish (1987) said children have a grasp of TV as object and as a message source before they are toilet trained and by 2½ years old, they view regularly and have clear expectations and viewing habits. Anderson and Collins (1988) noted the ability of preschoolers to discern central content and to engage in many inferential activities, at least for short programs. However, preschoolers have greater difficulty with, and more frequently misinterpret, full-length dramatic programs. Anderson and Collins suggested that children's improved comprehension of lengthier and more adult programs as they get older is due more to their increased experience with media and to their growing general knowledge of the world than to shifts in their ability to discern central content or to make inferences.

Clifford et al. (1995) found less perceived realism regarding drama as viewers get older, but not invariably so; it depended on specific program elements. They also found that single episodes were insufficient to generate significant changes in children's perceptions of the real world, and suggested that programs with relevant content may in fact stabilize beliefs that were unstable or changeable.

Stimulus Modalities

The modality involved in the television input is an important component of comprehension as it was with attention. Differences in comprehension appear to be due in part to differences in the types of stimuli to which children of varying ages attend, and there is controversy about the relative importance of auditory versus visual stimuli to young children in their television viewing. Some (e.g., Anderson & Lorch, 1983; Pezdek & Hartman, 1983) have emphasized the importance of auditory stimuli in helping a child to monitor television content while doing other things. Others (e.g., Hayes & Birnbaum, 1980) have suggested that the fragmentary comprehension of preschoolers may be due to their reliance on visual rather than auditory input, and they appear to ignore large parts of auditory input, or process it superficially, and pay greater attention to visual stimuli.

Hoffner, Cantor, and Thorson (1988) reported that 5- and 6-year-olds may have more difficulty understanding and integrating visual input than auditory input whereas older children (8–9 and 10–12) appear to understand equally well in either format (Hoffner et al., 1988). When the younger participants in the Hoffner et al. study were in an audiovisual condition, however, and they were given both visual and auditory input, they could sequence sentences as well as the older participants. The authors suggested that the older children may have formed a visual representation while listening to auditory input, whereas the younger children may have needed visual support as well (Hoffner et al., 1988). Similarly, in a study of 4- and 7-year-olds' comprehension of audiovisual and audio-only presentations (Gibbons, Anderson, Smith, Field, & Fischer, 1986), the visually presented actions were associated with better performance in the younger children but not in the older ones. The younger children also understood dialogue better when it was presented in the audiovisual condition than in the audio-only condition.

Children attend most when both visual and auditory presentations are used, and narration improved visual attention and comprehension of visual content in one study (Rolandelli, Wright, Huston, & Eakins, 1991). However, children could understand the verbal content without looking; that is, their comprehension of auditory material did not depend on looking. If there was no narration, auditory attention predicted comprehension of visual content; that is, auditory monitoring of content occurred, but visual attention was most critical for understanding when there was no narration. The authors concluded that the findings provided some support for visual superiority, but the visual modality does not appear to mediate the auditory modality.

Girls attended more to the auditory modality than boys, and boys were more dependent on looking. Narration enhances visual attention and comprehension, it mediates attention and comprehension, and it seems to make programs more understandable and interesting for young children because it is appropriate to their language ability (Rolandelli et al., 1991). However, the researchers found that the auditory component is important independent of visual input. Older children process more auditorily and they understand better, but both young and old did better with narration. They concluded that "auditory attention contributes, both uniquely and interactively with visual attention, to children's processing of television." (Rolandelli et al., 1991, p. 120). Other researchers (Calvert, Huston, & Wright, 1987) concluded that there is modality-specific processing of information, and visual presentation does not interfere with linguistic processing.

Inconsistencies in findings of children's relative abilities in these areas may be due to the fact that specific visual information may be relatively easier to remember, but deriving meaning from complex visual sequences or scenes may be harder for young children than deriving it from verbal descriptions (Hoffner et al., 1988). Young children also may lack adequate language skills to describe the meaning they get from complex visual material. As some films and many programs for children are essentially nonverbal (mostly action-adventure), however, with little dialogue, young children may have difficulty interpreting their content (Hoffner et al., 1988). Moreover, children may remember those programs without having been able to derive complex meaning from them.

Formal Features

The levels of comprehension children are capable of are not a function solely of viewer age and maturity or developmental level, however; they are also influenced by specific characteristics of television content. Features such as pace, for example, may affect not only attention but also comprehension, and in unexpected directions at times. Wright et al. (1984) found that fast pace may actually interfere with comprehension, as fast-paced shows are harder for children to integrate than slower paced ones. In addition, format of the show (e.g., story vs. magazine) appears to be more important than fast pace; and high-continuity programs such as stories result in increased attention, better comprehension, and better recall than shows with low continuity like a magazine format (Wright et al., 1984).

Salience of the stimuli also affects young children's comprehension and retention of television information. Young children attend to salient input because they do not have the necessary strategies to recognize and retain information that is less salient (Wright & Huston, 1981).

Hayes and Kelly (1984) suggested that the formal features of radio or television, such as sound effects and zooms, may serve as "punctuation" and may influence attention to particular aspects. If these are clear and consistent, comprehension and recall might be facilitated. If shifts are not marked by perceptually salient features, however, comprehension might be negatively affected. In either case, young children attend primarily to certain aspects of the television experience; to the extent that other aspects are ignored, their understanding is distorted and limited.

Realism of Content

Much of the literature suggests that realism in television content and children's ability to distinguish real from fantasy material are important factors in their comprehension of television information and in television's effects on them. Young children have difficulty distinguishing television content from real-world experience and may overgeneralize. They first attribute equal reality to everything they see. They are high on the *Magic Window* dimension, the degree to which the belief is held that television content accurately and literally represents real life (Potter, 1986, 1988). First-grade children in one study (Van Evra, 1984), for example, did not see television as a separate world. They appeared to be sufficiently egocentric as to assume that whatever happens in their own family is also what occurs more generally in other families both in real life and on television.

Nonetheless, young children do develop competence even without special training, and studying the development of their viewing skills shows how they try out and revise various hypotheses until they can make sense of television information (Gardner & Krasny Brown, 1984).

Prawat, Anderson, and Hapkeiwicz (1989) studied preschoolers, second graders, fifth graders, and graduate students to see what criteria they used for determining the reality of specific items. There was significant variation across this age range, influenced strongly by the type of item that was being judged. The authors concluded that if there are specific criteria available, one does not have to rely on abstract ones, which is more difficult. For example, classifying dreams was hard compared to classifying dolls (Prawat et al., 1989).

There is some disagreement in the literature on the age at which children can distinguish reality from fantasy, but in general there is a negative relation between age and perceived realism over the elementary years (Rubin, 1986a). By age 5 or 6, children have a rough sense of what is realistic and what is not. According to Gardner and Krasny Brown (1984), however, children's major continuing task, a more complex one, is to see how much something that looks real is actually staged. Although initial decoding is accomplished by the time of school entry, more complex questions continue, as is also true with other aspects of television viewing (Gardner & Krasny Brown, 1984).

Children do develop knowledge of a distinction between pretend and real before they develop one between apparent and real; and even 3-year-olds do better on the former than on the latter (Flavell, Flavell, & Green, 1987). However, children show a huge increase at age 4 or 5 in their ability to understand the differences between appearance and reality, and by age 4, most children can see what is real (Adler, 1991). Before that, they believe that what they see is real. Therefore, things that look scary arouse fear in preschoolers, whereas for older school-age children who can discriminate better between what can and cannot occur, there is more fear in response to things that actually could happen regardless of appearance (Cantor & Sparks, 1984). Thus, we would expect younger children to be more frightened by ghosts, monsters, and other imaginary creatures that they see on television. Older children might well be frightened by such events as a kidnaping, which they perceive as an actual possibility, even though the perpetrators of the crime conveyed the threat calmly and subtly. Younger children would likely miss the more subtle danger. As Potter (1986) noted, perceived reality is more likely correlated with individual differences than with the actual television content. As children appear to be most affected by things that they consider to be realistic or plausible, young children's difficulty distinguishing real information from fantasy material may cause further distortion and poor comprehension of television messages.

Others place the age for making this distinction at a higher level. In Dorr's (1983) study, for example, children seemed generally unable to explain what they meant by something on television being real until about sixth grade. As they got older, they were better able to explain, and there was an increase in the number who meant "possible" when they said "real." For older children (age 16) and adults, "real" more often meant "probable" or something that had happened to someone they knew. In any case, even when viewing time is reduced, television is more likely to have an impact on children who see it as realistic.

Even adults blur the line between fantasy and reality when comedians play themselves in other programs, or real people such as newscasters have cameo roles on sitcoms, or celebrities play other celebrities, or sitcom characters make reference to real people. This makes the material part real and part unreal with a mix of celebrities, images, entertaining news, and "newsy" entertainment (Lacey, 1993).

Thus, as with attention, comprehension is increasingly influenced by the prior experience and knowledge that a child brings to the situation and it is less bound to explicit television stimuli as the child gains experience (Wright & Huston, 1981).

Methodological Issues

Methodological weaknesses may have resulted in inaccurate conclusions in previous studies. For example, the important difference between linguistic competence and linguistic performance is very relevant in this context. Young children's relatively poor performance on many tasks may well be due to their inability to express their mastery of a concept or an idea rather than to their inability to understand it. Or, in the case of lengthy programs, they may have difficulty remembering particular components. When Pingree and her colleagues (1984) used stimuli that were short and simple and a method designed to maximize children's ability to communicate, for example, the results were quite different. When 3- and 5-year-olds in that study were asked to reconstruct an 8-minute television program with dolls in order to avoid reliance on verbal performance, the children's versions were not as rich as those of adults, but they did not have a qualitatively different meaning.

RETENTION

If it is important to ascertain which variables affect a child's attention to and comprehension of television content, it is even more essential to consider what factors lead to retention of that material, as one might assume that what is not remembered has little long-term effect. Discerning the most significant variables in this process is not as easy as it may appear at first glance. Retention is related not only to a child's age and level of cognitive development, but also to features and characteristics of the television information, to methods of measuring retention, and to interactions among many variables.

Mediating Variables

The mediating factors and intervening mental processes involved in the memory of television messages are still a source of some controversy. Some (e.g., Reeves & Thorson, 1986) consider memory to be mediated by the processes of attention and mental effort, and these processes are determined by both the structure of the message and the processing strategies of the viewer.

Formal Features.   Formal features, such as pace and continuity, also influence recall and recognition. Shows with a slower pace and greater continuity tend to be remembered better than fast-paced shows (Wright et al., 1984). As high continuity is associated with better recall, one would expect poorer recall in young children who are unable to integrate material to increase its continuity. In addition, J. L. Singer and D. G. Singer (1983) argued that the very rapid pace of television may minimize chances for reflection and effective storage and retrieval, although the salience of the information affects recall positively (Kellermann, 1985).

Campbell, Wright, and Huston (1987) found better recall and recognition scores among kindergartners for easy versions of messages about nutrition and poorer for difficult ones, with only slight variation in attention as a function of difficulty. Participants were given a child form and an adult form, and each form had three levels of difficulty. The authors concluded that formal features influence the level of processing independent of content, and that formal features probably signal appeal and comprehensibility which affects attention, processing, comprehension, and recall (Campbell et al., 1987).

Another significant factor in children's memory is the importance of the content to the child. As Lorch, Bellack, and Augsback (1987) pointed out, usually young children's memory for relevant information in TV studies is said to be poor and little differentiation is made between important and unimportant information. They found that importance affected recall, however, especially for 6-year-olds when compared to 4-year-olds, and the effects were not a function of mode of presentation or formal features. The authors cited the results as consistent with the notion of children as active viewers, and claimed that this is one of the first studies to establish a basis of comparison for information that varies in relevance to the child viewer.

Auditory Versus Visual Input.   Many researchers have found consistently higher levels of memory in younger children for visual aspects than for verbal aspects (e.g., Hayes & Birnbaum, 1980; Hayes & Schulze, 1977; Perlmutter & Myers, 1975; Sadowski, 1972; Watkins, Calvert, Huston-Stein, & Wright, 1980; Zuckerman et al., 1978), even though attention to auditory stimuli may be greater (Pezdek & Hartman, 1983).

Thus, as Hoffner et al. (1988) suggested earlier, children may remember specific visual material better, but they need verbal information to derive meaning and understand complex visual information. It appears that supplementary auditory information, either in the form of spontaneous labeling by the child or labeling by an adult, facilitates the reception of input through that modality when stimuli are primarily visual. Perhaps such labeling increases attention and helps the child encode the information (Watkins et al., 1980). Perhaps some of the inconsistencies in the literature, then, regarding the relative importance of visual and auditory input in children's comprehension result from a confounding of these processing components.

Developmental Differences.   Developmental level is, again, a very significant determinant of the differences that have been reported. Verbal encoding of auditory input appears to lead to the best recall, but such encoding is an age-related skill that is not available to young children who rely more heavily on visual input and hence show poorer recall of auditory information.

Other researchers have found that the different format variables that are involved in various media have more effect on younger children than on older children. For example, in one study (Meringoff et al., 1983), preschoolers' memory of figurative language was much improved when a story was read to them compared to their language recall after they viewed a television story. However, older children may remember language from television and stories equally well, but they may also be more sensitive than younger children to how that language is delivered (Meringoff et al., 1983).

Oyen and Bebko (1996) embedded a memory task for 4- to 7-year-olds in a computer game and compared performance on this task with performance that followed simple instructions to remember. Significantly more rehearsal—nearly double the amount—was observed in the game context, but the effect was not so huge if covert rehearsal was also included. Those who rehearsed in either context remembered more, but there was less recall in the games than in the "lesson" condition. The authors concluded that the games were more interesting but may have been distracting or more difficult because of other competing goals. Just changing task and interest value, then, may not lead to spontaneous rehearsal in children not so inclined (Oyen & Bebko, 1996).

Meadowcroft and Reeves (1989) found that 5- to 8-year-old children with advanced story schema skills showed less processing effort, better memory for central content, and better attention and memory coordination. Bea-gles-Roos and Gat (1983) concluded that young children appear to acquire basic television skills quite early; after that their general cognitive skills, which are not medium specific, are more important. For example, children's increasing ability to verbally encode information facilitates not only their comprehension of that material, but their recall of it as well.

Effective learners use both types of processing in a smoothly integrated process that involves visual recognition and verbal encoding, but older children process linguistic presentations more easily, encode them more efficiently, and remember them better. Finally, somewhat surprisingly, and against their prediction, Beentjes and van der Voort (1993) found that television stories led to more influential learning than print stories. More-over, print stories were recalled as well as television stories when immedi-ate retention was tested, but retention of television stories on delayed tests was superior to that for print stories.

The type of material being recalled varies also. In a study of younger children, Hayes and Casey (1992) found that preschoolers' mention of affective states of characters on Sesame Street or The Cosby Show seg-ments was very low when retelling the stories, constituting less than 1% of the reactions they recalled. Recognition lasted longer for human portray-als than for muppet and cartoon shows, and accurate description was higher for basic emotions than for complex ones. Even when verbal labels were provided, the children could not remember cartoon or muppet emo-tional states, and they rarely mentioned affect or physical states in retelling the stories (Hayes & Casey, 1992).

One very significant age-related difference in the viewing experience between adults and children noted by Winn (1985) is in the background of actual experiences they can bring to bear on their viewing. According to Winn, adults have a vast number of experiences, fantasies, and relationships that can be used to transform the television material into something they need. The experiences of young children, on the other hand, are limited, and television viewing for them is more of a primary activity. Children's real experiences may even stir memories of television content rather than the reverse, as is the case for adults (Winn, 1985).

Recognition Versus Recall

The suggestion from the literature that young children remember little of what they see depends in part on the measures used to assess their retention. Young children typically perform better on recognition tasks than on tests of recall, and many researchers have reported significantly better recall of television content by older children (Meringoff, 1980; Odom, 1972; Roedder, 1981). If both kinds of measures are not included, younger children who focus on visual input are penalized by the typical open-ended verbal recall measures. If recognition of material they had viewed was measured, as opposed to recall, one would expect their performance to improve. Hayes and Kelly (1984), in fact, did find better retention of visual material when a recognition measure was used rather than a recall measure.

Young children are less able than older children to encode the information verbally, but they might recognize it as familiar. Therefore, when various comparisons are made, and where age is important, one should look carefully at the measures used. It may be that a recall task was used, whereas television's advantage, especially for younger children, is in its visual components, which are more important in recognition. Finally, Cullingsford (1984) noted that recall is voluntary and recognition is not; he claimed that children recall little of television but recognize a lot because television includes much repetition and familiarity.

Motivation for Viewing

Motivation for viewing television also affects recall, although there is no simple one-to-one relation between motivation and recall (Kellermann, 1985). According to Kellermann, watching television to relax leads to different mental activities than watching it to seek some specific information. Children may approach television programs with an attitude of not feeling it necessary to remember; that is, they approach it differently than they would if they thought it was significant (Cullingsford, 1984). The amount remembered, according to Cullingsford, is inversely related to the amount watched, because those who watch more pay less close attention and do not try to remember. Moreover, Kellermann noted that motivation interacts with attention to determine what message is received and the structure of the message affects how the information is encoded and retrieved (Kellermann, 1985).

LINGUISTIC AND HOLISTIC ASPECTS

Research indicates that not only do certain specific features and forms of television affect attention and comprehension, but that verbal encoding and storage is essential to efficient processing of information and to recall of that material. For the most part, however, visual and auditory features have not been broken down any further or separated into other groupings. And yet, doing so can help to pinpoint which specific factors make a significant difference and how and why they do.

Auditory and visual aspects of television stimuli can be distinguished and refined further; for example, on the basis of their linguistic or sequential features as compared with their more holistic and spatial ones. Terms such as linguistic and sequential can be used to connote stimuli that are largely objective and informational; that rely heavily on language, verbal encoding, and logical thought or reasoning; and that are usually thought to be processed largely in the left hemisphere of the brain. The terms holistic and spatial, on the other hand, can be used to connote those stimuli that are not encoded verbally; that are reacted to as wholes; that are more dependent on images, moods, and impressions than on information; and that are usually thought to be processed largely in the right hemisphere of the brain. Thus, one can broaden and refine opportunities to understand children's television experience by conceptualizing expanded stimuli groups: visual–linguistic, visual–holistic, auditory–linguistic, and auditory--holistic.

Distinctions such as these can be helpful in explaining some of the rather paradoxical and seemingly contradictory findings discussed earlier. Moreover, linguistic and holistic features of the stimuli interact with the viewer's age, gender, cognitive level, and experience.

Most research to date has focused largely on either what an individual did, such as using visual recognition or verbal encoding (i.e., the kind of processing the individual engaged in), or on specific aspects of the television stimulus itself, such as the modality involved (visual or auditory) or the formal features employed. Clearly, however, all manner of interactions occur among various aspects of both the stimuli and the viewer's processing. For example, one cannot verbally encode visual–holistic information unless labels are applied. Similarly, long printed messages are not visual in the same way or with the same effect as are more salient visual stimuli such as animation. The grouping of all visual techniques together and all auditory techniques together, and the consequent reporting of children's attention to visual features or auditory features of the television presentation, then, masks important differences.

Furthermore, analytic or sequential processing is more common with verbally encoded stimuli, and global or holistic processing is more common with salient, holistic stimuli, but each type of processing can be applied to other stimuli. One can, for example, cast a critical, analytic eye on holistic content, although one is not likely to do so automatically. These variations are indicated in Fig. 1.1.

Stimuli–Processing Interactions.   Thus, there appear to be two similar and parallel but quite different issues involved, that are significant to our understanding of children's comprehension of television and its impact on them. One focuses on the TV content and one on viewer processing characteristics. First, a distinction can be made between linguistic and holistic characteristics of the television input within each

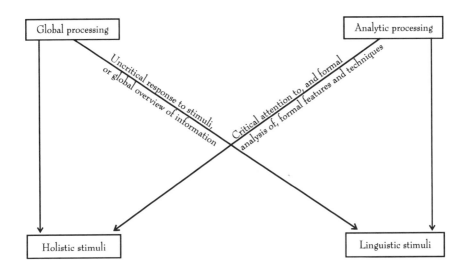

FIG. 1.1.   Interactions of processing style and type of stimuli. Older and more mature children can use all four combinations; younger ones rely largely on holistic processing of any of the data. Even among older children, however, reactions may vary at different times and with different content.

of the visual and auditory modalities. Second, there is the differentiation between largely analytic and largely global processing of the material. The first distinction has to do largely with the television stimuli presented and the second with differences in the viewer's processing of that information.

The interaction of the television stimulus characteristics, then, with the types of processing leads to four very broad categories of processing activity: visual–holistic (viewing much TV salience), visual–analytic or sequential (as in reading either from text print or TV), auditory–holistic (attending to salient auditory messages), and auditory–analytic or sequential (listening to verbal presentations, explanations, and dialogue). These categories are depicted graphically in Fig. 1.2.

Although this characterization is admittedly oversimplified, this conceptualization can be helpful in understanding children's television experience. Clarification of many of the complex, interesting, and at times contradictory findings reported in the literature might well be enhanced by a consideration of such distinctions.

Differentiation of types of visual or auditory stimuli (linguistic vs. holistic), or of the type of analysis required by the child, including processing differences (analytic or global), and varying levels in the capacity for such analyses by different gender and age groups, have not been reported. Young children, for example, are better able to process holistic aspects of both visual and auditory information.

MODE OF PROCESSING		
	Analytic	Holistic
Visual	(1) Linguistic stimuli (e.g. reading print in text or on television)	(2) Holistic stimuli (e.g. viewing logos, animation, scene changes)
Auditory	(3) Linguistic stimuli (e.g. listening to explana- tions or dialogue)	(4) Holistic stimuli (e.g. attending to jingles, slogans)

FIG. 1.2.   Summary chart of types of stimuli and modes of processingand their interaction. *Note.* Younger children rely primarily on (2) and (4); older children can use (1) and (3) more effectively as they gain experience with the medium and as they develop generally more mature cognitive abilities and strategies.

The less efficient holistic processing that young children use is also the kind of processing that television relies on to a large extent. It often emphasizes quick overviews of material with less depth of processing or analysis of content and less reflection because of the quick pace and content changes. The growing ability of older children to use verbal encoding and more analytic approaches to cognitive information, then, also means that they can pay less attention or view less and still derive as much meaning as younger children who view more; older children are more efficient viewers.

Younger viewers are less able to discriminate relevant and irrelevant information, and have fewer schemata and less complex codes to use in processing what they see. Their viewing experience, then, is quite different from that of older children in terms of what content they understand and retain. When confronted with auditory stimuli, there is often little verbal encoding done by young children, whose language skills are less well-developed. They likely do not understand or retain the information conveyed through adult narration or conversation (linguistic) as well as they understand and retain that conveyed by sound effects (holistic).

One could hypothesize, then, that among young children, adult dramas might be poorly understood when compared with comprehension of cartoons not only because of the content and the less developed cognitive capacity of younger children, but also because of the mode of transmission or format. Adult dramas rely heavily on verbal interaction and conversation, and they are much less dependent on the perceptually salient features that are a mainstay of cartoons.

Although the content of these programs is very different, the form in which that content is presented also varies significantly and further affects its comprehensibility to children and, hence, their preferences and level of attention.

This conceptualization of the interplay between more specific stimulus characteristics and processing strategies raises some interesting questions and possibilities. The reported fragmentation in comprehension that has been attributed to young children's difficulty integrating information temporally (Anderson & Collins, 1988), for example, may be due in part to the difficulty they have integrating linguistic and holistic components of that information. Moreover, important age–gender interactions in the relative importance of these perceptual components are likely as well, and would further affect the impact of the child's viewing experience and the kind of content information that is derived from it.

Analytic and holistic processing differences also interact with cognitive style. According to Smith and Kemler Nelson (1988), analytic processing is associated with controlled and effortful cognitive processes, whereas holistic processing is associated with a more automatic kind of processing. One might ask further whether similar differences exist between normal children's processing of television information and their processing of print. If children feel that print is "hard" and television is "easy," and if we could help children learn cues to distinguish the formats that are hard and require more effort from those that are easy, their learning from television could be enhanced (Salomon, 1984).

As linguistic stimuli are likely to be perceived as more difficult and requiring more complex processing than holistic input, learning to make the distinction between them may facilitate learning for children. They might become better able to adapt their level of effort to the demands of a specific task or type of material, for example.

Differences in Retention.   A further question that needs to be addressed concerns how all of these factors interact with different measures of memory. Holistic stimuli, for example, whether auditory or visual, would be expected to be more highly related to recognition, and linguistic or sequential material, whether visually or auditorially presented, would be expected to be more highly related to recall. As the linguistic or sequential material requires a higher level of processing and more extensive verbal encoding, recall is more efficient with older children who are more capable of such encoding. The recognition scores of young children who rely more heavily on holistic aspects of television input are higher than their recall scores; and their retention of holistic stimuli is higher than their retention of linguistic, verbal information, whether it is presented visually or auditorially.

Most reports suggest that young children's better performance on recognition tasks compared with recall tasks is due to their reliance on visual stimuli. Preschoolers may in fact ignore large chunks of auditory input (Hayes & Birnbaum, 1980) because it is more often linguistic and less frequently holistic. When the auditory stimuli are holistic (e.g., slogans, jingles), even very young children often demonstrate their retention by repeating the slogans or jingles, attending to them, and in other ways revealing their recognition memory of them. Older children, on the other hand, who are increasingly able to process or deal with linguistic or sequential features, also demonstrate more accurate recall.

Thus, level of retention varies depending not only on the gender and age of the child, or on the type of retention measure that is used, but on the relative weighting of linguistic and holistic components in the material. Distinctions between types of visual and types of auditory input, as well as processing differences, also might help to clarify the bases for some of the differences that have been reported in the literature between recall of information received from books and that received from film.

In addition, if age and gender differences emerge in encoding strategies and processing techniques, television's impact on these groups should also differ considerably. Might girls, for example, demonstrate an earlier ability to deal with, or be interested in and attentive to, more linguistic material such as adult dialogue and abstract material? Would they, then, be more drawn to and affected by soaps and situation comedies? Might boys, on the other hand, especially younger ones, be expected to favor and respond more positively to perceptually salient and holistic material such as cartoons, other animated presentations, or shows with more action for a longer period of time? Would soaps and other adult shows have less effect on younger children or on boys at later ages because they might be less attentive to them?

Further investigation of the impact of variations in the purpose of viewing, age differences, age–gender interactions, and the relation between specific content and kinds of processing is also needed.

SUMMARY

Which television information is actually attended to, understood, and retained by child viewers depends on a complex interaction of factors. These include the child's developmental level, past experience with television, interest in and motivation for viewing, and the content and format variables of the television programming. Young children are more stimulus bound and attracted by salience, although they are able to monitor some aspects of television input without full attention. Previous views of their level of comprehension, however, may have been underestimates if their limited verbal expressive skills or poorer recall of lengthy segments were mistakenly perceived as a lack of understanding. Newer research suggests that younger children have a basic understanding of much television information, but it is incomplete, frequently distorted, and largely forgotten.

Children are not just passive viewers who absorb information; they are active viewers whose processing of television material becomes more efficient as they get older. There is evidence to suggest that although young children remember visual information better, they require verbal input to interpret it accurately. Older children are less dependent on stimulus features, more able to focus on a central message, and better able to distinguish reality from fantasy. They increasingly use verbal encoding of television material, which enhances their comprehension and retention, and they use their past experience when possible to interpret television content.

A linguistic–holistic distinction within areas of auditory and visual stimuli and an interactionist position can facilitate our understanding of children's processing of television information and help explain and clarify some of the findings that have been reported in the research literature. Although the best learning comes from a smooth integration of both auditory and visual information and of linguistic and holistic components, such distinctions can be used to clarify developmental differences in attention and recall, programming preferences, advertising's impact, and other aspects of a child's television experience. Differences in processing style also interact with the characteristics of the stimuli, resulting in important differences in comprehension and retention of various components of television's messages. This perspective also serves as a fruitful source of hypotheses deserving further study and investigation.

2

Language, Reading, and Academic Achievement

Despite the clear significance of language in children's understanding and retention of television content, there is disagreement in the literature on the role that television plays in children's language development. Some have argued that television viewing impedes language, whereas others claim that it facilitates language acquisition.

Parents and educators also have worried about the possible adverse effects of excessive television viewing on children's academic achievement and its impact on their desire and ability to read. Evidence has suggested that their worries may have some basis in fact, but the relation is not simple or straightforward, and many variables interact to produce the results that have emerged. All of these issues are explored in this chapter.

LANGUAGE DEVELOPMENT

Television as Hindrance

The accusation that television impedes language development has often cited television's emphasis on action, short sequences, fast pace, and reliance on visual stimuli. Other qualities of television's language may be important as well. Doerken (1983) noted, for example, that television language includes much doublespeak and contradiction (e.g., dye your hair for a natural look) and slang and street language are part of many programs. Moreover, reliance on superlatives and exaggeration is the norm, which Doerken felt has an effect on cognitive structure. Doerken worried that we may program children in ways that make them less able to think about and articulate their own experience because of changes in the language itself. By narrowing word use or substituting jingles for thought, we may limit rational capacity, which is especially important for young viewers who are just starting to internalize language (Doerken, 1983).

26

According to Winn (1985), years and years of TV viewing have adversely affected viewers' ability to develop the verbal skills that a literate society requires, such as concentration, reading, and writing clearly. She argued that it is the commitment to language, as a mode of expression, not the acquisition of language, that suffers with heavy television viewing.

Television as Facilitator

Rice (1983), however, challenged the notion that television interferes with a child's acquisition of language. She set out to demonstrate the "link between the child as language learner and the child as television viewer" (p. 214). Given the well-documented ability of preschoolers to learn vocabulary incidentally, television dialogue should serve as a source of new words (Rice, 1983; Rice, Huston, Truglio, & Wright, 1990). Although programs vary greatly in their linguistic complexity, and in their dependence on visual or verbal material, some formats that are appropriate for young children include simple dialogue, redundancy, visual salience, and repetitions, according to Rice. Meanings are often depicted explicitly and visually, and children also are presented with a broad range of social contexts and the different language associated with them (Rice, 1983). Lemish and Rice (1986) likened the rich verbal interaction of the viewing context for children in the early stage of language acquisition to that experienced when parents read books to them. Seen thus, television is an important source of verbal stimulation and interaction.

Rice (1984) claimed that the emphasis on television's visual aspects is misleading because it ignores the auditory aspect, the verbal dialogue, and the important generic verbal codes that complement television's visual information. With increasing language facility, children can better understand television's language, and television can aid their language development (Wartella, 1986), but children need experience with the uniqueness of television's codes nonetheless (Rice, 1984).

Language comprehension also can be facilitated by television because it makes many of the same adjustments that parents make to adapt language to a child's needs, including a reduced rate, short comments, recasting of key information, and many comments about present referents (Rice, 1984). Television also can enhance language skills by teaching language and speech processes (e.g., sound blending) through animated visual displays of "invisible" components of reading. Such processes are hard to demonstrate with static material in the classroom (Greenfield, 1984b).

Age is likely an important variable once again, as rapid language development occurs during the preschool years, the time when heavy viewing of educational programs is prevalent (Rice, 1984). Rice and Woodsmall (1988) found that young children can learn new words while viewing television and this facilitates their language development. Moreover, this effect was not limited to those children who already had more advanced vocabularies, although 5-year-olds did appear to benefit more from the viewing situation than did 3-year-olds (Rice & Woodsmall, 1988).

Amount of Viewing

Some have argued that the amount of viewing is the most important variable and that heavy television viewing is negatively related to language development. In one study, for example, there was an inverse relation between viewing time and language performance in preschool children (Selnow & Bettinghaus, 1982). On the other hand, Harrison and Williams (1986) found light viewing habits among children who had higher vocabulary scores before television was introduced. This suggests that negative correlations between vocabulary and television viewing might best be interpreted as an indication that children with better vocabularies choose to watch less television rather than that television blocks or hinders vocabulary development (Anderson & Collins, 1988). In fact, bright and linguistically more sophisticated children tend to watch programs with more sophisticated language, whereas children with simpler language skills tend to watch more "language-poor" programs (Selnow & Bettinghaus, 1982).

Sesame Street and Language Gains

One of the debates that continues to rage is whether or not programs such as Sesame Street are effective in increasing cognitive skills generally and language skills in particular. The results of a 2-year longitudinal study by Rice and her colleagues (1990) offered solid evidence for the positive linguistic impact Sesame Street has on young children, particularly 3- to 5-year-olds. The researchers studied children in naturalistic settings that provided an especially strong test because of the possible interruptions, distractions, and competing activities. They compared language gains after viewing Sesame Street and after viewing cartoons and other programs. The data supported their hypothesis that Sesame Street contributed to vocabulary development, but other viewing did not have similar effects. Moreover, those findings were independent of family size, parent education and attitudes, and gender, and much of the learning occurred without direct intervention by parents. In fact, adults were present less than one quarter of the time, indicating that the cognitive gains after viewing were due to the content, not to the intervention by parents who encouraged children to watch as had been suggested by Winn (1985).

The vocabulary gain was especially pronounced for 3- to 5-year-olds, who are experiencing rapid development of oral language skills and who compose the target group for *Sesame Street*. The effect was weaker for 5- to 7-year-olds, who are learning more sophisticated vocabulary and whose interests are changing to other types of viewing. Rice and her colleagues (1990) suggested that one reason for *Sesame Street's* success lies in its format and techniques, which are intended to involve children, focus children's attention, use verbal and visual redundancies, and contain dialogue that resembles mother–child interactions, such as emphasis on the present, key words, and simple sentences, features not seen in other shows. Therefore, other shows are less likely to contribute to the language development of very young children (Rice et al., 1990). Although the results suggested that viewing *Sesame Street* led to vocabulary gains, Rice and her colleagues acknowledged that the data are correlational, and more evidence is necessary to demonstrate causality.

Pinon, Huston, and Wright (1989) found that children's viewing of *Sesame Street* increased from age 3 to 4 and then decreased. The amount of viewing, however, seemed more a function of family characteristics and opportunity and encouragement to view rather than cognitive change in the child. It was not related to parent education or occupation, gender, vocabulary level, interest in other media, or involvement with television. The researchers also reported that a working mother and time spent in day care or preschool correlated negatively with television viewing.

Parental Intervention

Although cognitive and language gains likely are not dependent solely on adult intervention, parent–child linguistic interaction is clearly important. For example, parents contribute to their children's linguistic processing when they watch television with their young children (6–30 months of age), take turns asking questions, label, and comment on the content, thus providing a rich combination of television dialogue, their own language, and comments about language and about television events (Rice, 1984).

When one studies the relation among amount of viewing, level of encouragement, and cognitive gains, however, one must consider the many potential confounding variables. In a naturalistic situation, for example, parents who encourage their children to watch *Sesame Street* in order to improve their skills are also likely to encourage them in many other ways. Surprisingly, however, Rice and her colleagues (1990) found that encouragement to view was negatively related to vocabulary acquisition, at least as measured by the Peabody Picture Vocabulary Test, despite the positive relation between actual viewing and vocabulary gain. Rice et al. suggested that the negative relation between encouragement to view and vocabulary gain may have emerged because parents who encourage viewing of *Sesame Street* may encourage other viewing as well, or because parents encourage slow language developers to watch the program because they consider *Sesame Street* to be educational. Children of parents with positive attitudes toward television in general had relatively lower vocabulary scores, perhaps because they were less likely to engage their children in nontelevision activities.

One of the important differences between television and reading in the stimulation of language is that unlike reading, talk about television does not require that time be set aside; it occurs along with other conversational events and other activities (Lemish & Rice, 1986). The children that Lemish and Rice studied watched television and talked while they played, while they had their diapers changed, and so on; and *Sesame Street* was especially likely to elicit television talk. Viewing television and talking about television are "extensions of nearly all forms of interpersonal communication that take place between family members" (Lull, 1988a, p. 246).

TELEVISION AND READING

Skill Acquisition and Reading Achievement

Many of the concerns about television's effects on achievement have focused more specifically on children's reading skills and on their reading habits and preferences. A study of a community before and after television was introduced indicated that although television does not result in the deterioration of well-established reading skills, it likely does slow the acquisition of those skills (Corteen & Williams, 1986). Heavy viewing was associated with poorer reading skills, and better readers more often used the print media than poorer readers.

Winn (1985) described the *lazy reader*, the child who reads but does so with lower levels of concentration and involvement, and she noted a change in the kinds of books children read in a trend toward reading "nonbooks" such as the *Guinness Book of Records*. According to Winn, these nonbooks involve a new style of reading. They are books without a sustained story or carefully sculpted arguments and they require little focus or concentration. They can be read in short segments or scanned, and they require no "getting into" (Winn, 1985).

Others see the use of television for escape and relaxation and as an easy way to learn as a healthy use of television that does not appear to interfere with either motivation to read or the reading process (Roberts, Bachen, Hornby, & Hernandez-Ramos, 1984). Those who see television as an easy source of learning may be more effective learners in general, with whatever medium they use (Roberts et al., 1984), or they may be minimizing television as a source of information and taking it less seriously than print. Children who were more bored and less involved with television had higher reading achievement scores. Such children may turn to print for information and stimulation, therefore showing a positive relation with reading achievement (Roberts et al., 1984). Comstock and Paik (1991) noted that the inverse relation between reading achievement and television viewing was greater among heavy viewers, children from higher socioeconomic backgrounds, children of higher ability, and viewers of mostly light entertainment content (comedy, cartoons, action-adventure).

Displacement Effect

Many have argued that television has a negative influence on achievement because television viewing displaces time that children could spend reading. Beentjes and Van der Voort (1988) reviewed research relating to the three main hypotheses put forward regarding television's impact on children's reading. They include television having a positive effect (facilitative effect), a negative effect (inhibition effect or displacement hypothesis), or no effect. They concluded that most evidence supports the inhibition hypothesis, although the relation between reading achievement and television viewing is complex and is influenced by several conditions. Children most vulnerable to the negative or inhibition effect are those who view heavy amounts of television, are socially advantaged, and are intelligent, although content is a factor also (Beentjes & Van der Voort, 1988). Beentjes and Van der Voort noted further that TV might also have a more indirect effect, such as displacing activities that facilitate general cognitive development, or it might weaken concentration abilities or persistence, though there was no direct evidence that television causes attentional difficulties with reading material.

Corteen and Williams (1986) suggested that the main variable accounting for the poorer reading of heavy viewers is the displacement of practice time and the resultant loss of fluency and automaticity, especially for those with learning disabilities or other difficulties with reading who most need the practice. In fact, some children may rely on television to compensate for their reading problems, and the viewing habits of children with learning problems are discussed more fully in chapter 8.

Comstock and Paik (1991) rejected displacement as the sole process. Rather, they concluded that the evidence suggests

> A three-factor process in which large amounts of viewing not only (a) displace skill acquisition but also (b) interfere with further practice, or skill development and maintenance, and (c) lower the quality or value by decreased capacity of practice done in conjunction with television. (p. 136)

In a longitudinal study on the issue of displacement and the effects of television on children's leisure-time reading, Koolstra and Van der Voort (1996) studied Dutch children who were in Grades 2 to 4 at the start of the study and surveyed them at 1-year intervals three times. They found that television viewing led to less comic book reading only from Year 2 to 3, but television viewing led to less book reading over both measurement periods. According to the researchers, television's effect is due to "(a) a television-induced deterioration of attitudes toward book reading, and (b) a television-induced deterioration of children's ability to concentrate on reading" (p. 4).

Several researchers have argued that television viewing primarily displaces other forms of entertainment and media use such as movies, radio, and comic books (Anderson & Collins, 1988; Mutz, Roberts, & van Vuuren, 1993). In a study by Mutz, et al. (1993), in which data were obtained before and after television was introduced to South Africa, the introduction of television affected time allocation for individuals but only for other media use (e.g., television viewing meant less time spent on movies and listening to the radio). After a year, television viewing decreased, but there was not a return to previous levels of the displaced activities (movies and radio). When the researchers separated individual and aggregate perspectives, they found that displacement continued through the first 5 years after the introduction of television, but overall, television's influence was modest and did not change the pattern of activities greatly, although there were slight decreases in reading, moviegoing, and listening to the radio.

Mutz et al. (1993) concluded that television led to restructuring of leisure time, which continued even when time spent viewing television decreased: "Displacement of time spent on some activity may likely also displace interest in that activity" (p. 71). Therefore, just cutting down on TV time to try to increase time spent on reading or other activities is unlikely to work on its own.

Simply reducing viewing time does not guarantee more reading, because individuals' choices about how they spend their time are determined by other factors, such as family education and attitudes, attitudes toward reading and toward television, and time available (Anderson & Collins, 1988). Anderson and Collins argued that there is no solid evidence that television necessarily displaces activities that are more cognitively valuable than television viewing, such as reading and home-work. Although some increase in reading occurs when television viewing is reduced, at least in the short term, most of the extra time that becomes available with such reduction in television time is spent on other recreational activities (Anderson & Collins, 1988).

Anderson and Collins (1988) maintained that displacement studies should look at why children spend time watching television and whether they actively choose it, in addition to considering all of the other factors (e.g., parent education, attitudes toward reading, weather conditions, and alternatives) that are probably more important than television availability in determining the total number of "cognitively valuable activities engaged in by children" (Anderson & Collins, 1988, p. 39). Anderson and Collins noted further that many other activities, including homework, are often shared with television rather than displaced by it.

Finally, Ritchie, Price, and Roberts (1987) used data from a 3-year panel study to reappraise the relation between television viewing and reading achievement and found strong negative correlations that support past findings. When they used more sophisticated analytic techniques, however, and looked at the relation over time and controlled for initial reading levels, the relation became weaker and less clear. That is, their simple correlations supported a displacement hypothesis, but when previous levels of the dependent variables were included, relations were weaker, although in the hypothesized direction.

Changes in reading skills or time spent reading did not seem related consistently to TV viewing time, and reading nonschool content was not related to improved reading skills. Significant relations were mostly for older children, and it was not clear whether younger ones were less affected or benefit from more television viewing. Ritchie et al. (1987) suggested that the results could be due to a number of factors: earlier effects (before the age of their participants); subtle cumulative effects of TV viewing over time; and complex, conditional processes and interactions, such as why they watch, choice of content, and environmental characteristics, which contribute differently for different children (Ritchie et al., 1987).

Harris and Williams (1985) also found that children's reasons for playing video games were associated with age, amount of time and money spent, and gender, which were all positively related with each other and negatively related to English grades. However, study time was not correlated with any of these variables, so that was not the cause, a finding that does not support a displacement hypothesis.

Neuman's (1988) analysis of data from eight states revealed little difference in reading scores, comprehension, vocabulary, or study skills scores with amount of viewing in the majority of children who watched for 2 to 4 hours a day. Over that, however, negative effects emerged and became increasingly harmful. She noted that this is a correlation, however, and may reflect differences in the characteristics of heavy and moderate viewers or in parental expectations and supervision as well as parent example. In an earlier comparison of heavy and light viewing and heavy and light reading, Neuman (1986) found that children internalize media attitudes and behaviors from their parents. Parents who watch more entertainment programs with their children may be encouraging more indiscriminate viewing and discouraging reading as an alternative activity (Wright et al., 1990). In addition, use of better measures than just the number of hours might yield stronger relations (Neuman, 1988). Neuman also explained that television viewing serves different needs and gratifications than sports, leisure reading, or time with friends, and viewing time decreases as children get older because of increased social activities and greater school demands.

Conclusions

After reexamining the research, Reinking and Wu (1990) concluded that regarding displacement, there is a positive relation if TV delivers strong educational content and a negative relation if TV displaces more educational activity, or no effect. For example, findings might vary if parents with high socioeconomic status (SES) park their children in front of the television set and low-SES parents join their children there. Reinking and Wu suggested that the study of these relation needs a more sophisticated approach than is usually used because they found that the negative relation between amount of time spent viewing TV and reading achievement was nonsignificant when relevant variables were controlled and more sophisticated data analysis was performed. Reinking and Wu reported that moderate television viewing does not have an adverse effect on reading achievement and may even help in some populations (e.g., disadvantaged children) by giving them background information and supplanting nontelevision experience.

Positive Effects of Television on Reading

Other researchers have gone beyond looking at potential negative effects from television viewing and have put forward a positive view of television's influence. They have suggested that although television may displace study time, or affect reading habits or study skills, it also can stimulate interest in new topics, provide background material for school projects, and stimulate classroom discussions.

Wright et al. (1990), for example, reported that older children who had watched adult informative programs, whether or not they watched with parents, subsequently used print media more. That is, children who watched more demanding and informative programs also liked to read, and those who watched more child entertainment programs like cartoons or other entertainment were less interested in reading books.

In addition, even when children are viewing fiction, there is likely to be some information that is academically relevant, although it can be either accurate or inaccurate (Anderson & Collins, 1988), and Bianculli (1994) claimed that television can be used to increase literacy if the right kinds of TV are watched. He spoke of "teleliteracy" and insisted that TV and books can exist alongside each other and can supplement each other, for example, using pertinent TV content to supplement classroom material, as it stimulates interest in new topical areas. He stated further that some barriers make it seem as though television and literature are mutually exclusive, but TV's accessibility and popularity mean it is a primary conveyor of information, including literature, and media studies are now included in many classrooms. Finally, because television exposes children to so much so fast—music, sports, literature, and so on—its potential for use outweighs its potential for abuse.

Finally, "Living Books" for computers, with which children can click on characters or objects and bring them to life with sounds and images and movement, adds to the fun of reading them (Hodges, 1996). It makes reading a highly interactive medium for learning (*Adventures in Learning*, 1992) and could increase motivation in children who are having difficulties. These and other programs allow children to have words pronounced repeatedly, go back to troublesome words or concepts, and generally to add to their reading experience by bringing highly salient and entertaining elements into it.

TELEVISION AND ACADEMIC ACHIEVEMENT

Parents' worries about the possible adverse effects of excessive television viewing on their children's grades and general academic achievement may have some basis in fact. Average 18-year-olds have spent over 2 years of their lives in front of television, and they have spent more hours watching television than they have in formal classroom instruction (Hearold, 1986). The relation is not simple or straightforward, however, and many variables interact to produce the results that have emerged.

A large assessment program in California in the early 1980s (California Assessment program, 1980, 1982) revealed a general inverse relation between amount of viewing and achievement. Heavy viewers of television scored lower on tests of reading, written expression, and math than did students who viewed little or no television. This was true for different socioeconomic levels and at both elementary and high school levels, although the relation was more pronounced for 12th graders.

There were no significant gender differences. This negative relation between achievement scores and heavy television viewing held regardless of the amount of time spent doing homework or reading for pleasure, and the sharpest decline in achievement scores appeared in participants who viewed more than 6 hours of TV daily. Not surprisingly, students who read the most and watched the least television earned the highest test scores (California Assessment Program, 1980).

An interesting socioeconomic interaction was apparent, however. Although achievement declined at all socioeconomic levels for students watching more than 5 or 6 hours of TV daily, those children at the lowest socioeconomic level who watched up to 3 hours a day actually improved in achievement. Viewing more than that, however, was associated with lower achievement. Although heavy television viewing did affect school achievement, then, the effect was most pronounced for more socially advantaged students (Fetler, 1984).

According to Fetler (1984), the difference in effect between the socioeconomic levels may be a function of the fact that television is less stimulating intellectually than many of the alternatives and resources available in affluent homes where many books, magazines, and other materials are routinely provided. In less affluent homes, on the other hand, television is more stimulating and educational than what is readily available and might well lead to some academic improvement.

According to Greenfield (1984b), all children learn how to watch television and get experience with its codes. Research in different countries and on different subcultures shows that children who suffer an educational disadvantage regarding books and lectures are not at the same disadvantage regarding learning from television. Therefore, if used properly, television can help raise minimum and average educational levels. Television is democratic and can reduce the advantage that middle-class children have because children from disadvantaged homes can still learn from television programs, such as *Sesame Street*, whereas they may have quit school (Greenfield, 1984b).

Comstock and Paik (1991) cited more recent studies that confirm CAP outcomes regarding television viewing and academic achievement, and a CAP follow-up study in 1986 showed a similar phenomenon beyond basic skills to include an inverse relation between amount of television viewed and achievement in history, social science, and science (CAP, 1988). As to whether television viewing is the cause or effect in this inverse relation, Comstock and Paik observed the following:

> The inverse associations between socioeconomic status and reading, and between mental ability and reading, the turning away from television toward print with the passage from childhood to the teenage years, and the special population that apparently makes up young people who are very light viewers lead us to believe that young people who are able and

especially those who are highly efficient at reading will come to watch less television. Thus, some of the negative association between viewing and reading and other achievement is caused by the behavior of brighter young persons who are able or highly proficient readers. (p. 134)

Comstock and Paik (1991) concluded further that children of lower intellectual ability, those who are in greater conflict with parents or peers, those in whose homes television is more central, and those who see no other activity as more rewarding or necessary, watch more television. All of those factors, however, are ones that we would associate with lower achievement because they interfere with skill acquisition and task completion, and because parents in whose homes television is more central are less apt to emphasize reading, homework, and achievement. The authors noted that at all ages there is a negative correlation between viewing television and achievement, regardless of the amount of time children spend on homework or reading for themselves.

On the other hand, children in both age groups studied (8–9 and 14–15) by Clifford et al. (1995) considered science on television to be beneficial, appreciated that important information was conveyed, and felt that science should be part of prime-time programming, not just school programs or minority channels. However, they watched such programs less as they got older. Clifford et al. did find gender differences, but in the opposite direction than conventional stereotypes would predict. Girls agreed more with positive statements and less with negative statements about science programs than boys did. Children can learn from those programs when they do watch them, but whether they do so depends on what skills and knowledge they bring to the viewing situation and how information is presented (Clifford et al., 1995). The authors concluded that even if children have normal processing ability, if they are not motivated and engaged, programs have little impact.

The relation between viewing and achievement, then, appears to be a curvilinear one (Fetler, 1984; Williams, Haertel, Haertel, & Walberg, 1982). Viewing fewer than 10 hours a week had a slightly positive effect on achievement and viewing more than 10 hours a week had negative effects that increased up until 35 to 40 hours, after which there was little further effect (Williams et al., 1982).

Children also may transfer some of the lower levels of information processing that television requires, such as chunking and encoding, to independent tasks such as problem solving that actually require higher levels of processing (Williams, 1986). They may use strategies that they developed to process television content for nontelevision tasks, such as reading. For example, they may use their tendency to make quick shifts in focus from television viewing to processing print. Such strategies may be inappropriate for the second activity, however; if so, processing will be less effective. In the case of transferring quick attentional shifts to reading print, one would expect the focus and concentration required for reading to suffer.

TELEVISION AND OTHER SKILL DEVELOPMENT

Television has also been implicated as a negative influence on children's listening and writing behaviors. According to Doerken (1983), children's listening skills are adversely affected by television because children get used to talking over television as background noise, and they then carry that tendency over to school, where they frequently interrupt teachers and peers and may be inattentive to what others are saying. Moreover, children carry over their television style to writing as well, with the result that their writing is often choppy, it jumps around, and in that respect is more like television than it is like material in which main points are developed in a logical sequence and arguments are built point by point (Doerken, 1983).

They may also transfer other strategies, such as divided or partial attention, that they use with television, to the school situation, with resultant inappropriate attentional patterns (Anderson & Collins, 1988), or they may have difficulty separating visual attention from auditory attention and may have difficulty listening if there is not visual input simultaneously (Anderson & Collins, 1988).

Postman (1985) raised other concerns about television's "style of learning," which he claimed is, by its nature, hostile to school learning or learning from books. Postman made a distinction between what he called the television curriculum and the school curriculum. He claimed that television's philosophy rests on three commandments, the influence of which can be seen in every kind of programming:

1. There shall be no prerequisites. Television "is a nongraded curriculum...[that] undermines the idea that sequence and continuity have anything to do with thought itself" (p. 147).
2. There shall be no perplexity, which would cause a viewer to change channels. "This means that there must be nothing that has to be remembered, studied, applied or, worst of all, endured" (p. 147). The assumption is made that viewer contentment and satisfaction are more important than viewer growth.
3. There shall be little or no exposition in the form of reasons, discussion, and argument. Rather, the teaching is more in the form of storytelling. "The name we may properly give to an education without prerequisites, perplexity and exposition is entertainment" (p. 148).

Moreover, according to Postman, the school curriculum is being strongly influenced and determined by the character of television.

Many scholars (e.g., Cullingsford, 1984; Doerken, 1983; Medrich, 1979; Williams, 1986) have suggested that television's impact on achievement comes not only as a function of the time spent and the displacement of other activities, but also as a result of habits of passivity and decreased efforts and involvement that it engenders. Anderson and Collins (1988), on the other hand, argued that this hypothesis has not been strongly supported in the research.

SCHOOL VERSUS TELEVISION

Hodge and Tripp (1986) suggested that there is a two-way interaction between school culture and television culture, such that the heavy viewer comes to school with more emphasis on television culture and therefore may be at a disadvantage in school, where the television culture is less "legitimate." Such children tend to view more television, do less well in school, and are more often from poor, less well-educated homes in which there are fewer cultural or material resources and less privacy (Medrich, 1979). They are less likely to question television's message and more likely to watch "whatever's on," to watch as much as they want, and to watch because there is "nothing else to do." This makes television the dominant force for them outside of school and hence, especially powerful (Medrich, 1979).

Increased viewing also may lead to other school-related difficulties. Some have worried about television's effect on children's curiosity as well as its influence on their verbal ability and cognitive development. Harrison and Williams (1986) found that children in a town where television was introduced for the first time earned higher creativity scores initially, but 2 years later had scores similar to those of children who had grown up with television. Some worry that television's fast pace may lead to a negative effect on learning habits and attention span (Zuckerman, Singer, & Singer, 1980).

On the other hand, others have claimed that the growing fear of TV as a resource is not deserved and that we should use television's potential rather than avoid it (Bianculli, 1994). Research by Jerome and Dorothy Singer has demonstrated that preschool children watching Barney, which was beating out Sesame Street and Mister Rogers in Nielsen ratings (cited in deGroot, 1994,) showed improved cognitive and attitudinal skills including better number skills, vocabulary, knowledge of shapes, colors, neighborhood locations, and manners, and the creation of positive feelings. Their findings were true of preschoolers of all cultures and races (de Groot, 1994). However, regular viewing of Sesame

Street and *Mister Rogers* is also associated with improved vocabulary and greater learning, as well as positive behaviors (de Groot, 1994).

Recently, in fact, many features and purposes of television and the schools have become blurred. School, once the bastion of the three Rs, now includes affective, emotional, and value-laden issues, and much effort is expended to stimulate, entertain, and hold the interest of students in unique and varied ways. Television, on the other hand, although seen largely as an entertainment activity, also can be very educational. Children learn much about the world from their television viewing, and study of television's techniques can be fascinating for young viewers in addition to helping them to become more literate, less vulnerable viewers. Once they see how specific television effects are achieved and how various subtle messages are communicated, they can view TV more critically and better understand the television programming and advertising they see. Critical and analytical skills from school can be used to take a closer look at TV content and debate the reality and desirability of the values presented.

Conversely television's inherent fascination and interest for children can be used well in the classroom. Some classrooms, for example, devote time to studying a movie, play, or TV program as part of the reading curriculum. Some researchers have used television scripts as reading material for children whose motivation lags (Lee, 1980). Others have encouraged children to dissect television plots, to debate the merits of the strategies used by characters to solve problems, to identify stereotypes, and to separate fact from speculation; in other words to deconstruct television and develop more informed viewing skills. Reinking and Wu (1990) noted further that teachers can use children's television to promote reading instruction without worrying that there will be negative side effects. For example, children can watch programs to get background information and show new words they learned from television.

Because of its strong visual component and capacity for compelling graphics, television can explain complex concepts in ways not possible in a regular classroom. Multimedia presentations can be exciting and stimulating for all learners and in fact reflect the reality of learning in the world today. Television has much to offer academically and educationally when used sensibly and creatively.

Schools also can use television's intrinsic appeal to encourage discussion of important societal issues, such as violence, stereotyping, and advertising. Critical thinking skills developed in school can be applied to the analysis and evaluation of TV content and stimulate debate as to the reality and desirability of the values presented.

Television is only one factor in a context of many other cognitive, socialization, and experiential variables, all of which interact to produce both television viewing and achievement behavior. School personnel, parents, peers, and television characters all serve as models of social behavior for children. They provide many behavioral options, both appropriate and inappropriate. Although the modeling is usually implicit, rather than explicit or direct, children learn ways to solve problems, interact with others, obtain what is important to them, and "get ahead." How strong an influence, normal or deviant, each of these models has on children, however, is controversial.

Nickerson (1995) pointed out other ways that technology can be used to enhance learning, not by just using more technology in the classroom, but by providing the opportunity to develop new approaches to teaching. Technology allows exploration of various aspects of the world through simulation and helps identify misconceptions, it can facilitate active learning and discovery, and it can provide visual representations of processes happening (e.g., supernova explosion), at different times and in different levels of detail, controlled by the user, providing a wide range of information sources and tools, all within a nonthreatening environment (Nickerson, 1995).

Fortunately for today's students, increasingly widespread interest in media literacy is helping children to understand and evaluate the impact of the media on them and to soften the sharp, often adversarial, line between children's viewing experiences and their school experiences. The best aspects of each should be used to capture and foster children's enthusiasm for learning and facilitate their healthy development.

METHODOLOGICAL ISSUES

Some also have criticized the methodology in studies relating television and school achievement or reading skills. Roberts et al. (1984) argued, for example, that typical studies of television use and school performance use "amount" of viewing as a critical variable despite the fact that children are poor estimators of their viewing time and despite the fact that the notion of an additive effect, in which more television viewing leads to a greater effect, is too simple a view of television behavior. According to Roberts and his colleagues, such a practice ignores mediating variables such as different attitudes, uses made of television or gratifications sought, and others that affect behavior. Moreover, school achievement is usually represented by test scores; however, as with television, reading is only one part of a larger pattern of attitudes, behavior and cognition related to reading. It is not just a matter of skills, but of what is read, how much is read, and family attitudes (Roberts et al., 1984).

Anderson and Collins (1988) suggested that correlations between low achievement and heavy television viewing may be a result of a third factor, namely imitation of parents who do not have a strong interest in reading, and modeling of television viewing as an alternative leisure activity. Even if excessive television viewing interferes with school performance, however, one cannot isolate television itself as the cause, as the same could be said for any other activity such as sports that occupies too much of a child's out-of-school time (Hodge & Tripp, 1986).

Both television viewing and school behavior are part of a larger context of social behavior and relationships that must be taken into account (Fetler, 1984). In fact, television's major impact educationally may be through children's social learning—their learning about society and about themselves—which may also affect their academic learning in school and depends on the child's social context (Ball, Palmer, & Millward, 1986).

SUMMARY

Although there is not unanimous support for television's positive role in children's language development, many feel that television can enhance children's language in various ways, particularly when parents are involved with them in the viewing situation. Programs such as *Sesame Street* in which modifications are made to approximate parent–child verbal interactions seem most likely to facilitate vocabulary gain, whether or not a parent is actually present. Excessive television viewing may interfere with the acquisition of reading, listening, and writing skills, and it may affect reading preferences as well.

Research into the relation between television viewing and academic achievement suggests that it may be largely a curvilinear one, but the amount of viewing interacts with socioeconomic level and IQ. Children who view some television, especially those from deprived or disadvantaged backgrounds, often show improved achievement. However, viewing more than 5 or 6 hours a day is associated with poorer achievement in all groups. Television appears to have a more negative effect on the achievement of socially advantaged students than on disadvantaged ones, presumably because it displaces other, more beneficial alternatives. For disadvantaged students, however, television may provide some compensatory information.

Finally, rigidly separating school learning and learning from television seems increasingly counterproductive. Rather, the intrinsic appeal of television and its capacity for transmitting information in complex and stimulating formats can be used in classroom settings. Similarly, the critical thinking and analytic skills developed in school can be used to understand and evaluate television content.

3

Comparisons With Other Media

One of the most important age-related variables in children's processing of television information is their increasing efficiency in understanding what they see. Several authors (e.g., Gardner, 1983; Meringoff, 1980; Salomon, 1979; Winn, 1985) have emphasized the important role that varying symbol systems play in differences among levels of comprehension. Some have focused on the language of television and others on the exclusivity or accessibility of television's content. Some have gone further and compared symbol systems across media in order to discern how differences in the emphases of various media affect comprehension, attention, and recall.

TELEVISION CODES

Wartella (1986) claimed that form and content are inseparable in a meaningful audiovisual experience. However, the information is patterned in representational codes that connect form and content and that children actively interpret. Moreover, production techniques guide them in making sense of programs. According to Wartella, three kinds of codes are used: *iconic* (presentation of a visual image), *medium-specific* (particular patterns of production and editing, such as zooms, replays, etc.), and *generic* (such as language), and there is much variation in how language is used. Generic codes interact with iconic and production ones to influence attention and comprehension. Knowledge of these codes changes with age, as does children's understanding of the content. The ability to deal with visual input makes the iconic code easiest to interpret (Wartella, 1986).

One cannot "assume that the 'grammar' of verbal language is the same as a visual language or that there is only one grammar of visual language" (Hodge & Tripp, 1986, p. 46), nor that children use only one grammar to decode auditory and visual television messages or to send their own. Hodge and Tripp suggested that we interpret the two and use a "metagrammar" as in their example of a boy who said "you sorta listen with your eyes" (p. 47). That is, we must look at varying levels of a message, varying media, and varying codes.

Carpenter (1986) suggested that radio, television, and film are new languages with as yet unknown grammars, each with different codes and each with its own language. For example, radio and television both have short and unrelated programs with commercials in between, all together in a knot, without antecedents or consequences, rather than having a linear form. Carpenter argued that media do not just communicate an idea in different ways, but that specific ideas or insights belong primarily to one or another and are best communicated through that one. Television language, for example, is closest to drama (with music, art, language, and gestures), and it retains uncertainty. It goes quickly, with no time to go back. Angle and distance shift continuously, and gestures convey inner experiences that cannot be expressed in words. Thus, each medium communicates a unique aspect of reality and gives a different perspective (Carpenter, 1986). Television language, then, conveys some ideas more effectively than others to children, resulting in varying degrees of impact of a message.

Television also relies on other codes, such as broadcast and narrowcast codes that are defined by the audience (Fiske, 1982). Broadcast codes are for a mass audience, and narrowcast codes are used for a specific audience. Broadcast codes are simple, have immediate appeal, do not require education to understand them, and the audience expects reassurance and confirmation. Narrowcast codes are aimed at or involve primarily a defined, limited audience, usually one whose members have chosen to learn the necessary codes and who rely on shared educational or intellectual experience and expect to be changed by the communication. They may be elitist or divisive (we–them) as compared with broadcast codes that stress similarities (us). If narrowcast codes reach members of an "outgroup" or a different group, "aberrant decoding" results and produces a different meaning, something that happens often with the mass media according to Fiske (1982).

Broadcast codes, then, should be more easily understood by children because broadcast codes stress group similarities. They may make children's assimilation of and identification with the message more likely or easier. Where narrowcast codes are used, then, children, especially young ones, would be more likely to use the aberrant decoding that Fiske (1982) described.

Meyrowitz (1985) then used these distinctions to compare print and broadcast media and said that print has a "front region" bias, where we deal with formal stylized and idealized messages. Such messages require much decoding, which is related to education, age, and even wealth. Understanding of them fosters elitism and separate informational systems. The electronic media, on the other hand, according to Meyrowitz, have a "back region" bias, where the privacy of groups is invaded, and the distinction between private and public behavior is blurred. There are fewer restrictions as a function of age, socioeconomic level, or education. Those media break down discrete informational systems, which has a leveling effect and everyone has access to the same information, so we can treat individuals in high places as peers.

If one applies these concepts to children, then, the back region bias of TV greatly increases children's access to adult information. Television has made all knowledge equally available to viewers; the exclusivity of information that became possible for adults with the Gutenberg printing press is dissolved with television (Postman, 1982). However, if this increased access is coupled with children's greater likelihood of using aberrant decoding, the potential for misinterpretation is greater for children. In effect, they are seeing, and trying to interpret, the adult world through children's eyes and with children's cognitive capacities.

Newspapers and magazines also popularize knowledge, however, and thus break down discrete informational systems (Eaman, 1987). Moreover, the ability to understand electronic information messages also depends on our ability to put them into context; that is, it depends on our print media experience as well (Eaman, 1987). Eaman also pointed out that too much information, or information overload, can impede understanding, and often one would prefer less information if one could understand more of it.

SYMBOL SYSTEMS AND SCHEMATA

Salomon (1979) attributed the most important influence on cognition and learning to differences in the symbol systems used by the media to represent content rather than the media per se. Moreover, there are important differences in the cognitive structures of children that influence how they process symbolic material, and different symbol systems require different kinds of mental skills in order to process the information (Salomon, 1981a). Older children are more efficient in their processing of television material because they use symbolic codes that allow them to process the verbal information more directly and thus to comprehend with less than full and focused attention. According to Salomon (1979), they have less need, for example, to transform verbal information into nonverbal representations as younger children do.

The better the fit between the symbols presented and the child's cognitive structures, the more complete the child's comprehension of the content will be. For example, if the television content is presented simply, has clear and obvious symbols such as visual images, and does not have subtle linguistic messages, a young child will be able to understand the content more easily. If the content presented requires more reliance on verbal codes, however, or involves subtle or unusual language tricks, a young child is more likely to be confused by that content. The cognitive structures that children develop become increasingly complex as children mature and gain experience.

In the context of television, a very young child approaches programming content with different and less sophisticated or complex schemata or expectations with which to interpret that information than older children have. For example, a young child may assume, based on rather limited experience and simple cognitive structures, that large individuals are also strong individuals. Interpreting a scene, then, in which a small person is very strong or a large person is weak presents the child with a processing problem. If even more abstraction is required (e.g., a large person who is strong physically but weak psychologically or morally), a very young child faces inordinate and insurmountable problems in understanding. He or she then is likely to decrease attention, draw a simple and concrete but inaccurate conclusion, or otherwise misinterpret the information. It is too far removed from the child's cognitive abilities either to be assimilated or accommodated. If the material is within a child's cognitive reach (i.e., requires some accommodation of his or her schemata to make the material fit), the child changes the operative schemata and learns. If the material is far beyond his or her level altogether, accommodation does not occur and the material is missed.

Young children use schemata that are more limited, concrete, and often require imagery. Older children, who have developed more complex schemata that include imagery but also include language variations and verbal encoding, and who can take more abstract components into account when interpreting information, clearly can be more efficient and literate viewers. Thus, the child's schemata affect what is learned from television, but television content also affects the development of schemata (Salomon, 1981a).

With more experience, however, children's use of scripts can reduce processing demands progressively further (Hawkins & Pingree, 1986). That is, as they gain experience with the television medium, they develop ways of interpreting even relatively complex content more easily and more quickly. They may, for example, with experience, come to expect a scene change whenever the background music changes in a certain way. When a scene change occurs, then, they are taken less by surprise and are less confused by the switch than a younger, less experienced child would be.

Age is important in this process as the young, with a more limited *channel capacity* (amount of stimulation that can be picked up and retained) are less literate viewers and can process only a little in spite of many hours of viewing (Cohen & Salomon, 1979). According to Cohen and Salomon, limits of channel capacity depend on schemata used to process information and on competition one experiences with other informational sources.

Cohen and Salomon (1979) also suggested that some of the differences between laboratory and field studies may be due to the fact that participants may use closer to full channel capacity in controlled studies but may commit only part of it under natural conditions.

Amount of Invested Mental Effort (AIME)

According to Salomon (1981b, 1983, 1984), the amount of mental effort invested (AIME) in television viewing, which he defined as "the number of nonautomatic mental elaborations applied to the material" (Salomon, 1984, p. 60), is affected by a viewer's perception of what is demanded. Symbol systems on television require less mental effort to extract meaning (i.e., they emphasize experiential aspects, imagery), and they may allow "shallower" processing than reading, regardless of content. In fact this characteristic may be part of television's appeal (Cohen & Salomon, 1979).

In other words, the imagery and symbols on television generally allow viewers to derive meaning with less effort than they would require to derive meaning from reading. Reading requires more focused concentration, a greater facility with language and recall of vocabulary, and a mastery of all of the skills that comprise reading. According to Cohen and Salomon (1979), in reading, the mental schema, or perspective that a reader brings to the material affects the likelihood of remembering elements of a story, and processing with more AIME leads to better learning, recall, comprehension, and inferences.

According to Salomon, AIME depends on a viewer's perception of material, what effort it deserves, the likely payoff of more effort, and belief in one's own efficiency; that is, the issue of AIME indicates that children interact with the medium (Salomon, 1984). They must make judgments about the level of effort required for a task. Children do, however, use many cues to decide what level of processing is required to comprehend the information presented (Wright et al., 1984). Moreover, their assessment of how much effort is needed to understand material, either printed or televised, affects the depth of information processing that they actually use, and thereby fulfills their expectations (Salomon & Leigh, 1984). For example, they are likely to read comic books with less invested effort, making that particular reading activity more like television viewing. In fact, one might view comics, with their heavy visual and pictorial component, as more like television than they are like ordinary books.

Moreover, variations can exist even within television viewing. For example, watching an educational channel leads to greater AIME than entertainment channels (Salomon, 1981a). Comstock and Paik (1991) also suggested that the low invested mental effort may carry over to other programming besides entertainment, so children do not learn too much of an informational or cognitive nature, but they do learn about behavior. As self-perceived efficacy is positively associated with effort for print and negatively associated with television, the most self-confident children are likely to use less effective strategies for learning from television (Comstock & Paik, 1991).

In a *drip effect* one picks up knowledge and information even if one is viewing television primarily for entertainment. This suggests, according to Salomon (1981a), that perhaps repeated exposure to undemanding material makes it part of one's schemata and thus influences one to be exposed further to similar material. This is consistent with the cultivation effect proposed by Gerbner, Gross, Morgan, and Signorielli (1980), discussed more fully in chapter 9. The extent of such change, however, is strongly influenced by social reinforcement (Salomon 1981a).

In any case, depth of processing, and not just amount of time spent, strongly moderates television's effects (Cohen & Salomon, 1979). If children are asked to watch in order to learn (i.e., the perceived demand is changed), AIME increases and so does their inference-making performance. Thus, they can mobilize their abilities; when a deeper understanding is sought, they can also expend more effort for their processing of television information as well (Salomon & Leigh, 1984). If children are not instructed to react differently than usual, however, less effort is invested and little inferential knowledge is extracted. That is, they tend to respond and perform below their actual ability level (Salomon, 1983). Effortless processing of television information, then, is based on children's preconceptions and expectations, not on the inherent nature of television.

Children can change their processing, exert more effort, and show increased understanding when they are told that they will be tested for recall of content (Anderson & Collins, 1988). They can also be encouraged to invest more effort and to look at television programs with a more critical eye. The development of those critical viewing skills is discussed more fully in chapter 11.

COMPARISONS OF PRINT, TELEVISION, AND RADIO

Each communication medium emphasizes particular features and modalities and each has characteristic components. The print media are strictly visual or abstract visual (Rice, 1984), radio is totally auditory, and television is a combination of both. Films are animated and highly visual, whereas books that are read to children are more static pictorially, but they allow for more auditory attention, listening skills, and application of other knowledge (Meringoff, 1980). Moreover, the same medium (e.g., television) can be a vehicle for different symbol systems (language and visual imagery); and the same symbol system (e.g., language) can occur in different media, such as books or television. Gardner (1983), however, questioned whether information encountered in one medium (e.g., film) is the same information when it is transmitted by another system (e.g., books). One might also ask whether one symbol system (e.g., language) involves the same operations when it occurs in different media (e.g., books vs. television). Meringoff (1980) concluded that children's repeated experiences with specific media and their differential effects have important implications, because development of specific perceptual and cognitive skills may be affected by the relative amounts of visual and auditory information to which children are exposed in specific media and the nature of those stimuli.

Hayes and Kelly (1985), on the other hand, in a study of media similarities and differences in adults' and young children's apprehension of stories, found remarkable consistency in the story grammar reflected in the recall of both groups. Children and adults appeared to use the same kind of grammar to recall television stories as they did for oral and written ones, perhaps because they both require verbal encoding. There is also overlap between skills necessary to interpret print and radio, and there can be overlap between skills needed in reading and viewing television as well, but it depends on how the medium is being used (Greenfield, 1984a).

As the work of Rice and her colleagues (Rice, 1984; Rice et al., 1990; Rice & Woodsmall, 1988) has indicated, however, television programs also can incorporate repetition and other adjustments to facilitate language gains. Moreover, the rapid increase in the use of VCRs means that children now have increased control over the content that is viewed, the rate at which it is presented, and the amount of repetition as they have with books, although the tactile experience of holding books and turning pages is still missing. By the time they are in Grades 5 and 6, children see television, relative to print, to be more like real life and easier to understand and learn from; that is, less demanding (Salomon, 1984). Greenfield (1984a) concluded, however, that children learn television information more thoroughly than they learn what they have heard on the radio or have read, and she disagreed with others who say that reading leads to stronger learning.

These considerations have educational implications as well. A balanced education, for example, means using audio to stimulate imagination and to highlight verbal information, and using video to transmit information, especially action information (Greenfield & Beagles-Roos, 1988). As auditory information is retained better when it is accompanied by visual input, the combination of audio and visual may actually enhance listening (Anderson & Collins, 1988).

There are many differences between the learning that goes on with television as opposed to that with radio. According to Suzuki (1989), for example, television's reliance on visual images restricts what can be learned. As radio requires listeners to use their imaginations, it can explore the whole range of concepts and discoveries in science, for example, whereas television's scope is more limited; areas such as math, astronomy, geology, and molecular biology are rarely covered (Suzuki, 1989).

In the Greenfield and Beagles-Roos (1988) study, for information transmission television was associated with better overall retention, reinforcement by visual images, better recall of story action and details, and a more vague recall of characters than from radio. Radio, on the other hand, was associated with more recall of direct dialogue; surprisingly, there was no difference between radio and television for expressive or figurative language. Similarly, Gardner and Krasny Brown (1984) found that the 6- to 10-year-olds in their study remembered more story events after television than from a book, and the younger ones relied more on picture content. They were more likely to act out actions, and they showed an increased repertoire of imagery. More inferences were made, however, with an audio-only presentation such as radio.

In a later study by Greenfield and her colleagues (1986), children in Grades 1 and 2 and Grades 3 and 4 were given a story in a television format or a radio format to compare their ability to complete an incomplete story by introducing new elements. Those who had the radio format showed more imaginative completions, in words used and novel character references, than those with the television presentations. Moreover, there was a carryover effect in that when the television format was preceded by radio, the students showed more imagination; when radio was preceded by television, they showed less, perhaps because of expectations they had set up—relaxation for television and greater effort for radio (Greenfield, Farrar, & Beagles-Roos, 1986). The authors also suggested that the emphasis on listening in the radio format is more similar to the school situation and thus might add to the effort used.

These results also may be interpreted as an indication that the children's television completions were simply less repetitive and more concise, rather than less imaginative. Because the audiovisual version conveyed more information, less elaboration by the children was required (Anderson & Collins, 1988). Greenfield and Beagles-Roos (1988) concluded that children socialized by television may have more information but be less creative, show less precise verbal behavior, and be less active mentally than the generation brought up on radio.

Story content that children generate also appears to differ across various media. For example, in one study (Watkins, 1988) children in Grades 3, 5, and 8 wrote a "TV" story and a "real-life" story. At all three age levels, children who were heavy viewers gave less complex responses and were less invested in the task than those who viewed less television; they gave fewer details, they showed fewer insights into characters, and they placed more emphasis on superficial descriptions of observable action. Children in all three grades distinguished between television and real story content. Television stories involved more adults, distant relationships, and simple actions. The real stories made more use of real-life events and experience, frequently including characters or situations from the students' own experiences. Children who watched more television wrote differently than those who viewed less. Higher levels of viewing were associated with lower real-life complexity and higher television complexity. With the younger children, more viewing was associated with more similarity of real and television stories; for the oldest, more effort was invested in the television than in the real stories (Watkins, 1988).

Children still can enjoy television programs at a superficial level, without seeking to understand at a deeper level, but they do not learn as much from the experience (Salomon & Leigh, 1984). That is, they treat print more seriously and learn more from it. According to Salomon and Leigh (1984) and others, children rely more on their ability when processing print than they do when processing television information, and this appears to be especially true among high-ability children. The worst effects are likely to occur in high-ability children who have the most negative view of television, invest the least effort, and make the poorest inferences (Salomon, 1984).

SUMMARY

As they acquire greater familiarity and experience with television viewing, children develop more efficient strategies to interpret what they see. They use increasingly complex and sophisticated symbolic codes, which allow them to assess how much effort is required and to comprehend television's messages with less than full attention. They tend to invest less mental effort in television viewing than in reading and other school-related tasks. Comparisons of television, radio, and print media have revealed that children attend to and retain different information from each of them; and they use their growing cognitive skills differently to process the information. Many feel that children treat print more seriously, and invest more effort, but children can be directed to view television content in the same way.

II

Social, Emotional, and Behavioral Aspects of the Television Experience

4

Television Violence

Startling statistics have been reported for the number of violent incidents on television to which children are exposed. Lamson (1995) reported that prime-time programs average 8 to 12 violent acts an hour, that a recent study by the Annenberg School of Communication cited 32 violent acts an hour in children's programming—an all-time high—and *TV Guide* tallied 1,845 violent acts in 18 hours of viewing, an average of 100 an hour or one every 36 seconds (Lamson, 1995). In the study commissioned by *TV Guide* results showed more violence than ever and from more sources—cable, home videos, broadcasts and local stations—with reality shows, cartoons, music videos, and promos for violent movies being the worst offenders (Disney, 1995). Cartoons had the most violent scenes (471 in 1 day) of the programs monitored, and one in five of all violent scenes involved a life-threatening assault, most involving guns (Disney, 1995).

Some (e.g., Leonard, 1995) claim that the impact of television violence has been exaggerated, and that ratings concerns actually have led to a decrease in network violence and the airing of mostly sitcoms. Others (Donnerstein, Slaby, & Eron, 1994) maintain that the level of television violence has remained fairly constant over the past two decades, although cable television has added to it. They say most of the violence is presented without context or judgment about its acceptability and most morning and early afternoon violence is seen by children. Assuming 2 to 4 hours viewing a day, by the time a child finishes elementary school, he or she will have seen 8,000 murders and 100,000 other violent acts (Donnerstein et al., 1994): "For the television industry, issues of 'quality' and 'social responsibility' are peripheral to the issue of maximizing audience size—and there is no formula more tried and true than violence for generating large audiences." (Centerwall, 1995, p. 185).

Discovering possible links between viewing such large amounts of violence and aggressive behavior, as well as other behavioral effects, is clearly a very important undertaking.

RESEARCH TO DATE

The relation between television violence and real-life aggression is still a controversial topic, but one that has changed direction somewhat.

Much in the current press assumes a relation between TV violence and aggression. Those who are convinced of the impact of TV violence on children's behavior insist that it is inconsistent and nonsensical to assume that advertisers' 30-second spots effect behavior change but that a half hour of gratuitous television violence will not (Spicer, 1995). Others are quick to point out that many currently middle-aged individuals who watched violence on TV and in movies as children did not become violent, and many other countries that have had TV for over 40 years have far less violence than the United States (Cuff, 1995).

Most researchers agree that there is a strong association between viewing violence and behaving aggressively, but there is considerable disagreement about the nature and direction of that relations and its duration.

Television Violence as a Cause of Aggression

Many researchers claim that exposure to television violence increases aggressive behavior. Some report, for example, that research shows a positive relation between exposure to TV violence and aggressive behavior over many different kinds of measures and ages, and exposure seems not only to increase violence but to decrease prosocial behavior as well (Donnerstein et al., 1994). Centerwall (1995) claimed that his study proved that TV was responsible for doubled homicide rates 10 to 15 years after the introduction of TV, when the first children to view TV could commit crimes in adulthood. Just viewing violent television, even without a subsequent related cue, led to more aggressive behavior than viewing nonviolent television.

Viemero and Paajanen (1990) studied 8- to 10-year-old Finnish children's viewing habits, aggression, aggressive and fear fantasies, and fantasies and dreams about TV using self-rated and peer-nominated measures of aggression. They found significant positive relations for boys between aggression and TV viewing variables and a significant positive relation between amount of TV and viewing of violence, on one hand, and fear and aggressive fantasies and fantasies about TV content that they had seen on the other. These correlations occurred less often for girls, but held for all ages, although more frequently for older children. The authors concluded that the results support the information-processing theory that the more children watch television, the more they fantasize about the programs and replay the scenes they saw, which then leads to explicit aggressive behavior.

Paik and Comstock (1994) reported an updated meta-analysis that confirmed Hearold's (1986) findings with clearly positive relations between exposure to television violence and antisocial and aggressive behavior, with positive and significant effects for field studies and time-series studies. Moreover, there were significant positive relations between exposure to violence and seriously harmful and criminal acts.

In another meta-analysis, Wood, Wong, and Chacere (1991) looked at the effects of exposure to media violence on behavior in spontaneous social interactions. They found that exposure to violence was associated with more aggressiveness with strangers, friends, and classmates when aggregate findings were examined, but the effect was not consistent across studies. There were stronger relations with normal than with emotionally disturbed children and in laboratory settings over others.

Wood et al. (1991) noted that the effect size is important given that the behavioral assessment occurred during natural interactions. In addition, they noted that "Exposure to media violence may have a small to moderate impact on a single behavior, but cumulated across multiple exposures and multiple social interactions, the impact may be substantial" (p. 378). Thus, the impact over a lifetime might be greater than after only a few episodes. Wood et al. concluded that their analysis demonstrated a causal relation between media violence and aggression, but more research is needed on viewer selection of violent programs and the cumulative impact over time of exposure to such programs.

Laboratory and Field Studies

Others (e.g., Leifer, Gordon, & Graves, 1974; Murray, 1984) have argued that naturalistic and field data, as well as experimental studies of children from preschool to adolescence, support a consensus that viewing violence does influence a child's values, attitudes, and behavior, and that it is associated with increased aggression under certain circumstances. Frustration and provocation may increase the size of the effect, but frustration does not appear to be a necessary condition (Hearold, 1986).

Several researchers have pointed out, however, that laboratory studies reflect short-term effects and not long-term socialization effects of the sort that are examined in naturalistic studies (Lynn, Hampson, & Agahi, 1989; Wackman, Wartella, & Ward, 1977). Milavsky, Kessler, Stipp, and Rubena (1982) concluded that present evidence suggests that short-term effects do not lead to stable real-world aggression. At least findings of television's effects are weaker when more real-life methods are used or when long-term effects and generalization of effects are investigated (Dorr, 1986).

Friedrich-Cofer and Huston (1986) maintained that there is much evidence for a bidirectional relation between viewing violence and aggression, with consistent positive findings from the laboratory and modest but consistent findings from field studies. Others (e.g., Cook,

Kendzierski, & Thomas, 1983) have argued that there is less consistency in results regarding television violence and aggression than has been claimed, that biases may have inflated estimates in the past, and that television's role is likely small compared to other socialization factors. Lynn et al. (1989) found no supportive evidence for a causal relation between amount of television violence viewed and subsequent aggression, and in Sweden, researchers found a high positive relation between television viewing and aggression, although not causal (Rosengren & Windahl, 1989). Still others (Baron & Reiss, 1985; Lynn et al., 1989) have questioned how much impact, particularly long term, such viewing actually does have on behavior.

More recently Wiegman, Kuttschreuter, and Baarda (1992) reported that the possible correlation they found between television violence and aggression almost totally disappeared when they corrected for intelligence and starting level of aggression. They also noted several interesting cross-cultural gender differences. Correlations between television violence and aggression were significant for both genders in the United States and the Netherlands, only for boys in Finland, and for neither gender in Poland and Australia. If all the countries, and an Israeli kibbutz, are included, over half of the longitudinal findings were not significant, and the authors concluded that there was almost no evidence for a causal or bidirectional relation between aggression and viewing violence. Weigman et al. noted that Huesmann and Eron (1986) interpreted the data differently to mean that there is significant evidence to support such a relation; but, they say, Huesmann and Eron's conclusions have been partially supported only in the United States, not in the other countries.

In a review of many earlier studies, Freedman (1984) concluded that there was a small but consistent positive relation between viewing violence and behaving aggressively, but little evidence, at least so far, that viewing it in natural settings or over the long term causes individuals to become more aggressive. Freedman (1986) argued that laboratory effects tend to be magnified and have not been confirmed in field studies. He claimed that lab findings are not likely to generalize for several reasons, including the fact that there is no retaliation for aggressive behavior in laboratory studies, the aggression is not the same as it is usually defined, and it is sanctioned by the experimenter (Freedman, 1984). Moreover, according to Freedman, the effect of one program, or one chosen for an experiment, might be quite different from a mix of nonviolent and violent programming. Finally, as imitation is not total and indiscriminate, the effects depend on program context, such as whether the aggressive person is punished. If the aggression is rewarded, it may lead to an increase; if it is punished, it may lead to a decrease (Freedman, 1984). Although laboratory studies show that children can learn aggressive behaviors from watching television, and viewing violence can disinhibit aggressive responses, field study evidence on the relation between aggressive content and aggressive responses is less strong (Sprafkin, Gadow, & Abelman, 1992). Others (Baron & Reiss, 1985) have criticized the research methodology used in past studies and have claimed that the imitation effects that have been blamed on viewing media violence are statistical artifacts.

Conclusions From Research to Date

Clearly, any relation that exists between viewing violence and aggression is not a clear or linear one. At the very least, recent research dashes any hopes for a simple, unidirectional causal sequence in which viewing of television violence clearly leads to aggressive behavior, and it underscores the fact that previous claims and counterclaims may have been highly oversimplified. Both laboratory and field studies have demonstrated short-term effects (e.g., disinhibition, arousal, and contagion) more clearly than long-term effects (e.g., learning of attitudes, values, and habitual patterns of behavior; Friedrich-Cofer & Huston, 1986).

To be sure, television violence undoubtedly plays an important role in the aggressive behavior of children, and recent moves to reduce the level of violence in TV programming are laudatory indeed. However, many questions remain. Why does violence have such appeal to some viewers? What mediates the relation between television violence and aggressive behavior? What variables are important in this relation? Who is most vulnerable to the effects of television violence? Factors such as opportunity, control, rehearsal, perceived reality, and the presence of an adult affect a child's behavioral response to television and need to be considered. For example, aggressive behaviors and attitudes modeled from television may be acquired but not actually performed when adequate social controls exist (Joy, Kimball, & Zabrack, 1986).

Finally, schools, families, and peers also play important roles. Children learn how aggressive behavior is dealt with on the playground. Did teachers turn a blind eye or offer a protective response? Did they seize the opportunity to teach other alternatives to handling problems? What modeling goes on there? Parents also may model aggression, and the aggressive child learns by example. Peers can exert pressure and model behavior. The frustration of a child who is not learning contributes to that child's potential for increased aggressiveness.

Part of the difficulty in arriving at definitive conclusions in this field of inquiry lies in the definition of violence itself, and what is counted as violent varies from study to study. For example, Schneider (1989) cited Gerbner's broad definition of violence ("any antisocial behavior in goal seeking," p. 163), and said his results regarding the amount of violent content that children watch is less startling because it includes slapstick, pratfalls, and so on. Hess (1995) said Eron's definition of aggressive behavior is narrower, and includes behavior intended to irritate or injure. Most accounts of violence restrict it largely to physical injury and do not include the frequent verbal abuse, intimidation, aggressive humor, sarcasm, or other forms of verbal aggression of many programs, which may be quite upsetting to young children.

INTERVENING VARIABLES

Significant developmental and gender variables, family background and attitudes, and the quality and nature of a child's other experiences, as well as his or her perception of the television portrayal, are important factors that influence television's impact. Other factors that affect the likelihood of an individual actually performing a specific aggressive act include arousal level of the viewer, predisposition to act aggressively, whether the behavior is reinforced, the nature of the television content, and the viewing context.

In the following paragraphs we consider the many variables that are involved in the relation between television viewing of violence and actual aggressive behavior. We take a look at the developmental variables that influence who will react aggressively, as well as some of the television features that make a difference. We also consider some proposed mechanisms by which viewing violence might be translated into actual aggressive behavior (i.e., the "how" of the relation, and at some of the effects other than increased aggressiveness that viewing violence can have.

Viewer Variables

Developmental Level. The cognitive and social maturity of children at the time of viewing is a critical variable in any relation between viewing violence and aggressive behavior. As children's level of comprehension of television content and their own behavioral controls are not fully developed, the potential effect of violent portrayals may be considerably stronger for children than for adults. Moreover, younger children are more likely to be affected by specific aspects such as the more salient aggressive acts, whereas issues such as justification for those acts may be lost (Rule & Ferguson, 1986). In addition, whereas adults can distance themselves from violent television programs, young children feel very involved and see the images as real (Van der Voort, 1986), and are more likely to imitate aggression because they do not understand the consequences of that behavior as well as older children and adults do. They do not even understand that death is permanent (Cannon, 1995).

These factors become especially important when one considers that children frequently watch programs that are not child oriented but intended for an adult audience.

During the period between ages 9 and 12, an important one for changing perception and experience, children tend to watch more television and, hence, more violence (Van der Voort, 1986). By age 12 they are less inclined to view the violent programs negatively, and even when violence and aggressive behavior are not directly related, the effects of viewing violence may appear in the form of less civility and a decrease in affiliative and other prosocial behavior rather than more aggression (Van der Voort, 1986). As they mature, in the 9- to 12-year-old range, individuals understand better, they are less inclined to see television violence as realistic, they tend to be more detached and respond less emotionally, and they are less frightened by violence (Van der Voort, 1986).

On the other hand, Paik and Comstock (1994) reported a positive association between viewing violence and antisocial behavior regardless of age, from nursery school to adulthood. Preschoolers showed the highest effect size but are least capable of acting on it, although violence among preschoolers is as real to them as other violence is to adults, and long-term consequences need to be considered (Paik & Comstock, 1994).

Intelligence Level. Several sets of studies have noted a relation between intelligence and aggression. Weigman and his colleagues (1992) found a significant negative relation between intelligence and both aggression and viewing of television. Children who watched a lot of aggression and who also behaved aggressively were lower in intelligence. In boys, intelligence was related to less viewing of violence and less aggressive behavior. Correlations were in the same direction for girls, but were not significant. The researchers noted, however, the important difficulties in trying to compare various studies, as some that intended to measure intelligence actually measured only academic achievement; and school achievement is a less stable factor that may be influenced by television and by aggression.

Lynn et al. (1989) also reported significant negative correlations between IQ and both amount of viewing of violence and enjoyment of it, and similar correlations between families. However, when they examined within-family correlations, the relations dropped and none was statistically significant, leading Lynn et al. to conclude that the correlations were due to some other factor common to both intelligence and television viewing.

One report noted that children who have superior analytic and language skills are more likely to imagine different viewpoints, are less likely to use force to persuade others, are more able to foresee consequences of their behavior, and have a greater range of behavioral options to violence (*American Psychological Association*, 1995).

Huesmann and colleagues' (Huesmann, Eron, Lefkowitz, & Walder, 1984; Huesmann, Eron, & Yarmel, 1987) data collection over 22 years on the relationship between intellectual functioning and aggressiveness, found that aggression interfered with intellectual development and predicted poorer adult intellectual achievement. They hypothesized that lower intelligence increases the likelihood of learning aggressive responses early and then this aggressiveness makes continued intellectual development more difficult, and they considered both to be stable characteristics across generations and within marriages.

Gender.   Others have found that gender differences also exist in the relation between viewing violence and aggression. According to Turner, Hesse, and Peterson-Lewis (1986), the evidence supports a hypothesis that television results in a long-term increase in aggression in boys but not girls. Paik and Comstock (1994) found a consistent positive and significant gender effect, but only slightly higher for males in more realistic survey studies. Given the higher base rate for violence in males, however, Paik and Comstock considered this small gender difference to make the effect more troublesome socially.

Some (Van der Voort, 1986) have found that although viewing frequency is similar for males and females, they differ in their program preferences. Boys prefer violent programs, whereas girls prefer nonviolent ones. Girls enjoy violence less, approve of it less, and see it as less realistic. However, they also get frightened more easily, respond more emotionally, and watch in a more involved, less detached way (Van der Voort, 1986). Others have reported that boys seem more drawn to violent shows and are more agitated by them, whereas girls are more often repelled by them and saddened (Levine, 1995).

Finally, Lynn et al. (1989) reported more family aggression effects of viewing television violence for sisters than for brothers or brother–sister pairs, which suggests that girls may be more susceptible to influences of the family, including viewing violence on television. They stated further that boys and girls experience the same television viewing environment in the family and therefore differences in enjoyment of violence and in aggressive behavior must be due to factors other than environment. However, this view ignores the fact that the "same" environment is never really the same as there are subtle differences in cues for acceptability, much data regarding identification with same-sex characters, and other gender differences within the family.

Arousal Level.   Several researchers (e.g., Greer, Potts, Wright, & Huston, 1982; Huston-Stein, Fox, Green, Watkins, & Whitaker, 1981; Potts, Huston, & Wright, 1986) have tried to sort out the relative contributions of action (salience) and violence (content) in television's effects on the attention and social behavior of children. Although variation in content and in the viewing context affect children's comprehension as well, it appears to be the salience of violence on television that attracts attention and thus facilitates understanding and memory of the material (Rule & Ferguson, 1986). Younger children are more susceptible to the arousal effect (Hearold, 1986; Van der Voort, 1986).

Once a child's arousal level is increased, toys and other materials in the environment become especially important. In one study (Josephson, 1987), boys noted as characteristically high-aggressive boys showed more aggressive behavior after they had viewed violent television and after they had also been shown a related cue subsequently than did those boys who viewed violent television but did not receive a subsequent cue. However, both the violent content and the cue may have suppressed aggressive behavior in boys rated as characteristically low in aggression (Josephson, 1987).

In the study by Potts et al. (1986), aggressive toys elicited more generalized aggressive behavior but they led not only to more fantasy and object aggression, but also to more verbal and physical aggression in the boys' play. The authors suggested that the arousal phenomena may be most likely in an environment with few behavioral constraints. Thus, if Rambo toys elicit aggressive behavior after watching television, it may be due less to modeling of the television content than to general arousal, which is then followed by cuing of aggressive behavior by available toys; the aggressive behavior is activated by toy cues rather than directly imitated.

The difference between arousal and modeling hypotheses is that "arousal can increase the likelihood of behavior that is different in kind from the behavior shown by the model" (Greer et al., 1982, p. 611). That is, arousal is a motivational state that provides energy that is then directed by environmental, situational, or individual cues. The more that cues in real life approximate those on television, the more likely aggressive behavior is (Dorr, 1986). These observations assume even greater importance in the context of the new media that seem to be associated with higher levels of arousal and are discussed more fully in chapter 10.

Initial Levels of Aggression. According to Messaris (1986), data reveal the importance of preexisting aggressive tendencies in a child's response to aggressive television fare; the programs trigger rather than teach the aggressive behavior. Lynn et al. (1989) suggested that only those children with a genetic predisposition to behave aggressively will be affected by television violence.

In their longitudinal study on the effects of viewing aggressive and prosocial behaviors, carried out in the Netherlands, Wiegman et al.

(1992) found a significant positive correlation between viewing violence and aggressive behavior, but the relation all but disappeared when starting levels of aggression and intelligence were controlled. They concluded that their data could not support the social learning view that viewing violence leads to aggression.

Huesmann, Eron, et al. (1984), in a study over 22 years with data on the aggressiveness of over 600 children as well as their parents and children, showed that children who were more aggressive at 8 years old were more aggressive at 30 years old. Early aggressive behavior predicted later antisocial and criminal behavior, and the stability of aggression across generations within a family when measured at comparable ages was higher than it was within individuals across ages. Huesmann, Eron, et al. concluded that whatever causes it, aggression is a trait that is persistent and constant across situations once it has been established, although it may be influenced by situational factors.

In another study, boys who watched violence and identified with violent characters were more aggressive 2 years later no matter what their original level of aggressive behavior was. The degree of identification of the child with the television character, then, may be as important as the amount of viewing or exposure (Huesmann, 1986).

Furthermore, repeated exposure to violent solutions to problems may work to perpetuate high levels of aggression and work against society's demands for more controlled and mature behavior (Friedrich-Cofer & Huston, 1986). In addition, the motivational state of the viewer, such as frustration or anger, may also make him or her especially prone to imitating the violence seen (Huston-Stein & Friedrich, 1975).

Perhaps Chesterton, writing in the 1920s, said it best. In response to the furor over a child who had killed his father with a knife after viewing a silent movie, Chesterton wrote, "this may possibly have occurred, though if it did, anybody of common sense would prefer to have details of that particular child, rather than about that particular picture" (cited in Jensen & Graham, 1995, p. 109).

Viewing Variables

Perceived Reality.   Hearold (1986) conducted a meta-analysis, based on data for over 100,000 individuals, which involved over 1,000 comparisons and included laboratory experiments, surveys, and field studies from both psychology and communications. One of her conclusions was that television realism was the most important factor, at least for older viewers. This finding raises important developmental issues. Older viewers can more easily make distinctions between real and fantasy; younger ones cannot. If such developmental differences are not taken into account, many of the findings that have been reported may be misinterpreted. Preschoolers' ability to distinguish real and fantasy is an important concern as they are the ones who are most likely to be watching cartoons, including violent ones.

On the other hand, Wiegman et al. (1992) found that although children who saw more aggression scored higher on perceived reality, there was no significant relation between perceived reality and aggression. They concluded that perceived reality does not moderate the relation. Identification with characters, however, was significantly correlated with viewing violence; children who identified more with characters watched more violence and vice versa.

According to Hearold (1986) the least effect of television violence should occur after viewing cartoon violence in which aggression is punished, negative consequences are shown, and the perpetrator is a "totally bad person" or one who does not do anything good. Fowles (1992) also suggested that in cartoons the consequences of violence are not shown, and that children like to watch cartoons because they can behave aggressively vicariously, without repercussions. Fowles also said that it helps them cut tensions and that evidence that they stir children up is weak. He claimed that in the short term, television leads to decreased pressure and relaxation, as with adults, but long-term effects are still not known.

The greatest effects, on the other hand, according to Hearold (1986) should be with a newscast of triumphant soldiers or police putting down a riot; that is, real violence that is justified and followed by reward, with no negative consequences. Endlessly repeating brutally violent footage, such as the Rodney King beatings, is upsetting to people because it is real (Jensen & Graham, 1995).

Rubin, Perse, and Taylor (1988) suggested that people evaluate television content before they incorporate it into social perceptions, and if the violence is seen as unrealistic, it may be discounted. On the other hand, if it is perceived as realistic, the situation changes. We do know that the violence seen daily on the news can affect viewers. O'Keefe and Reid-Nash (1987) found that attention to television news led to greater fearfulness and more concern about protecting one's self from crime, likely because of the way in which television presents crime news and the nature of the audience's attention. The reverse was true with newspaper news, where greater concern about crime came first and led to more attention to the papers (O'Keefe & Reid-Nash, 1987). The fact that they found no overall relation between crime shows and fear as they found with the news was perhaps due to the fact that the viewers understand clearly that news is real.

What impact do these same shows have on young viewers? Young children, who have difficulty with reality–fantasy distinctions, would not likely be able to make a discrimination between news and crime shows. For them, the fear-evoking characteristics of both would be about equal. Moreover, their inability to understand subtle dimensions of the information, political intrigue, language intricacies, and many other aspects of what they view, makes their experience a very different one from that of older children and adults.

The realism of the violence, the degree to which the child feels that a program realistically and accurately reflects life, and the level of identification of the viewer with the victim or with the aggressors, are important factors in its impact (Eron, 1982). In Huesmann and Eron's (1986) study, the positive correlation between aggressive behavior and the perceived realism of television violence was significant for both genders, and both genders now perceive television to be equally realistic (Huesmann & Eron, 1986). As the perceived realism of violence decreases from Grade 1 to Grade 5, however (Eron, 1982), there may be less reactivity to it with age, both because of habituation and because of less identification with or sympathy for the characters.

Amount of Viewing.   Although the frequency of exposure is an important factor as well, its role in the association with aggressive behavior is not a clear-cut one. Lynn et al. (1989) suggested that the amount of time spent watching television violence is less important in later aggression than an individual's genetic predisposition and that an individual's reaction to violence, such as amount of enjoyment expressed about a violent show, is more important than the amount of violence viewed.

Socioeconomic level may be an interactive factor here as well. Van der Voort (1986) found that children from lower SES homes not only engaged in higher levels of viewing, but also showed more enjoyment of and approval of violence, identified more strongly with the television characters, and had lower achievement levels at school. They often are left alone with the TV as a babysitter (Scheer, 1995).

Family Background.   Family attitudes toward aggression also constitute a critical variable in television's impact. Parental influence through the medium of modeling, punishment, and choice of discipline, as well as through general attitudes toward aggression and toward the child, is strong. Many researchers have noted the relationship between parental discipline styles and aggressiveness in children. Singer and Singer (1986), for example, reported that children in high-aggression groups were more likely to have experienced power-assertive techniques, and harsh physical punishment has been associated with aggressive behavior in youth (Farrington, 1991; Pepler & Slaby, 1994; Straus, 1991). Wiegman et al. (1992) also found that parents' punishment style was related to children's aggression but not to viewing violence.

Others have noted the relationship between parental attitudes toward television in general and toward violence in particular, and aggressiveness in children. Children whose parents are less concerned about television violence's effects show a stronger preference for violence, respond less emotionally, tend to be more aggressive, and, although needing them most, are less likely to learn critical viewing skills (Van der Voort, 1986). Messaris (1986) suggested that children do not imitate television unless others have previously encouraged them, intentionally or not, to engage in the particular kind of behavior being imitated. Previous encouragement or discouragement of a behavior by parents may be the crucial factor in whether a child imitates it after viewing it on television independent of any intervention that the parent makes in the actual television experience.

On the other hand, Lynn et al. (1989) interpreted the low correlations between siblings on aggression to indicate a lack of shared family environmental effects such as amount of television violence viewed by families.

CAUSAL EXPLANATIONS

Although there is considerable agreement that an association between viewing violence and aggressive behavior exists, particularly in short-term laboratory studies, there is far less agreement on the nature of that relation or its causes, and several explanatory models have been put foward in an attempt to understand it better.

Modeling

The relation between violence on TV and aggressive behavior has often been attributed to modeling or social learning as the mediating variable. A particularly strong finding is the report of a significant increase in aggressive behavior, both physical and verbal, among children in a community with no television after television was introduced to that town (Joy et al., 1986). Those increases, still apparent 2 years after the introduction of television, occurred not just in children who were already aggressive, but in children who were low in aggression initially. Some children may imitate television violence whether or not their parents condone violent content because it gives them feelings of power and adventure ("Full of Sound and Fury," 1994).

Sawin (1990) studied preschoolers in small play groups to more closely simulate home viewing conditions and to study the influence of an adult's presence. Children were classed at baseline as low, moderate, or high in aggression, and Sawin looked at short-term effects of arousal as well as cumulative effects on learning. The children were shown violent and nonviolent content and became more aggressive during the exposure to the latter. They also showed increased aggression with an adult present, and these findings were true for both genders and for all baseline levels of aggression.

Sawin (1990) explained these rather surprising findings in terms of differences between the two programs in their tendencies to elicit imitation. Although violent content did not lead to more aggression, the violent content did have more influence on the play activities of the children, especially among the high-aggressive boys. Sawin explained that the violent content (*Batman*) led to fairly structured reenactment in later play and less hurtful aggression than in the more diffuse play after a nonviolent program. The children who viewed the nonviolent content were bored, showed fewer group fantasy activities, no alternative imitative behaviors, and more harmful aggressive acts.

There were interesting and important socioeconomic differences, however. The findings already described were for children from lower SES backgrounds. For children from middle class homes, the aggressive film led to a higher number of harmful and more diffuse aggressive behaviors without the less harmful imitation that the lower SES children had shown, and middle-class children engaged in more thematic play after the nonviolent content and reenacted it.

Sawin (1990) explained the greater level of aggressiveness with an adult present as seemingly due to the adult's passive role. The adult did not respond to aggression in the early stages, which may have been seen as approval and thus reinforced the behavior. Or, perhaps it was meant to force the adult to intervene, indicating that how adults respond is an important short-term influence on how much television violence affects children.

Comstock and Paik (1991) noted that studies with young children, such as Bandura's (1967) with the Bobo doll, have good external validity because young children do not understand experimentation and would not role play. That validity also is enhanced, according to Comstock and Paik, by more naturalistic studies that produce similar results, by studies of communities before and after the introduction of television such as the work of Williams (1986), and the many studies by Singer and Singer and their colleagues that showed positive relations between viewing violence and behaving aggressively with no evidence that other variables were the cause.

On the other hand, not all children who view violence become aggressive, and a simple social learning theoretical model does not explain why some children appear to be more interested in television violence, enjoy it more, and are more affected by it. Comstock and Paik (1991) said that factors or contingencies that play a role in media effects include four dimensions, and whatever heightens these dimensions increases the likelihood of similar behavior in the future. These are:

1. Efficacy, whether rewarded or punished.
2. Normativeness, whether justified, with consequences, intentionally hurtful, and so on.
3. Pertinence, similar to viewer, commonality of cues.
4. Susceptibility, predisposition to act aggressively, pleasure, frustration, anger, lack of criticism.

Factors that might facilitate effects include identification with the perpetrator, justification or reward for antisocial behavior, and cues that appear to exist in real life (Paik & Comstock, 1994). Wober and Gunter (1988) concluded that "a limited version of the theory can probably be said to be widely accepted—that some violence instigates violent actions among some viewers, on some occasions" (p. 17).

If a child who is very frustrated in his or her interpersonal relationships watches a good deal of violent content, for example, and if that child receives little other competing information to counter aggression as a solution, he or she may imitate it. Another child with the same interpersonal problem who learns alternate strategies from parents or peers or who is actively discouraged from using the aggressive techniques observed on television may not emulate the television models.

Wiegman et al. (1992) also found that in a naturalistic viewing situation, children view both violent and prosocial programs, so they are highly related, and discrimination between the two variables is difficult. Children who have seen a lot of prosocial models also have watched many aggressive models. The authors say this is important because social learning theory says modeling occurs only with a diet that is more or less pure. They found no evidence that the two types of television models influenced the children's aggressive or prosocial behavior, and they could not find children who watched mostly violent content. Because of this mix, the influence of viewing violence could not be separated from other effects of viewing television.

Selective Exposure

Some argue that not enough attention has been paid to the question of why viewers select some messages and programs over others, known as *selective exposure* (Zillmann & Bryant, 1985b). Although higher levels of viewing may lead to more aggressive behavior, it is also the case that more aggressive children select violent television more frequently (Eron, 1982; Friedrich-Cofer & Huston, 1986; Huesmann, 1986; Huesmann, Eron, et al., 1984). Children who are predisposed to behave aggressively and view aggression do act more aggressively afterward (Singer, 1980), but their aggressive predisposition may well determine their viewing preferences as well. In other words, there is selective exposure to television violence (Zillmann & Bryant, 1985b).

Cultivation Theory

Gerbner's cultivation theory (Gerbner, Gross, Morgan, & Signorielli, 1980), described in more detail in chapter 9, deals with the cumulative effects of viewing television violence. According to this view, heavy viewers of television share a commonality of outlook that is consistent with television portrayals, and may develop distorted and inaccurate perceptions of violence in the real world. There is also some evidence that people tend to change attitudes and behavior to correspond more closely with what they see on television, provided it is not counter to social prescriptions (Cheney, 1983). For example, women watching aggression do not immediately become aggressive, but men watching aggression become more aggressive.

Cognitive-Neoassociationist Theory

In his cognitive-neoassociationist theory, Berkowitz (1986) asserted that viewing aggression disinhibits viewers' controls on aggressive behavior. If the aggression is approved, the disinhibition increases, and aggression is more likely, although the aggressive acts are not necessarily imitations of the specific acts seen on television (Berkowitz, 1986). According to Berkowitz (1988), even neutral stimuli can evoke aggressive behavior when they are associated in one's mind with aversive conditions or events; that is, negative feelings evoke aggressive tendencies, and this process underlies the aggression that often follows frustration. In addition, later comments or objects may serve as retrieval cues for aggressive thoughts that occur during the viewing of a violent program through a system of semantically related concepts (Berkowitz, 1986; Berkowitz & Rogers, 1986).

Berkowitz and Rogers (1986) also noted the role of a *priming effect,* or the increased likelihood that an activated concept or elements of thought associated with it will come to mind again for some time after it has been activated. Furthermore, viewing violence can prime related thoughts, resulting in a greater likelihood that other aggressive thoughts will be recalled quite automatically and involuntarily (Berkowitz & Rogers, 1986). Later comments or objects then may serve as retrieval cues for aggressive thoughts that occur during the television viewing (Berkowitz, 1986).

When a child does not behave aggressively after viewing violence, it may be because he or she did not attend to or concentrate on the aggressive aspects of the material (Berkowitz, 1986), or because language and cognitive skills are not sufficiently developed for semantically related concepts to operate (Berkowitz & Rogers, 1986). Violent television content also may contribute to aggressive behavior by reinforcing and maintaining certain attitudes and beliefs about violence, or by justifying it and decreasing anxiety about it (Donnerstein et al., 1994).

Script Theory

The real-life experience of children is an important determinant of television's effect as well. As most viewers have little real-life experience with violence but much exposure to it on television, most of the knowledge and scripts about violence are likely derived initially from, and hence influenced by, television (Williams, 1986). If only aggressive scripts are acquired during the sensitive period when children acquire a network of behavioral scripts, they can only behave aggressively (Huesmann, 1986, 1988).

Huesmann and Eron (1986) suggested that children store aggressive solutions in memory and use them to guide their behavior. Those who watch lots of violence are more likely to develop cognitive scripts that entail violence or aggression as a solution, and they may be rehearsed in fantasy. Moreover, the more that children rehearse aggression in fantasy, the more likely they are to recall such scripts and the more aggressive their overt behavior becomes (Eron, 1982; Huesmann, 1988; Huesmann, Lagerspetz, & Eron, 1984). Individual differences in aggression after viewing violence are due to a cumulative learning process that strengthens the schemas or scripts for aggressive behavior (Huesmann, 1986). On the other hand, Lynn et al. (1989) found no increase in the correlations between violence viewing and aggression over the age range of 11 to 15 years old, which they felt is inconsistent with a cumulative effect of viewing violence.

According to Huesmann (1988), aggressive behavior usually has negative consequences, including decreased popularity, poorer achievement, and parent–teacher intervention. For most children these expected consequences lead to an inhibition of aggressive scripts. For some, however, negative consequences lead to more aggression. As aggressive behavior becomes a habit, it interferes with social and academic adjustment and leads to greater frustration and more aggressive behavior (Huesmann, 1988; Huesmann & Eron, 1986).

Social-processing deficits also may interfere with creative conflict resolutions and individuals with such deficits tend to generate fewer solutions and more aggressive ones (Geen, 1994). If aggression is learned early as a problem-solving technique, it is very resistant to change (Eron, 1980, 1986; Huesmann, 1988).

Habituation and Desensitization

One of the most alarming aspects of television violence is its potential to habituate and desensitize people to violence and aggression after significant exposure over a long period of time Drabman & Thomas, 1975; Himmelweit, Swift, & Jaeger, 1980; Huston-Stein & Friedrich, 1975; Van der Voort (1986). According to Van der Voort (1986), heavy viewers are less likely to see violence as "terrible." They enjoy and prefer violence, they are more likely to see it as justified, and they show less emotional reactivity to repeated viewing of violent programs. A decrease in physiological arousal and emotional intensity after frequent exposures to violence has also been demonstrated (Rule & Ferguson, 1986). Griffiths and Shuckford (1989) suggested that desensitization occurs because stimuli lose their novelty and importance for the viewer because of changed expectations through conditioning associated with viewing violence.

Linz, Donnerstein, and Penrod (1984) suggested that these changes in perceptions and emotional reactions to violence can lead to less emotional response or intervention when actual aggression occurs, which may be as important as the decreased inhibitions against behaving aggressively, findings which are consistent with other studies that have been done with children (Linz et al., 1984). Worries abound that perhaps children of our violent media culture will not only become more aggressive, but may also be slow to help victims of real-life aggression.

Much research does show callousness toward female victims, especially rape victims, after exposure to violence or sexually explicit content, with perhaps an even greater effect on younger viewers who do not have critical viewing skills or experience to negate such portrayals (Donnerstein et al., 1994). After continued exposure, then, alterations in perception and affect may carry over to real-life situations. Rock videos are likely to be as influential as other TV programs, maybe moreso because of their slick and addictive quality, their rhythms, and their appeal for teens and preteens with VCRs (Lefrancois, 1995).

Jerzy Kosinski's (cited in Sohn, 1982) recounting of an experience he had while teaching is a rather disconcerting one. Video monitors were installed on either side of a blackboard in a large classroom to which several 7- to 10-year-old children had been invited. As he sat reading them a story, he was attacked by an intruder (a prearranged event), who rushed into the room and began hitting and pushing him and arguing with him. Cameras filmed the incident and the reactions of the students. To his dismay, most of the students rarely looked at the actual happening in the room; rather, they watched it on the television monitors, which were easier for them to see:

Later, when we talked about it, many of the children explained that they could see the attack better on the screens. After all, they pointed out, they could see close-ups of the attacker and of me, his hand on my face, his expressions—all the details they wanted—without being frightened by "the real thing" (or by the necessity of becoming involved, the kids were less interested in the actual assault than in what the TV cameras were doing—as if they had paid to see a film, as if the incident had been staged to entertain them! And all during the confrontation—despite my yelling, his threats, the fear that I showed—the kids did not interfere or offer to help. None of them. They sat transfixed as if the TV cameras neutralized the act of violence. And perhaps they did. By filming a brutal physical struggle from a variety of viewpoints, the cameras transformed a human conflict into an aesthetic happening, distancing the audience and allowing them an alternative to moral judgment and involvement (Sohn, 1982, pp. 356, 359).

Genotype–Environment Correlation and Interaction Theory

Lynn et al. (1989) claimed that their genotype–environment correlation and interaction theory takes into account two important factors not included in other explanatory models: a) the genotype–environment correlation (the way parents pass on characteristics to their children through genetic and environmental means), and b) the genotype–environment interaction (the idea that genetic predispositions cause children to act differently within the same environment). The genotype–environment correlation tends to increase similarities among siblings of a family, whereas the genotype–environment interaction tends to decrease similarities. Lynn et al. suggested that such a model differentiates among passive viewers of violence (children who watch with the whole family) and active viewers of violence (children who seek out violent programs). In their model, viewing of violence affects only those individuals who are predisposed genetically to choose aggressive TV characters as models. They claimed that the enjoyment of television violence is the significant variable, not the amount of viewing. They believed that the results from their study of more than 2,000 children in Northern Ireland are hard to explain by a sociological or social learning theory, but that the theory is salvageable if it is reformulated in terms of their genotype–environment correlation and interaction model.

Conclusions

After reviewing the vast literature on theoretical points of view, including modeling and imitation, disinhibition, arousal, and more recently, the perception of aggression as normative, Geen and Thomas (1986) concluded that:

- Children may learn aggressive behaviors but not act them out without reinforcement.
- Modeling does not account for aggressive behaviors that differ from those observed, but these may be explained by a cognitive associative perspective.
- Media violence may increase arousal and lead to subsequent aggression.
- Viewers who see "justified" aggression may feel that aggression is an appropriate response to provocation.
- There is little evidence for a catharsis view that viewing violence actually leads to a decrease in aggressive behavior.
- Field studies yield a mixed picture, and the search today is for complex intervening processes.

Of the many interacting factors, Sawin (1990) said, "Exposure to television violence results in increases in aggressive behavior for *some* children in *some* situations, but there are insignificant or no direct instigating effects on the behavior of other children in other situations" (p. 175).

Different responses to violence result from variations in children's cognitive development, social learning, and situational variables. "The cumulative evidence indicates that these antecedent, concurrent, and subsequent subject and situational variables serve as filters of media content, and as modifiers of television's effects" (Sawin, 1990, p. 176). Rather than looking at television's effects on children's behavior, Sawin urged further study of children's learning and cognitive developmental factors to see how they modify response to television.

OTHER EFFECTS OF VIEWING VIOLENCE

Behavioral Changes

Viewing violence on television can affect behavior in other ways than aggressiveness, including materialism and unlawful behavior (Hearold, 1986), and physical effects such as obesity (Dietz & Gortmaker, 1985; Kolata, 1986). In a poll of over 70,000 *USA Weekend* readers, 86% reported changes in their children's behavior after watching a violent show, but they also reported that sometimes the children became more detached, "spaced out," and passive (Levine, 1995). In addition, a report by the National Health and Education Consortium described limits on cognitive development, less ability to form close relationships, and disturbed physiological functioning as consequences of children's increased exposure to televised and real-life violence. It claimed that violence also diverts children's attention from learning in school to protection of self and families (American Psychological Association, 1995).

Fear and Anxiety

One common reaction to television violence is fear, which has received a good deal less attention than aggression despite its importance. In one discussion of television violence with some 10-year olds in a downtown Toronto fifth-grade class, virtually all of them reported having seen things on television that terrified them. They recalled nightmares, worries about parent behavior after watching abusive parents on television, and fears that scary things that happened on television could happen to them (Waisglas, 1992).

In one study (Ridley-Johnson, Surdy, & O'Laughlin, 1991), parents were as concerned about television contributing to fear and passivity in their adolescent children as they were about aggression-related effects. There was also a gender difference in parental concerns: Parents were as concerned about the fear-related effects for girls as for boys, but there was more concern about aggression-related effects among parents of boys. Ridley-Johnson et al. said this is consistent with learning theory as well as current socialization practices, because both genders can learn about aggression from TV violence, but whether those attitudes and behaviors are actually expressed depends on other variables such as expectations and consequences, and how the boys and girls are socialized and reinforced differently for aggressive behavior. TV violence also may have more of an effect on boys because they model the aggression as acceptable and see the world as threatening (Ridley-Johnson et al., 1991).

On the other hand, Cooke (1995) pointed out that concerns about harmful media effects arose before television and date back to the 1930s and 1940s, when studies warned of radio's negative effects on school performance and on children's ability to distinguish reality from fantasy and blamed comic books for poor reading skills.

INTERVENTION STRATEGIES

Whatever the final outcome of research on the relation between viewing violent television content and aggressive behavior, no one has argued that heavy viewing of violence is a desirable behavior or one that enhances a child's development, and there is virtually no evidence to support a catharsis view in which viewing violence leads to a decrease in aggressive behavior by draining off a child's aggressive tendencies in fantasy. Although other variables clearly interact with the amount of violence viewed, there are still strong reasons, both cognitive and behavioral, to reduce excessive amounts of violence viewing.

Reducing Levels of Television Violence

Research to date does indicate strongly that reducing levels of viewing of such violent programming would be a worthy aim. How this might be accomplished is less clear, but there is widespread concern about the level of violence and there are many moves afoot to limit it. Options include voluntary reductions of violence by networks, regulatory controls, enforced rating systems, and technological devices for television sets.

In Canada, for example, 200,000 Canadians petitioned the Canadian Radio-television and Telecommunications Commission (CRTC) after the Montréal massacre in 1989 in which 14 young women were gunned down at their university; 1.3 million signed a petition demanding legislative action against violence, circulated by a young woman whose sister had been raped and murdered; and 350,000 teachers also had urged action (Spicer, 1995). According to Keith Spicer, former head of the CRTC, the Canadian approach to violence was to try to reduce it on a number of fronts: 80% by way of public education through various groups and associations, 10% through technological devices such as the V-chip (described more fully in the next paragraph), and 10% through voluntary codes. The hope was to balance creative expression and children's health through consensus and cooperation, rather than through regulations and new laws. One author noted that when voluntary guidelines on violence were announced by the networks in 1992, reporters could not find any producers who thought those guidelines would require any changes in their programming (Centerwall, 1995). In addition to trying to reduce violent content, the CRTC also aimed to encourage more creative and intelligent children's programming.

Programs also have been developed to reduce the effects of exposure to violent content. Huesmann and his colleagues (1983), for example, studied first and third graders who had high levels of exposure to violence. Over a 2-year period, they gave some a treatment condition developed to reduce the likelihood of them imitating the aggression they had seen. A control group got comparable but neutral treatment. After 2 years, the experimental group showed significantly less aggression as rated by peers, and there was a weaker relation between viewing violence and behaving aggressively (Huesmann, Eron, Klein, Brice, & Fischer, 1983).

Rating Systems

Centerwall (1995) advocated violence ratings for TV, which would not impinge on anyone's freedom of expression but would help parents judge how violent television programs were without having to watch them. The newest ratings in the United States, carried on all of the major networks and some cable stations, began January 1, 1997 and appear on screens at the beginning of shows (New York Times Service and Staff, 1997). Moreover, television sets that have the V-chip can be set to block shows considered unsuitable for children. The ratings include the following:

1. TV-Y, All children–Appropriate for all children, but designed specifically for preschool-age children, ages 2 to 6, and not expected to frighten them.
2. TV-Y7, Directed to Older Children—For children 7 and older, better for children who can distinguish fantasy from reality. May include mild comedic or physical violence, and might frighten younger children.
3. TV-G, General Audience—Appropriate for all ages. Not designed specifically for younger children but alright for them as there is little or no violence, strong language, or sexual situations or dialogue.
4. TV-PG, Parental Guidance—May contain material unsuitable for young children and parents may want to be present if younger children are viewing it. May contain some strong language, suggestive situations, and limited violence.
5. TV-14, Parents Strongly Cautioned—May contain material unsuitable for children younger than 14 and parents should monitor it carefully and not let younger children watch. May contain mature themes, sexual and more violent content, and strong language.
6. TV-M, Mature Audience Only—Designed specifically for adults and may be unsuitable for those younger than 17. May contain graphic violence, explicit sex, mature themes, and profanity (*The New York Times* Service and Staff, 1997).

The whole issue of classification is controversial, however. Some have argued, for example, that classification ignores the context of content, that providing an objective rating or assessment of content is impossible, and that some valuable and acceptable programming would be banned as a result of an "objective" rating of the content (King, 1995). Donnerstein et al. (1994) encouraged parents to use the rating system often, and they said cable operators and videocassette distributors should prominently post ratings for films they are broadcasting or renting.

According to Donnerstein et al., the problem with the current rating system is that content is rated according to what's been seen to be offensive traditionally rather than what has likely to be harmful to children. For example, they suggested that violence should be rated separately from factors such as mature themes, profanity, or sexual content. They pointed out that the system also rates explicit sex more restrictively than violence. Short sex scenes can lead to an R rating, whereas many gory scenes can still occur in PG movies. The system pays little attention to context, stressing amount and explicitness instead (Donnerstein et al., 1994). Moreover, as much of what children watch is aimed at adults, in order to regulate what they watch, controls would have to be very pervasive.

Others are concerned that certain boycott groups would try to control content by threatening advertisers of programs with ratings over their approved level, which would lead to undesirable uniformity and lack of choice (King, 1995).

Technological Aids

One new, and rather controversial, weapon in the war against violence viewing by children is the V-chip. Designed by a Canadian man, Tim Collings, who was determined to deal with TV violence without restricting creative freedom, the V-chip is a technological device that flags programs that exceed a chosen level of violence, language, or sexually explicit content and screens them out. When the system becomes fully operational, every program will have classification signals encoded so that viewers can edit out programs that exceed their specified limits without actually having to view the shows (Atkinson, 1996).

Some concern has arisen that use of the V-chip would mean that broadcasters could then increase levels of violence and explicit sexual content, and children would be exposed to even higher levels. Parental monitoring and responsibility for their children's viewing clearly is still essential, and one problem with devices such as the V-chip is that those parents who use it are likely the ones who already are monitoring or limiting their children's access to violent programming.

As television has been found to be "an effective and pervasive teacher of children and youth" (Slaby, Barham, Eron, & Wilcox, 1994, p. 451), it should be used to contribute to solving the violence issue according to Slaby et al. (1994). They suggested that to accomplish this, the Federal Communications Commission should require limits on dramatized violence during prime time when children are likely to be watching, that television programs be used in educational programs and activities to prevent violence, and that the film rating system be revised to flag violent content more adequately.

Coping with Fear

Wilson, Hoffner, and Cantor (1987) studied the cognitive strategies of three age groups: 3- to 5-year-olds, 6- to 7-year olds, and 9- to 11-year-olds. Cognitive strategies to deal with fear from the media, such as "tell yourself it's not real," increased with age. Noncognitive strategies, such as playing with a toy or eating or drinking, which may distract children from a scary program or provide physical comfort (e.g., hugging a blanket), were more effective for younger children and decreased with age. Sitting near parents was popular with all age groups, and avoiding looking at frightening stimuli (e.g., covering one's face) was not popular at any age. In any case, scary shows were popular with children and fright reactions were common (Wilson et al., 1987).

Some aspects of socialization may affect which coping strategies viewers use, and coping strategies such as avoidance or interpersonal comfort were used more by girls than boys in one study, although both used cognitive coping strategies more equally (Hoffner, 1995).

SUMMARY

The impact of viewing television violence on various facets of social behavior is a critical, but extraordinarily complex, area of investigation. The relation between viewing violence on television and subsequent aggressive behavior appears to have been oversimplified frequently in the past. Issues of realism, salience, arousal, toy cuing, strength of identification, family attitudes and behavior, habituation and desensitization, past experience, situational variables, behavioral controls, amount of viewing, and purpose of viewing, as well as gender and age differences, all interact to determine whether an individual will actually behave aggressively after viewing violence. *conclusion*

Newer research suggests that although television viewing of violence frequently has been associated with increased aggressive behavior, at least over the short term and in laboratory studies, its long-term effect in naturalistic settings is less clear. However, repeated exposure may serve to maintain a short-term effect. Many writers view the relation between viewing of violence and aggression as bidirectional, where increases in aggressive behavior follow such viewing, but aggressive children, or children predisposed to act aggressively, more frequently select violent programs as well.

Children can be helped to deal with their reactions to television violence, and various technological aids and ratings systems are now available to help parents control their children's television viewing.

Viewing television violence affects children in other ways as well, with increased fear as the most common effect. Parents need to monitor their children's viewing, decrease the amount of violence their children view, and help them develop coping strategies when they are exposed to material that frightens them.

5

Television and Other Behavior

Although much has been written about television's negative impact, it clearly can be a positive force as well. It can stimulate the imagination as long as a child does not depend on it for imaginative activity (Singer & Singer, 1986). It can be used to increase creativity and tolerance (Rosenkoetter, Huston, & Wright, 1990). It can teach prosocial skills (de Groot, 1994; Forge & Phemister, 1987; Potts et al., 1986; Rushton, 1988), and it can move extraordinary numbers of people to act charitably, as was demonstrated very dramatically by the success of the Live Aid concert and the number of other "aid" concerts that followed. It can provide dramatization of experience, a view of history unfolding, solid entertainment, and an increasing sense of community (TVO, 1985). It can facilitate the location of missing children, and it can be used to strengthen family ties and values. It can provide role models for children and teach coping skills, as well as reverse negative images and stereotypes (Hattemer & Showers, 1995b; Liebert, Sprafkin, & Davidson, 1982).

PROSOCIAL BEHAVIOR

Studies in both laboratory and naturalistic settings have demonstrated that television can lead to increased generosity, cooperation, adherence to rules, delay of gratification, friendliness, and decreased fear (Rushton, 1988). Research also has shown that children learned nurturance, sympathy, and persistence from watching Mister Rogers (de Groot, 1994). Even prosocial cartoons elicited more prosocial behavior in preschoolers than neutral ones (Forge & Phemister, 1987). Similarly, with prosocial cues, children increased the number of requests and suggestions for rules in an apparent attempt to verbalize their preferences rather than to aggressively force them on others (Potts et al., 1986). Some suggest that prosocial programming is more effective with children who lack family, church, or school models and teaching (Hattemer & Showers, 1995b).

Other studies have given less reason for optimism about the efficacy of prosocial content in increasing prosocial behavior. Wiegman et al.

(1992), for example, in their longitudinal study of the impact of both aggressive and prosocial models on children's behavior, found no significant positive correlations between viewing prosocial behavior on television and prosocial behavior in children. Interestingly, however, there was a strong correlation between viewing violence and viewing prosocial behavior; that is, the children who saw many aggressive models also saw many prosocial models because they were heavy viewers.

Others have found that the presence of an adult or adult mediation may be a critical variable, at least with very young children. In one study of 3- and 4-year-olds (J. L. Singer & D. G. Singer, 1976), children were influenced by the presence of an adult who engaged them and gave them immediate feedback on their own responses. J. L. Singer and D. G. Singer (1976) concluded that television's prosocial or cognitive benefits may occur only with some mediation by an adult.

Wright et al. (1990) found that viewing adult entertainment was positively correlated with low levels of prosocial behavior in younger children; for older ones, having a history of watching child-informative programs was negatively related to prosocial behavior. Wright et al. offered several possible explanations for these findings. First, parents who view large amounts of television with their children may have quite different values than those who view infrequently, and their children may reflect these. Parents may not consider actions in children's programs to be as value laden as those in adult programs and therefore provide less commentary.

Including prosocial content in children's programming and advertising is an important administrative decision. Prosocial behavior or positive characteristics can be included in commercials as well as programs, and now, new possibilities for increased prosocial program delivery exist because of the increase in cable channels with greater ability to provide special programming for narrower target audiences (Johnston & Ettema, 1986).

It is clearly necessary to produce attractive prosocial programs, however, if children are to choose them over other ones. Some (e.g., Kunkel & Murray, 1991) claim that children's needs get a short shrift because of broadcasters' need to get the largest possible audiences for their programs. On the other hand, the potential for prosocial effects from commercial television may be greater because it reaches a much larger audience (Sprafkin et al., 1992). Television, then, could be used to strengthen values such as cooperation, family stability, gender equality, nonviolence, and other positive behaviors in the same way that it can undermine them (Lefrancois, 1992).

STEREOTYPES

Stereotypy is said to occur when a group is portrayed in a way that implies that anyone in that group has similar characteristics and attitudes or life situations (Liebert & Sprafkin, 1988). In many ways, television both reflects —and affects —our world. Many argue that the proportion of individuals and families portrayed in the various lifestyles on television does not accurately represent reality and that what is presented is based too heavily on stereotyped views of behavior. Of concern is the possible cumulative effect on children of repeated exposure to such "information."

Television can play a significant role in a child's developing beliefs and attitudes about what it means to be male or female in the world, and about appropriate gender-role behavior. Television can also influence children's developing attitudes about other groups or populations such as racial minorities and the elderly.

There is a considerable amount of research on gender-role stereotyping on television and its effects. Racial stereotypes persist also, however, and portrayals of the elderly, although improving, are still largely stereotypic. Because stereotypes of any kind are based on preconceptions, television content may confirm those ideas through biased presentations and information.

Gender-Role Stereotypes

The importance of children's attitudes about gender-role behavior is not limited to such concrete behaviors as choice of clothes to wear or toy selection; the significance of such attitudes lies in the fact that they strongly influence what opportunities children see for themselves, how they think about the world, and what they remember of what they see. In fact, "television's messages about sex-roles are among its most pervasive and stable features" (Morgan, 1987, p. 270).

Television's presentation of women in limited and outdated roles, despite daily evidence to the contrary, and the effects of such a presentation on a new generation of viewers, are important areas of investigation.

Despite gradual improvement over recent decades, highly stereotyped portrayals of men and women are still evident when specific TV behaviors are counted (Huston & Alvarez, 1990). Women shown on television are typically younger than men, and although the variety of roles for women has increased, women of all ages are still underrepresented. They appear in far fewer numbers than men with the exception of daytime soaps, in which women appear as often as men (Kimball, 1986). Women, when they are seen, are most often portrayed in unimportant, limited, and devalued ways (Signorielli, 1987). Thus, women are still low in both recognition (sheer presence) and respect (status or importance) in today's television programming (Liebert & Sprafkin, 1988). In short, despite the presence of some less traditional women on television, conventional, traditional images of women generally have been maintained (Signorielli, 1989).

Occupational Stereotypes

Television too frequently also portrays a distorted and stereotypic picture of occupational choice for women and reinforces traditional roles. As recently as 1983, Cheney reported that television provided only five occupations for half of the women on television: model, nurse, maid, secretary, and entertainer. Although there have been some changes in occupational opportunities depicted on television (e.g., women lawyers, policewomen, doctors), many of these are still limited and unrealistic (e.g., only young and beautiful lawyers, policewomen, and doctors), and they still do not reflect society realistically. It is rare to see women over 35 years old, or in supervisory positions; and despite the fact that they are at their peak of personal power, the presence of 30- to 40-year old women in television dramas has dropped 10% across the board (Ambrose, 1991).

We know all too well how the narrow views of women and minority groups and their capacities severely limited occupational avenues and opportunities for self-fulfillment in the past. If children paid little attention to these television portrayals, one could dismiss them as inaccurate annoyances, but children do attend to and respond to them. They do obtain significant occupational information from television (Wroblewski & Huston, 1987).

Racial and Ethnic Stereotypes

Similar stereotyping occurs for racial and ethnic minorities. Minorities, for example, are still underrepresented on television and often misrepresented as violent or generally portrayed in less desirable ways, perpetuating racism and stereotypes (Donnerstein et al., 1994). More important than specific counts of how many Blacks or members of various ethnic groups appear on television is the way in which they are portrayed and the context of their behavior (Greenberg, 1986).

There are considerable data to indicate that Blacks use television to learn about life and about themselves (Greenberg, 1986), they are likely to watch shows that include Blacks, and they do so with a strong sense of identification. As characters stand out for them and they react both cognitively and affectively to them, there should be more variety and heterogeneity in their presentation (Greenberg, 1986). Moreover, according to Greenberg (1986), Hispanics, despite their rapid increase in population proportion, seem to be portrayed inconsistently and perhaps even less often than previously. There is also a need for more research regarding the impact of television's content on the perceptions of the majority world by minorities, as well as on minority perceptions of, and attitudes toward, other minorities (Greenberg, 1986).

Effects of Stereotypic Portrayals

As we see in chapter 9, children who lack experience and information in an area and look to television for that information are particularly vulnerable to the influence of its portrayals. If those portrayals are biased or stereotyped, viewers who depend on them are more likely to develop stereotypic attitudes. Gerbner, Gross, Morgan, and Signorielli (1986), for example, found that most heavy viewers scored higher on their sexism scale when other characteristics were held constant. Some would argue, however, that a positive correlation between viewing stereotypy and exhibiting stereotypic attitudes could as easily indicate influence in the other direction: that children who hold sexist views tend to watch more television, perhaps to confirm their views.

Gunter (1985) cautioned, however, that descriptive content analyses of stereotyped television portrayals that do not also take into account audience perceptions of portrayals and social norms may not be a reliable indicator of television's potential to cultivate gender-role stereotypes. Perceptions of stereotyped content, in terms of limited choices and alternatives, for example, may be strong determinants of behavior, regardless of the objective "reality" of the content as indicated by content analysis counts (Gunter, 1985).

According to cognitive developmental theory, children at about age 5 or 6 recognize gender as an invariant characteristic, despite superficial changes in hair or clothing (Ruble, Balaban, & Cooper, 1981). Their interest in same-sex models and sex-appropriate behaviors increases, according to Ruble et al., because of their new sense of gender inevitability rather than the reverse. The researchers' findings indicated a direct connection both between watching television and sex-typed behavior and between a child's cognitive developmental level and the impact of gender-related television information. Ruble et al. (1981) suggested that gender constancy may be a developmental stage in which children actively seek information about sex-appropriate behavior and then act accordingly, making television content especially relevant for them.

A child's *scripts*, or shared expectations, about certain situations and outcomes are also important in relation to television content. To the extent that television scripts deal with conventional aspects of life, in areas where the child has had actual experience, the content is interpreted in terms of that child's existent scripts (Durkin, 1985). Television, then, is likely to confirm rather than initiate, sex-role beliefs that children are learning in a broader context, although unconventional scripts may have more influence than those that are more routine (Durkin, 1985). Moreover, Durkin noted that although content is largely stereotyped, some of the material is not; in that case more frequent viewing would also mean a greater likelihood of children seeing diverse viewpoints.

Developmental and Gender Differences

Children's awareness of stereotyping improves with age and is learned from exposure to television and from other experiences with gender-role stereotypes (Huston et al., 1984). Durkin (1984) found that 4- to 9-year-old children already had clear and consistent information about gender-role constraints that are allegedly overrepresented on television. Others have found that although young children may perceive television to be more realistic, by the time they are in fifth and sixth grade, children do tend to see television occupations as more stereotyped than real-life ones (Van Evra, 1984; Wroblewski & Huston, 1987). Moreover, girls who showed interest in 'feminine' television occupations also watched more programs with traditional gender roles (Wroblewski & Huston, 1987).

The cognitive processing of the stereotypic television information is affected by other aspects of a child's developmental level and experiences. Normal developmental and nontelevision factors must also be taken into account, as children tend to demonstrate more gender-typed behavior at certain ages than at others in nontelevision activities as well (Van Evra, 1984).

According to Durkin (1985) there is no strong evidence for a linear effects hypothesis, in which more viewing is straightforwardly associated with a greater effect. That hypothesis neglects variations in the contribution of other factors—such as school, siblings, and peers—that are not constants. Moreover, according to Durkin (1984), children do not simply absorb television information; they actively process it and impose their own interpretations and expectations. It is very difficult to disentangle television's effects from other societal influences and informational sources in a child's life, (e.g., books, peers, school, and parents) or to make causal inferences (Kimball, 1986). Kimball (1986) did find, however, that students' sex-role perceptions, and their attitudes and beliefs about appropriate and typical sex-role behavior, did become more stereotyped after television was introduced to their community, even though they had already been receiving traditional messages and models through their parents, school, peers, and books. That is, television's introduction added enough to the messages that they were already receiving from other sources to lead to increased sex-typing (Kimball, 1986).

Family Background

There has been surprisingly little research attention paid to the influence of a child's actual family models on the impact of television's stereotypic portrayals. There are no systematic or frequent reports of differences in the effects of stereotypic portrayals on children who come from traditional and conventional homes and those who come from homes in which the family members are engaged in less stereotypic activity. One might expect, intuitively, that children from less stereotypic homes would be less susceptible to, or less affected by, television portrayals of stereotyped roles; that they would view stereotypic portrayals with less credulity; and that they might engage in less stereotyped behavior themselves. One of the most important questions in this regard involves how much children identify with television's characters, imitate them, or are influenced by them (Durkin, 1985). One would also expect the influence of family members who are more significantly related to and involved with the child to be much stronger than that of contrived and experimental models.

Holtzman and Akiyama (1985) urged study of the relationship between a group's perceived status in a society and the way in which that group is portrayed on television. If television is a significant socializing agent that affects customs and attitudes, even indirectly, and likely influences ideas regarding the status and importance of various groups, findings of frequency and mode of presentation are important (Holtzman & Akiyama, 1985). Underrepresentation of social groups or minorities, according to Signorielli (1987), "signifies restricted scope of action, stereotyped roles, diminished life chances, and underevaluation ranging from relative neglect to symbolic annihilation" (p. 256).

Counterstereotypic Portrayals

Exposure to nontraditional or counterstereotypic gender portrayals can make a difference, and changes in attitudes toward racial minorities can also be affected by counterstereotypic presentations.

The child's initial level of gender-role stereotypy is an important variable. List, Collins, and Westby (1983) found that gender-role stereotypes affected third-grade children's processing of television portrayals, but the children did remember counterstereotyped information as well as stereotyped information.

According to Durkin (1985), counterstereotypic portrayals offer a more diverse view of human potential. Even though these portrayals may constitute only a "drop in the bucket" in terms of what else an individual sees, they can be recognized and do affect responses to gender-role tests, a finding that has important implications for real-life interventions. Durkin said that counterstereotypic portrayals alone are probably not enough, however; verbal articulation, explicitness, and debate are likely necessary to increase the effect.

Simply viewing a few commercials, then, is not likely to have a pervasive effect in real life, in the face of other experiences and a long history of other messages, but perhaps frequent repetitions over a long period of time would have a significant impact.

Attitudinal Versus Behavior Change

Research evidence suggests, however, that there are very significant differences between effects on attitudes and effects on actual behavior. Morgan (1987), for example, found that over time television contributed to gender-role attitudes but not necessarily to behavior. He concluded that adolescents who spend more time watching television are more likely to express traditional gender-role attitudes. Although he found complex interactions between viewing and gender-role attitudes, he found no relation between amount of viewing and gender-role behavior. As television is part of a child's broader social context, the family's modeling of behavior, as well as the discussion of television content, are important in mediating and either reducing or increasing program messages (Durkin, 1985). The potential for changing such attitudes, then, has some support in the research literature, although no one knows how much behavioral change actually will occur, nor how long-term any changes will be.

OTHER VIEWING EFFECTS

Cognitive Skills and Learning

Kubey and Csikszentmihalyi (1990) noted that watching television does not require a lot of cognitive effort, but that may make continuing to concentrate more difficult rather than easier. Over time, they said, people may miss being challenged and involved and feel worse and more passive. They found that heavy viewers found their experience less rewarding and, because there was little concentration and alertness, perhaps more desensitizing.

Television also may affect children's ideas about problem solving. Selnow (1986), for example, suggested that television viewing may be related to children's perceptions of problem resolution just as it is seen to be related to other beliefs such as ideas about violence or the elderly. He said that heavy viewers see much repetition for problems that are introduced and then solved rather promptly according to a few set patterns. Selnow said the content of the problems and solutions does not matter; it is the rules underlying story lines that do. Therefore, according to Selnow, it may be the ease and speed and predictability of TV solutions that lead to concern for children who expect the same in the real world, and it is important to ask whether expectations about TV's solutions influence the perceptual framework the child uses to evaluate real-life events, predict activities and judge success or failure, especially if they see their own lives falling short of TV's ideal (Selnow, 1986).

Behavioral Controls

In one study (Singer, Singer, & Rapacynski, 1984), children who spent more time watching television, especially violent programs, were less likely to show the self-restraint necessary to sit quietly for a few minutes, and heavy television viewing in elementary children was correlated with later aggression, restlessness, and belief in a "scary" world (Desmond, Singer & Singer, 1990; Singer et al., 1984), as well as reading recognition scores (Desmond et al., 1990).

Some heavy viewers in the Desmond et al. (1990) study watched more than 7 hours daily, and their restlessness and aggression scores were the highest in their sample. They recommended no more than 1 hour a day for preschoolers and no more than 2 hours a day for children in the early elementary years.

Social and Emotional Functioning

Heavy television viewing also can affect the quality of a child's social interaction (Argenta, Stoneman, & Brody, 1986; Burton, Calonico, & McSeveney, 1979; Landsberg, 1985; Singer, 1980), and the specific programs viewed clearly affect the social interaction and toy play of preschoolers.

In one study (Argenta et al., 1986), because of the rapid visual and auditory sequences, cartoons were attended to most, with consequent decreased social interaction. Although Sesame Street was visually attended to less than cartoons, it elicited the most verbal imitation and seemed to encourage social interaction and active play with toys, especially for boys. Situation comedies were visually attended to least and were also the least favorite program, but they involved social behavior that was similar to that occurring during Sesame Street because both allowed children to divide their activity among the television, toys, and peers, and to remain active and involved. Only the cartoons led to them being mesmerized and stopping other interaction or involvement. Thus, the social context of television viewing varies with different programs, a finding that has important implications for monitoring children's viewing (Argenta et al., 1986). Moreover, if one worries about the effect of a single program, one ignores the usual viewing situation in which several programs are viewed over a single session, providing a variety of messages that dilute any single portrayal (Gunter et al., 1991).

Caughey (1986) noted that many viewers become attached to media figures because they seem real, and cultural cues are used to identify social situations, roles, and personalities. Viewers come to believe in the actors as the actual characters. Viewers may identify with characters on the screen, or live vicariously through their heroes. In fact, viewers may become involved with media figures even after the set is turned off, as when they become "fans." The media figures then can influence goals, values, and attitudes, and thus have a significant influence on social behavior (Caughey, 1986).

Kubey and Csikszentmihalyi (1990) also found that heavy viewing might be motivated by loneliness. As heavy viewers tended to experience solitude more negatively, and heavy viewing sessions often were preceded by solitude, those feelings could be avoided while viewing. The researchers warned that heavy viewing may so acclimate viewers to rapid changes and continual sights and sounds that they may become dependent on it and less able to fill leisure time without it. The causal direction for this is hard to pin down: Heavy viewing might lead to an inability to tolerate unstructured time, but discomfort with unstructured time may lead the person to watch a heavy amount of television. Finally, the condensation of time that occurs on television and in films may make the normal speed of one's life seem slow compared to that of people living before the advent of TV, perhaps leading to impatience and an increasing desire to keep going faster.

In addition, the fact that viewers may not be thinking directly about television when they are away from the set does not mean that television has its only impact during viewing. Rather, it can affect how they think or feel or behave away from it in subtle or unconscious ways (Kubey & Csikszentmihalyi, 1990). In one study of the effect of television viewing on children's daydreaming, Valkenburg and Van der Voort (1995) found that watching nonviolent programs led to a more positive and less aggressive daydreaming style, whereas watching violent dramatic programs led to a more aggressive and heroic, less positive style. That is, children daydream more frequently about themes consistent with frequently watched television content. Valkenburg and Van der Voort found that their daydreaming had no long-term influence on their viewing behavior, and that content not only stimulated certain kinds of daydreaming, but reduced others.

Music Videos

Greenfield and her colleagues (1987) looked at the cognitive effects of music videos and rock music lyrics. They found that understanding of lyrics increased with age but lyrics often are poorly understood, especially by younger children who lack experience and knowledge and are at a concrete level of cognitive development. Music videos were enjoyed less than songs alone and had a negative impact on imagination. Songs alone evoked more feelings than music videos (Greenfield, Bruzzone, & Koyamatsu, 1987).

Music videos, with their gangsta rap lyrics and graphic sexual and violent content, are a concern to many as well. By 1995, MTV had over 54 million subscribers. It is the most frequently watched cable channel among college students and is becoming the favorite of much younger 9-to 11-year-olds, introducing them to the most undesirable elements of the "grown-up" world, including abuse of women, sexism, racism, bigotry (Hattemer & Showers, 1995a), casual sex, violence, (especially against women) and negative messages about marriage, family, and work (TVO, 1985).

Gow (1996) looked at MTV's *Top 100 of the 90's, So Far* and found very different depictions of the two genders in the popular music videos. They continue to underrepresent women and emphasize their physical appearance rather than musical talent. Women also appear in fewer lead roles and in a narrow range of roles. There is less emphasis on physical characteristics for men, who are dominant in these videos. Few studies have been done, however, because the content often is too violent or pornographic to show to children deliberately (Hattemer & Showers, 1995a).

Positive Effects

On the other hand, Gunter and his colleagues (1991) emphasize the positive effects that television can confer. They noted that it can encourage reading and other activities, give insight into possible coping strategies, give information about all kinds of topics from gardening to health, discuss new developments in science and technology, and give news updates. Its effects depend on how children use it. Fowles (1992), in a chapter titled "Television is Good for Children," noted that preschoolers learn vocabulary, general knowledge about how things work, nonverbal information (e.g., how to treat pets, how to shake hands, how close to stand next to someone, etc.), and real-world information that is lacking in their lives (e.g., when a child living on a farm learns about taxi behavior).

POLITICAL SOCIALIZATION

Much has been written about television's role in the political socialization of children. According to Atkin (1981), *political socialization* is usually defined as the developmental process whereby children acquire attitudes, values, cognitions, and patterns of participation in their political environment. According to Atkin, effects occur in cognitive, affective, and behavioral domains. Cognitive effects include awareness of and knowledge about political matters; affective effects include general interest as well as evaluation of leaders and institutions; and behavioral effects include interpersonal discussion about political events as well as actual participation. It seems reasonable to assume, then, that children respond differently to political information and messages, depending on their information-processing abilities, experience, and family background. Parents are also important in facilitating or constraining, supporting or counteracting, the attitudinal effects of incoming messages from the media (Atkin, 1981).

Although parents, peers, schools, and the print media clearly contribute in important ways to this process, television has a very significant role to play as well. News from everywhere in the world now is brought into our living rooms daily, exposing children to political figures and events with unprecedented immediacy and vividness.

Despite rather widespread viewing of news there also appears to be some skepticism regarding the reliability of the news reports that are viewed. Gilbert (1988) reported that only about one in three (36%) Americans believes that news organizations take care to provide unbiased reporting, and they feel that reporters still interject their own opinions too frequently. Even seventh graders in one study (Rubin, 1976), although indicating that their main source of political information was the mass media, were somewhat skeptical about the reliability of that information. Moreover, the comprehension, interpretation, and assimilation of television information is affected further by age and developmental level, cognitive skills, socioeconomic level, information-processing abilities, family background and attitudes, as well as gender and racial identity.

Such interactions affect which components are attended to, what is actually understood and remembered, and how attitude changes are mediated. Thus, very young children, who lack the necessary schemata and cognitive and linguistic skills to process fully the information conveyed in news broadcasts may be affected much less politically than older children or adolescents who may be moved to greater involvement or action. Young children may be affected in other ways by the same content, however. Because of their greater attention to salient aspects and less attention to the attitudes represented by those events or to subtle messages, young children's focus may result in incomplete comprehension of the information at best and perhaps confusion or fearfulness.

Exposure to news may stimulate children to discuss issues with family members or peers, and viewing political information can stimulate children's interest in political issues generally, perhaps increasing the likelihood of their participation or attitude change. Television can also increase children's awareness of specific issues and can serve as a factor in changing beliefs about those issues. In short, television news and public affairs programming is a major informational source for children, but it is mediated by developmental, educational, interest level, and other variables.

SUMMARY

Television has been shown to facilitate prosocial behavior but there are many inconsistencies in research findings. Parental mediation and viewing patterns appear to be important variables, but the long-term effect of prosocial portrayals has not been established.

Television still perpetuates a high level of stereotypy. Women are underrepresented, and men and women are depicted in very different ways. Television does not appear to accurately reflect reality, either in demographic terms or in the nature of the portrayals, although there has been some recent improvement. Similar findings have been reported for ethnic and racial minorities and for the elderly. Developmental and gender differences, however, as well as children's own past experiences, their level of identification with television characters, the frequency of their viewing, and their families' attitudes all influence the impact that those portrayals actually have on behavior. Exposure to nontraditional or counterstereotyped behavior can effect attitudinal changes, at least short-term ones, but the long-term impact of such programs, especially in behavior change, has not been established.

Television also may have an effect on other behaviors and attitudes, including fearfulness, anxiety, dysphoria, imagination, creativity, problem solving, and social interaction. Finally, viewing television can affect children's attitudes and affective responses toward political figures and issues, and may influence their actual political involvement and participation.

6

Television Advertising and Behavior

More ads are currently directed at children than in the past, especially for toys and food—especially sugary food and fast foods—in that order (Comstock & Paik, 1991). Most commercials are 30 seconds long and children are exposed to 20 to 30 per hour. If the average viewing time is 4 to 5 hours a day, a child might see about 130 commercials a day, or more than 900 a week, 45,000 a year, or 7.5 hours worth per week (Himmelstein, 1984). In Kunkel's (1992) study, toys and breakfast foods made up over half of all ads observed, and adding sugared snacks and drinks boosted it to 74%. Healthy foods, on the other hand, were represented in only 2.8% of all advertising directed to children. Clearly, study of the effect of all of these commercial messages is essential.

According to Kunkel (1992), who studied advertising during children's programming on three types of channels (broadcast networks, cable networks, and independent stations) there are different patterns across them. Broadcast networks, for example, had the most advertising and cable had significantly less. Independent stations showed the most toy ads, but cable networks advertised the widest range of products, including phone messages aimed at children. Cable and independent stations are less cautious in advertising, which became possible after the demise of the National Association of Broadcasters' self-regulatory code and its basic standards for children's advertising (Kunkel, 1992).

Children's advertising is big business. One writer estimated that an advertising decrease of just 1% would cost the television industry $250 million annually in lost revenue (Centerwall, 1995). In the 1970s the networks dominated the advertising market, but changes during the 1980s included more independent broadcasters and targeting of smaller niche audiences including children. Cable became a bigger competitor with the networks, serving as another advertising avenue (Kunkel, 1992). Bianculli (1994) cited a phrase that Fred Friendly used when testifying in the 1960s when public TV was being debated and developed: "In commercial television, the networks make so much money doing their worst, they can't afford to do their best" (p. 114). Since then, Friendly said, costs and profits have risen significantly but quality has not (Bianculli, 1994).

The means by which advertising has an impact on children and their families in both direct and indirect ways has generated a considerable amount of research involving a wide range of variables in both cognitive and affective areas of functioning. Many studies have focused on the ability of children of various ages to distinguish television programs from commercials, their ability to understand the persuasive purpose or intent of advertising, and their ability to evaluate commercials objectively and critically. Other studies have tried to ascertain such emotional and attitudinal responses to advertising as trust, liking, believability, and desires for advertised products. These studies have sought to determine the actual impact of advertising on parent–child relationships and on the buying behavior of both sets of viewers, although some feel that only a small number of the thousands of ads children see actually lead to requests to their parents (Fowles, 1992).

MEDIATING VARIABLES

Developmental Variables

Age, as an index of developmental differences, is an important component in how children are able to deal with commercial information. Studies indicate clearly that children's comprehension of television advertising and its persuasive intent increases with age, presumably as a result of their increased exposure to and experience with commercials and of their greater cognitive maturity (Robertson & Rossiter, 1974). Their recall of content also increases with age (Roedder, 1981). Children younger than 7 or 8 years old show very little awareness of what a commercial actually is and its persuasive intent and appear unable to deal with commercials appropriately (Blosser & Roberts, 1985; Ward & Wackman, 1973).

Young children do not have the critical viewing skills that older children and adults can use, and they are unable to understand subtle cues and messages, making them significantly more vulnerable to advertising techniques. Children's discrimination between reality and fantasy is made more difficult by the fact that the frame of reference used can change (Young, 1990). For example, if a topic is personally relevant to a child (as would be the case with many commercials), that child uses a different frame of reference to make the judgment than if he or she is judging television more generally.

Thus, levels of cognitive development or maturity interact with the process of attending, and this interaction affects the reception, processing, and memory of commercial content. Cognitive ability clearly is a very important component in children's level of understanding of advertising and in their subsequent responses to it. When interpreting age differences in comprehension, however, one must be careful not to confuse children's inability to express or explain something clearly with their actual level of comprehension (Levin, Petros, & Petrella, 1982).

Formal Features

Age and developmental differences among children are relevant in the context of formal features as well. Most of the special effects in children's commercials that have been reported, such as fast-cutting visual techniques and music, are largely holistic and designed to create moods, images, and impressions rather than to convey accurate information about a product and its uses and benefits. Advertisers know that such features as music, repetition, jingles, slogans, visual effects, and animation command greater attention in viewers of all ages, but are especially attractive to young viewers who rely most heavily on such perceptually salient cues to derive meaning or to gain information from the television input. Salient commercials spread throughout a program, rather than clustered at the beginning or end, command greater attention (Greer et al., 1982).

The effectiveness of advertising lies in its reliance on recognition memory (the only one available to the very young) rather than on more active retrieval of information stored previously (J. L. Singer & D. G. Singer, 1983). Holistic material, either visual or auditory, is more easily recognized and remembered.

As young children are more likely to watch programs that include cartoons, animation, animals, and other rapid-paced and highly salient material, and as advertisers also rely frequently on similar techniques, young children may have considerable difficulty distinguishing programs from commercials. The ability to make a distinction between programming and advertising also improves with age (Meringoff & Lesser, 1980; Ward & Wackman, 1973), and location of the commercial relative to the program influences their ability to make that distinction (Hoy, Young, & Mowen, 1986). Even when they are able to discern differences between programs and ads, however, young children still show very limited knowledge of the commercials and their purpose. Finally, with elaborate and sophisticated computer technology and editing techniques such as morphing, there can be endless mutations of toys into live-action characters, movie scenes, and back to toys again. This confuses young children even further, and some ads even fool most adults (Saunders, 1996).

Advertising's "Information"

Young (1990) noted a further difference in advertising from other forms of 'balanced' presentations in education and other media areas. He said: "Advertising is a particular form of discourse where only the best side of a case is put forward so that the virtues of the topic are presented, to the relative neglect of the vices" (p. 291). Young said it takes certain skills to understand that advertising is advocative and the intent is persuasion, skills that emerge along with others in middle childhood and through early adolescence. One of these skills, for example, is knowing that a literal interpretation is not the only one and learning to "read between the lines." In addition, the interests of the advertiser are not the same as those of the one receiving the message, the child. Young mentioned studies conducted in the United States that show increased cynical and negative attitudes toward advertising with more experience, but not all children do become cynical and advertisers can reestablish credibility by creating new types of ads (Young, 1990).

There is a relative lack of hard product information such as material, price, performance, or construction information, and much more reliance on action, appearance, fun, or newness features in most commercials (Barcus, 1980). A theme of fun or happiness was involved in just over one quarter of the ads in Kunkel's (1992) study, and were predominantly in commercials for fast foods. Taste/flavor/smell and product performance each accounted for an additional 18%. Thus, those three themes accounted for nearly two thirds of all advertising. Least frequently used as a principal strategy to advertise products were quality of materials, safety, and peer status.

Both live action and animation, used frequently in advertising directed at children, are highly visual, largely holistic techniques, often used to convey an image of fun or action rather than to provide information about the actual characteristics or virtues of a product. Studies have documented the importance of nonverbal elements in advertising that may have an influence in the information they provide, the way information is processed, or the way affect is used or induced (Edell, 1988).

Premiums clearly are an important determinant of children's response to advertising (Comstock & Paik, 1991; Kunkel, 1992). Kunkel (1992) reported premiums appearing in 10% of ads, whereas contests were reported in only 3%. Children recall premium offers more than attributes of a product, and they are more important to younger children in choosing a product (Comstock & Paik, 1991). The younger children also recalled attributes less well than older viewers (Comstock & Paik, 1991). Not only would an attractive image or impression of a toy be expected to influence buying behavior more strongly, but products that are less attractively presented command less attention and hence are not remembered as well.

Kunkel (1992) reported that about half of the commercials he looked at included at least one disclaimer and almost 10% had two or more (e.g., parts sold separately, some assembly required, get your parents' permission). Half were conveyed by auditory messages only and about one third were conveyed only visually despite research that shows that children's understanding is greatest with both.

The form of presentation for such disclaimers as "batteries not included" or "sold separately" or "some assembly required" determine how salient such messages are for a viewer. Qualifiers and disclaimers would rarely, if ever, be presented in a highly salient manner as, for instance, with a catchy jingle. Because they tend to be the "small print" of the commercials, they command far less attention. In fact, they may go largely unnoticed, something the advertiser may hope for, as an unassembled product or one without batteries would be far less attractive to potential buyers. Moreover, recall is affected by the form of presentation of such disclaimers (Meringoff & Lesser, 1980). When wording that was appropriate to the children was used ("you have to put it together" instead of "some assembly required"), the children did much better (Liebert, Sprafkin, Liebert, & Rubinstein, 1977).

Gender Differences

Despite the likely importance of gender differences in attention to and recall of advertising messages, surprisingly few have been reported. Gender differences in responses to advertising may be related to the degree of gender-role stereotyping of a child, the interaction of that stereotyping with the particular advertisement, the willingness to admit persuasibility, the cognitive levels of processing of commercial information, and the different information-processing styles of boys and girls. Gender differences do emerge in older children regarding the reported impact of the commercials on buying behavior, however negatively these commercials are viewed by both genders (Van Evra, 1984). The impact of television advertising on children's behavior depends on many complex processes, and negative attitudes toward advertising do not necessarily predict behavioral effects.

Amount of Viewing

Some researchers have implicated amount of viewing as a critical variable in attention to commercials. Although heavy viewing does not seem to accelerate or slow understanding of television advertising, heavy viewers pay more attention to commercials, trust them more, and have more positive attitudes toward advertising and the products advertised than do light viewers (Adler et al., 1979; Rossiter, 1980). They are also exposed to hundreds more commercials because of the high number of viewing hours. Moreover, the more commercials they view, the more likely they are to see content that provides them with information they seek (Van Evra, 1995).

Viewer Needs

Advertising effectiveness also depends to some extent on why viewers are watching television. If they have a need for a specific product, such as when they are feeling miserable with a cold, they likely will be more receptive to messages about cold remedies than they would be when they are feeling fine. Moreover, if they view a particular ad repeatedly when they are feeling well, they are more likely to remember it later when they do have a need for that type of product (Van Evra, 1995). In the end, advertising's impact likely depends on how well the information it offers fits with a child's need for that particular information, (i.e., its relevance for the child) and what other sources the child has for information that competes with what he or she sees on the screen (Van Evra, 1995).

STEREOTYPES IN ADVERTISING

Advertising still tends to perpetuate many stereotypes. Women, for example, are presented much more frequently as silly, helpless, dependent, passive, lacking in competence, weak, and competent mainly in trivial roles. As recently as 1993, *Sports Illustrated* was running ads using female models to sell male products such as deodorant, and some of the most sexist ads are for beer companies who are also big sponsors of sporting events on TV (Jollimore, 1993). Exceptions are some of the larger-than-life female heroines.

To be fair, there are commercials that portray competent women, or women as successful business types. Despite some improvements, however, these are still rather few and far between. The demographics in advertising do not accurately reflect women's actual presence in the real work world. Moreover, women are much more likely to be shown puzzled by consumer choices to be made, to seek advice, often from a man, and to speak in irritating and whiny voices. As recently as the late 1980s, men's voices were heard in over 85% of television commercials (Ambrose, 1991).

Advertising content can be discriminatory and sexist in other ways as well. A few years ago, a Reebok ad featuring prominent female athletes was noteworthy in its exceptionality to the usual role of women in ads and their usual nonsports or nonathletic portrayal, and significantly lower numbers of female athletes in ad campaigns (Jollimore, 1993). Other data indicate that the heavy imbalance in the number of male versus female voice-overs, and males in authority or expert roles continues despite an absence of data to demonstrate their greater effectiveness in such roles (Canadian Advertising Foundation, 1987).

Even the formal features (e.g., pace, sound effects) of television can be used to enhance stereotypic content and they may come to have connotative meaning as when masculine and feminine content is presented with different forms. An example of this synthesis of form and content occurs when an ad for tissues or deodorant, aimed at women, is presented with soft lights, hazy and muted colors, and a filmy, slow-paced voice-over, as opposed to an action-packed, loud beer commercial directed at men.

IMPACT OF ADVERTISING

Advertising affects parent–child interactions as advertisers try to win the consumer dollar by appealing to children who then put pressure on parents to buy the advertised products. Even though commercials may not direct a child explicitly to ask parents for advertised products, children's exposure to advertising does lead to such requests, especially for toys and cereals (Liebert et al., 1982). Cross-cultural studies, however, reveal wide differences in parental reactions to such requests. In one study of U.S., English, and Japanese children (Robertson, Ward, Gatignon, & Klees, 1989), researchers looked at the relation between amount of viewing and product-recognizing behavior and between frequency of requests and parent–child conflicts. Their findings revealed differences in the level of authoritarianism of the three cultures and baseline data that suggested more family rules in Japan than in the United States or England. There also was less viewing and less demanding, less communicating, and less independence in Japanese children when compared with the other two groups. U. S. children were the most independent and made the most purchase requests and hence showed higher levels of conflict. Some older children, on the other hand, may not even have to ask for particular products because their parents already know their preferences and buy accordingly (Isler, Popper, & Ward, 1987).

Advertising can affect viewers in other ways as well. Comstock and Paik (1991) suggested that advertising can adversely affect self-esteem in three ways: a) by portraying achievements that viewers are not capable of b) by portraying others as better off in some way than the viewer and c) by portraying individuals who are like the viewer in socially inferior roles. Conversely, the obverse occurs when portrayals show achievements that viewers are competent at, or persons like the viewer are shown as better off, or viewer roles are portrayed as superior, all of which lead to enhanced self-esteem. However, as the researchers pointed out, these would all be more common for males than females given the content of most advertisements.

THE NATURE OF ADVERTISING'S APPEAL

Product Information Versus Images

The primary goal of advertising is not necessarily direct persuasion, but to put awareness of a product in the viewer's conscious mind and to have him or her associate it with something good or desirable (Cheney, 1983). According to Rutherford (1988), advertising is not usually very informative regarding the characteristics and price of a product, and the amount of "hard information" has decreased since the early years. Advertising has instead become an art form (Rutherford, 1994). The aims are to create an image or impression rather than to provide information, to persuade through emotional rather than rational argument, and to have the viewer associate a product with positive attitudes or things (Carpenter, 1986).

Advertisers want to shape their message to those viewer needs and experiences. Commercial messages are meant to resonate with a viewer's feelings, and they trigger emotions that are then labeled for the viewer or associated with the product name (Nelson, 1987). At times, viewers can be hard pressed to see any logical connection between some of the components of a commercial because of the abundance of associations and images.

Rather than conveying information about product characteristics, then, advertising offers information on lifestyles and about viewers; and ways are presented to solve discontent about one's appearance or status (Rutherford, 1988). Older "plot ads," which were more linear and informational, are disappearing. They are not as engaging as the more visual and emotive ones that are also being used increasingly in political campaigns (Nelson, 1987). The fact that there are increasing numbers of such ads, as compared with more informational ones, may mean that children, who rely on and respond more to such techniques, will be even more vulnerable to advertising messages. When children are processing a very strong and immediate stimulus, then, they may not be able to invoke their generalized distrust of commercials, despite their understanding of them (Goldberg & Gorn, 1983). Furthermore, with the evasive action now available with VCRs, commercials more and more frequently are developed to merge with nonadvertising, to be so entertaining and appealing on their own that they will be "zapproof" (Miller, 1987).

Logical, critical components may have far less impact than those that make a more emotional appeal through the use of images and impressions. For example, in one study, background music succeeded in creating a positive outlook toward a brand being advertised and affected recall of its characteristics (Macklin, 1988). Thus, rather than objectively considering a product's merit, viewers respond in less rational, more emotional ways. They may suspend rational analysis temporarily as a direct result of advertising's appeal to strong, but vaguely and poorly defined needs to succeed or to belong. Viewers may respond emotionally in spite of a need to be rational because of the powerful persuasive impact of the advertisement.

In viewers of any age, then, television programming and advertising can manipulate or override analytic and logical processing of the information. This persuasive effort is often facilitated or accomplished through the use of half-truths and fallacious logic, such as reports of so-called scientific research or extensive surveys used in association with highly salient images. Such a combination may make us think that we are responding rationally when in fact we are responding emotionally on the basis of the images.

Television advertising helps us to support our buying decisions by providing us with some apparent logical basis for our behavior, even though on closer examination the logic does not stand up. With increasing age, we may become more aware of the weak or nonexistent logical base of an advertisement and reject the message, but the emotional side or appeal of the advertisement may still override that logical decision and lead to yielding behavior. This seems to have occurred in Grade 7 girls in one study who freely expressed negative attitudes toward advertising and verbalized their awareness of being exploited or manipulated, at the same time acknowledging that they were still very much influenced by it in their buying behavior (Van Evra, 1984).

Celebrity Endorsement

Children's response to television commercials also is affected by the person delivering the commercial message. The mere appearance of a character with a product can affect the child's evaluation of the product significantly, depending on how the child views the character. In one study (Ross et al., 1984), for example, children who watched ads in which a celebrity endorsed the product believed that the celebrity was an expert about the product (toy), and the children showed an increased preference for it. When live action was included, estimates of the actual properties of the toy were exaggerated and the 8- to 14-year-old male participants were more likely to think that the advertisement had not been contrived or staged.

The younger boys in the sample, 8- to 10-year-olds, were more reliant on the endorser's advice than the older boys, and they seemed more vulnerable to the perceptual tricks used in the ad. However, there was no significant difference between them in affective response or in preference; and there was no evidence of greater resistance on the part of the older boys.

The combination of a famous presenter with perceptually exciting and dramatic material from his "real" world would be a powerful message for children who are prone to believe adults, aspire to emulate heroes, and are literal-minded in their interpretation of sensory information (Ross et al., 1984, p. 187)

Celebrities whom children associate to some degree with activities represented by a toy were seen as more credible or reliable experts than those who had no such association. Moreover, "synthetic" celebrities (e.g., someone dressed as a football player but not really one) may well have the same influence, especially if live action is included (Ross et al., 1984). The practice of using live action to fill time that might have been used to view the actual product instead, however, serves no legitimate informational purpose and tends to mislead children about the product (Ross et al., 1984).

Program-Length Commercials

Programs also can reinforce commercials and almost serve as "ads" for the commercials (Himmelstein, 1984), as when they include a lifestyle in which an advertiser's product would fit. Other programs are populated by licensed characters that began as toys and later had programs developed around them in what are sometimes referred to as *program-length commercials* (Engelhardt, 1987; Kunkel, 1988). The main goal of such shows is to sell toys through the heroes of the show. Merging programs and commercials for toys, however, as when a program is in fact a half-hour commercial for a toy, may enhance the cuing effect (McIlwraith, 1987). Many have argued that this takes unfair advantage of children as the practice makes separation of program and advertising less clear and harder to discern (Kunkel, 1988). In fact, some have argued for a long-range goal of abolishing children's advertising altogether to protect children from commercial exploitation (Huston, Watkins, & Kunkel, 1989). Others suggest federal guidelines that would require commercial-free programs with educational or cultural merit for at least 1 hour on Saturday mornings, that no advertising directed at younger children be allowed, and that premium offers, so attractive to young children, should be looked at carefully (Comstock & Paik, 1991).

CRITICAL VIEWING OF ADVERTISING

Brucks, Armstrong, and Goldberg (1988) used nondirective probes instead of direct questions with 9- and 10-year-olds to evaluate their knowledge of advertising and the effect of a cue on their thoughts while watching television. Brucks et al. claimed that the number of counterarguments produced by the participants indicated that they were using cognitive defenses. Having knowledge about advertising, however, did not result in more counterarguments unless there was a cue present to activate their knowledge. Brucks et al. said that direct questions actually activate knowledge about advertising, and thus overestimate children's use of cognitive defenses. Knowledge about advertising provided in instructional films led to more critical and skeptical answers to direct questions, but this orientation was not consistent with participants actual thoughts while viewing. That is, children's knowledge did not generate critical thoughts unless cues were given to activate their knowledge; they did not spontaneously retrieve their knowledge.

Brucks et al. (1988) concluded that their results show that children of this age need more than a critical or skeptical attitude toward advertising; they need more knowledge about how advertising works and cues to use that knowledge. Simple cues will work; and schools could teach about advertising and parents could provide cues regarding watching advertisements carefully (Brucks et al., 1988).

In addition, even young children can be taught to discriminate between factual information about a product and persuasive advertising techniques. Peterson and Lewis (1988), for example, studied children ages 6 to 10 in an after-school day-care center who learned to discriminate information and advertising techniques after being shown ads that were relevant to the day's learning module. Learning modules included information (factual content of the commercials) or advertising tricks or persuasive techniques. A control group did not show the same learning. The researchers concluded that even young children can learn to distinguish between information and advertising techniques, and they learned it in a "quasi-classroom" setting. Critical viewing skills are discussed more fully in chapter 11.

"ADVERTISING" CAMPAIGNS IN OTHER AREAS

Although much of the research on advertising's effects has been done in relation to buying behavior, advertising also can affect other behaviors. Some do not consider this to be "advertising," but rather promotion or public action campaigning. Nonetheless, many of the techniques that serve advertisers well can also convey these other messages. Advertising, then, has been used to discourage smoking, drinking and driving, shoplifting, drug use, and other behaviors, and to promote sound nutritional practices.

The number of such ads in television and print media is strong testimony to the perceived effectiveness of such advertising. The actual impact on behavior of this use of advertising, however, is inconsistent. In one study of the effects of television advertising on drinking among teenagers (Atkin, Hocking, & Block, 1984), for example, the relation between ad exposure and drinking liquor was a strong positive one, with a moderate relation for beer and a weak one for wine. Interestingly, peer influence was more important in the latter two. Moreover, the relation between drinking and advertising was stronger than the relation between drinking and parent influence, gender, age, social status, or seeing alcohol in programming. Atkin et al. cautioned, however, that that relation may be caused by other factors such as dissatisfaction with life, which might lead to viewing more television ads and more drinking.

Pronutritional ads have not been very effective in increasing the consumption of nutritional foods (Jeffrey, McLellarn, & Fox, 1982; Peterson, Jeffrey, Bridgwater, & Dawson, 1984). When pronutritional messages for high-nutrition foods were used with kindergarten children, followed by measurement of recall, information learned, preferences, and behavioral assessments, recall and information were the only areas with significant results (Peterson et al., 1984). The children apparently attended to and learned the message and the nutritional concepts, but they did not change their preferences or their consumption practices; rather, consumption was a behavior that depended on many factors including, but not restricted to, preference. Several researchers have noted the relation between television viewing and obesity (Dietz & Gortmaker, 1985; Kolata, 1986). Given the number of food ads directed at children, especially for sugary cereals, some have called for a ban on such ads (Dietz & Gortmaker, 1985).

Winett (1986) reported the same problem in his discussion of the impact of prosocial programs on behaviors such as health practices and energy conservation. Although some programs, such as Feeling Good, in the mid-1970s, included motivational objectives as well as informational ones, changing even simple behaviors was still difficult. Clearly, changing information and recall is easier than changing intent or actual behavior (Winett, 1986).

These results are consistent with other findings mentioned earlier of a frequent lack of a relation between knowledge about advertising itself and its actual impact on behavior. For actual behavior change to occur, as in nutritional practices, for example, viewers must be shown specific substitutions to be made at the supermarket, and how to prepare desirable and appealing meals (Winett & Kramer, 1989); that is, behavior change must be modeled.

Recent research also underscores the need for relevance to the viewer in changing behavior. Roser (1990) found, for example, that attention to messages could affect recall, but did not affect attitudes or behavior directly because they were influenced by viewer perceptions of relevance. It seems unlikely, then, that children's behavior would change unless they saw the messages being delivered as providing significant and relevant information for them (Van Evra, 1995). As with other aspects of advertising, complex interactions exist that operate to influence behavior, and consumer behavior is no exception.

Because the forms used in advertising vary greatly among shows, children's viewing patterns, as well as age, gender, and social class differences, might well be expected to result in differing impact levels of television advertising. As children get older, they are better able to understand verbal or linguistic stimuli and become less reliant on, perhaps less attentive to perceptually salient stimuli than they were when they were younger. At the same time, however, if they watch mainly shows directed at younger children, they are exposed to different types of commercials than their peers who watch more age-appropriate programming, and may be attracted to them as well.

Although little attention appears to have been paid to the relation between children's viewing patterns and their favorite programs, on the one hand, and the attitudes of those children toward advertising on the other, it is an area worthy of some attention.

Gender differences in the commercials themselves also should be investigated further to determine whether advertisers actually take into account age and gender differences in the processing of commercial information. When, for example, do advertisers use more highly perceptually salient and image-oriented advertising for some target groups and more logical, authoritative content for others? Do these variations make a difference? Answers to such questions would shed light not only on advertising's effectiveness with different groups, but also on differences in the cognitive processing of television information by children of both genders and at different ages. As children's developmental levels strongly determine their understanding of and response to television advertising, it is essential that researchers learn precisely how developmental processes govern their responses to advertising and how they can learn to deal with it competently and realistically.

SUMMARY

Advertising's influence on children's behavior is not as straightforward as one might expect or as advertisers might hope. As children grow older, they develop an increasing awareness of how advertising works, but it still influences their buying behavior. Young children are more vulnerable to the perceptual salience of most commercials and do not have the cognitive capacity to evaluate them critically. They have more difficulty than older children distinguishing commercials from programs, and they do not view commercials as selectively as older children do. Moreover, advertisers' use of premiums, contests, animation, and other appealing tactics make actual product attributes more difficult for children to discern or evaluate.

Most ads rely on holistic stimuli to command attention and create moods and images rather than providing solid information about a product, and many stereotypes are still apparent in advertising content.

Advertising can also affect children's interactions with their parents and their self-esteem. However, children can be taught to view advertising more critically and thereby to reduce their vulnerability to its persuasive tactics.

Advertising's techniques have been used to modify other behaviors such as smoking, shoplifting, impaired driving, and nutritional habits. The effectiveness of these programs is not clear because actual behavior change is determined by a very complex interactive network of variables. Conveying information is easier than effecting actual behavior change, but these advertising campaigns undoubtedly make a positive contribution.

7

Television and the Family Context

The context in which children view television and their interaction with family members and peers also moderate television's impact in important ways. In fact, the home environment is a major contributor to the different uses that are made of television by individuals (Lull, 1980, 1988b). According to Lull (1988), the viewing situation becomes a social setting in which family members can communicate: "'Watching television' is a family activity that involves an intermeshing of the constantly changing personal agendas, moods, and emotional priorities of each family member with the fluctuating agenda of programs that emanates from TV sets" (p. 17).

TELEVISION AND OTHER FAMILY ACTIVITIES

Television often has been criticized for undermining important aspects of family life by displacing other important family activities. Concerns exist about the activities TV displaces, such as families talking and interacting together, children playing with their siblings, and others. Some (e.g., Winn, 1985) have argued that although television has kept family members from dispersing, it dominates their time together and can destroy the qualities that distinguish one family from another, such as unique activities, games, and rituals. Winn (1985) felt that despite the fact that families still do special things together, television diminishes their ordinary daily life together, because it is a regular, scheduled, and rather mechanized daily activity.

Robinson (1990) maintained that television has taken time away from 'functionally equivalent' activities like reading fiction and movie attendance as well as from nonmedia activities like gardening or sleeping, and most importantly has been associated with decreased social interaction outside the family. He said that television viewing is associated with a less active lifestyle and that there is little support for the idea that viewing television together increases family cohesion or discourse.

According to Kubey (1990), family television viewing is less challenging and less activating than family time in other activities, and heavy viewers in his study felt significantly less activated when they were participating in non-TV family activities. He suggested that clearly some family members would benefit from engaging in more direct interaction and in more creative and active pursuits, and noted that it is especially problematic when some family members, such as children, have to compete with television for parental attention.

On the other hand, such views neglect the fact that television has become an important way to bring family members together in an era when demands on them differ significantly from those of pretelevision times. According to Rubin (1986a), most children watch television with their parents. Kubey and Csikszentmihalyi (1990) concluded that television viewing is in harmony with family life: Heavy viewers spend more time generally with their families and feel better with them than lighter viewers. They further noted that even though viewing levels drop off in adolescence, television viewing is still a common activity that offers the opportunity for shared experiences with other family members. In other words, they found little support for the idea that heavy viewing by adolescents is associated with poor relationships with the family; if anything, it seemed to convey a preference for spending time with family members. Similarly, Brown and Bryant (1990) claimed that rather than destroying family interaction as many have claimed, newer studies suggest that television viewing may even increase a family's togetherness.

With more than 70% of women now working outside of the home, both parents are often tired; and more families prefer to stay home for entertainment rather than going out (Lull, 1988a). According to Lull (1988a), the trend toward staying home has not been caused by television, but television adds another strong reason to do so and it interacts with other social, cultural, and economic factors to create this trend.

Finally, Wright et al. (1990), noting the increasing control of socialization by television, maintained that television is often a background to other family activities. Although the television set may be on for many hours in a day, family members actually watch fewer hours than that and often engage in other activities at the same time.

TELEVISION MODELS OF FAMILIES

Douglas (1996) noted that domestic comedies, not dramas, generally show a traditional family model with families managing their relationships and conflicts quite effectively. Parents are generally portrayed as providing appropriate models for the children in the family, and implicit rules are as prevalent as explicit attempts to influence activity. There are generally positive and cohesive family relationships, although children in families are shown more negatively and in less satisfying relationships. Relationships between and among siblings were evaluated as less effective than ones involving adults, and there was more conflict and less support among siblings. Douglas (1996) said the results are consistent with real family life: "These results are significant, in part, because domestic comedy often is seen as real and is especially likely to influence family cognition" (p. 696).

In addition, however, Douglas and Olson (1996) note that children's experiences on television seem to have deteriorated over time. The general environment of modern families was rated as more conflictful and less cohesive and parents were less able to socialize their children or manage daily life effectively. Siblings were seen to be more hostile, less cohesive, and less effectively socialized. Douglas and Olson suggested that real and TV families' experiences may converge so viewers expect to see child-centered programs and to interpret the experience of children on television negatively. Television families appear to behave in ways viewers understand and can relate to, but more study is needed of how much viewers integrate family life on television into their own.

The way in which members of a family perceive what families should be like and what is appropriate and desirable behavior may be influenced by television's portrayals of families. Brown and Bryant (1990) pointed out that children who watch many families on television tend to believe that those families are supportive and show concern for each other; if they watch those shows with their parents and discuss the content with them, they are more likely to have positive views about families.

COVIEWING WITH PARENTS

Benefits of Coviewing

The viewing context, especially whether children watch alone or with friends, siblings, or parents, greatly affects TV's impact. Although television is an important source of values at school age, children often have difficulty integrating its components, which may lead to a distorted view. The presence of parents or siblings can help (Van Dyck, 1984; Wright et al., 1990). Direct parental communication and discussion help to shape the child's perception of families in the real world, which then are used to assess the realism of the television world (Austin, Roberts, & Nass, 1990). Parent coviewing also can provide children with a role model for appropriate television viewing behavior (Anderson & Collins, 1988). Coviewing with adults can enhance children's understanding of television content if the parents offer comments about it during and after viewing a program, and they can reinforce content children learn during educational programs (Wright et al., 1990).

One of the significant aspects of the viewing context lies in its role as a source of alternate information. If parents watch with their children, they can provide other views to supplement, alter, modify, or refute information that their children are receiving. They may, of course, still provide alternate information even if they are not coviewing; but it comes to the children in other contexts, then, and perhaps has less direct association or immediate relevance for the child. Moreover, if the information does not come in other contexts, television serves as the major source of that knowledge. One of the reasons that adult intervention and discussion about television enhances its impact is likely because such comments and discussion make the viewing experience an informational session in which parents can offer alternative, and, perhaps, competing information.

According to Wartella (1986), the interpersonal context is also important for interpreting the codes of television and making sense of television is frequently an interpersonal process for children. Their interaction with parents and siblings directly and indirectly affects their learning. Families not only counter television's messages, then; they are important in determining what the messages will be (Hodge & Tripp, 1986).

Anderson and Collins (1988) concluded, however, that there is little evidence that coviewing is used extensively for cognitive interactions between the child and the parent or that it significantly modifies television's cognitive effects. As Anderson and Collins pointed out, the effects of coviewing may not be directly related to the time spent together with the television anyway. They likely have more to do with actual comments and explanatory behavior of parents, such as making a comment when entering or leaving the room (Anderson & Collins, 1988), or with the degree of control exerted by parents.

Levels of Coviewing

Coviewing is an important aspect of the viewing situation, but many studies indicate low levels of coviewing (Desmond et al., 1990; Dorr, Kovaric, & Doubleday, 1989; Wright et al., 1990), and age and developmental level of the child need to be taken into account. For example, in one study of over 300 3- to 5-year-olds (St. Peters, Fitch, Huston, Wright, & Eakins, 1991), the majority of children's programs were watched without parents and coviewing declined with age. Further, children of parents who encourage television viewing watched more child informative programs. Dorr et al. (1989) found that coviewing family series on television occurred most frequently when parents believed television could affect their children, when they explicitly encouraged coviewing with older children, and when their own orientation was positive.

Coviewing occurred least often with younger children who need parental mediation the most. Dorr et al. concluded that the coviewing was motivated by similar interests or preferences rather than mediation of children's viewing experiences.

In one study of children from 6 to 17 years old (Lawrence & Wozniak, 1989), participants spent two thirds of their television time with family members, most frequently a brother or sister. When they did watch television with parents, most often it was the father; it was rare for whole families to watch together. Family characteristics did not affect this: coviewing was similar across age, income, education, and other variables including rural versus urban.

Finally, there are age, gender, racial, and cultural differences as well. Brown, Childers, Bauman, & Koch (1990) surveyed 2,056 children 12 to 14 years old and found that Blacks and girls spent more time with radio and TV than Whites and boys, although TV use decreased with age. Not surprisingly, children spent more time with TV and radio when there was less access to parents either because the mother worked or because there was no father in the home. Blacks, who were more likely to live in father-absent homes, used radio and TV more than White adolescents regardless of gender, age, SES, or parent education.

Parental Mediation and Commentary

Simply coviewing with an adult is not enough, however; comments from significant others can facilitate learning, and interaction and talk about a show are essential (Corder-Bolz, 1980; Greenfield, 1984b). Desmond et al. (1990) said their data point to the need for parental strategies for discussing, explaining, and setting rules about television.

> Children who dwell in such a positive atmosphere of family communica-
> tion are less fearful of being harmed, less aggressive, and more willing to
> wait patiently than are children from families who simply comment on
> televisions' [sic] array of people and events. (p. 304)

Lawrence and Wozniak (1989) urged more research on the verbal interactions among family members while watching television, and on which interactions enhance learning. The best situation occurs when parents watch with their children, talk about programs with them, and help their children relate the TV content to their own lives.

Desmond et al. (1990) observed not only that parental mediation during viewing is rather rare, but also that it can sometimes have an adverse effect on children's experience. For example, if calling attention to the screen is a characteristic mediation activity, but a parent does so during a violent scene with a "look at that" comment, the child's attention is heightened, and the parent may be conveying tacit approval of the content. At the very least, the parent in that situation is heightening the salience of that scene, which the child is viewing out of context and may or may not understand the meaning and significance of.

Messaris (1986; Messaris & Kerr, 1983) has done a considerable amount of work in the study of families' influence on children's television experience. Messaris and Kerr (1983) looked at mothers' comments to children about television content and how the patterns of those comments varied with the more general styles of communication in families.

According to Messaris (1986), parents are very involved in their children's learning from television, and children rely on their parents or other household adults to construct a picture of the world from television in three ways. First, the child needs to learn to distinguish one program type from another (e.g., fantasy vs. documentaries) and then to distinguish the difference between television content and reality. Cognitive developmental level and parent intervention both play a part here. Second, by parents judging the accuracy of a program's portrayal and engaging in frequent discussion, they play an important role in children's use of television to explore the real world and to evaluate the accuracy of its portrayals of both negative and positive situations and events.

According to Messaris (1986) conversations with mothers help to decrease the unrealistic expectations in overly positive or exciting portrayals, and parents are protective regarding negative information or events, although they usually confirmed the accuracy of the information. Parents also use these conversations to try to strengthen their own families, such as by playing down differences that are threatening or playing up ones that are to their advantage.

The third way that parents and sometimes siblings interact is to supplement the information that the child receives from television by providing "background" information when the child is confronted with unfamiliar material. Messaris (1986) found this to be a very common television experience, mentioned by 80% of the mothers interviewed. Information was either such that all of the children would acquire it as they grew up or it was "specialized" information such as scientific information or information about specific ethnic or occupational groups.

Socioeconomic level needs to be considered when looking at the ways in which such parental discussion affect children's television experiences, however, as mothers in different social classes make different comments about television content to their children. Messaris and Thomas (1986) found that both middle-class and working-class mothers gave additional information about a stimulus and said that television shows were not real. Working-class mothers, however, were more likely to confirm the realism of programs that involved a negative portrayal of crime and other undesirable behavior in order to discourage their children from following that model. They were more explicit in urging imitation of some behaviors and discouraging imitation of others. Upper middle-class mothers, on the other hand, made more nondirective comments to their children to show their position, but then they let their children work out the implications.

In an interesting program developed by TV Ontario in the mid-1980s, television was used to stimulate parental awareness and to facilitate family discussion on many aspects of family and child development. The series was not classified as entertainment, but rather as a vehicle to bring several generations together to discuss various topics, and additional information was provided as needed. Topics included socialization; physical, cognitive, language, emotional, and moral development; discipline; play; learning disabilities; and child abuse. It was intended for viewing by parents with or without their children. True-to-life programs, using actual situations and not actors, portrayed real-life situations and problems. A companion guide suggested discussion topics and points to watch for while viewing the programs. A list of supplementary reading material and a list of community resources were also provided. Parents could buy the handbook, watch the programs and follow the advice and other activities. They could also choose to take advantage of an interactive component by filling in questionnaires and getting individualized feedback (TVO, 1985).

Gender Differences

The relatively low incidence of adult mediation is rather troubling given the strong research evidence that confirms its importance. In their study of kindergarten and first-grade children to see how much family communication mediated the children's understanding of television and the series of cognitive skills necessary for such understanding, Desmond, Hirsch, Singer, and Singer (1987) found that certain family mediation styles were more effective for boys than for girls. Withdrawal of love and power-assertive disciplinary techniques were used somewhat more frequently with boys. Withdrawal of love was associated with heavy television viewing, negatively associated with general mediation, and strongly related to aggressiveness and restlessness in boys but not in girls. Power-assertive discipline was associated with ability to distinguish fantasy from reality and with knowledge about how television achieves some special effects.

Desmond et al. (1987) concluded that as boys generally receive more power assertive techniques, withdrawal of love represents less discipline for them whereas it is usually used more with girls. When the researchers looked at the genders separately, however, a different pattern emerged. Mediation specific to television was much more effective for boys, and there was no strong relationship for girls. As there were no variations in the amount of mediation received by each, Desmond et al. attributed the differences to developmental differences between the boys and girls in the sample. The girls started out with a better understanding than the boys and thus had less to learn. Nonetheless, Desmond et al. concluded that there is a need to mediate viewing for both genders.

COVIEWING WITH SIBLINGS

Although coviewing with parents has been found to be an important mediating variable in children's television experience, coviewing with siblings is the most common viewing context (Lawrence & Wozniak, 1989; Reid & Frazer, 1980; Wright et al., 1990). Wright et al. (1990) found that only children viewed a lot of child informative programs, whereas when children viewed with siblings, the pattern of viewing depended on the age of the siblings. Children with older siblings stopped watching child informative programs fairly young, and they watched more entertainment programs and comedies, more often without adults present. Children with younger siblings viewed child informative programs for longer and usually with an adult present. In one study (Pinon et al., 1989), the presence of younger siblings increased viewing of *Sesame Street* and the presence of older ones decreased it.

In an interesting study by Haefner and Wartella (1987), coviewing with older siblings did not influence Grade 1 and Grade 2 children's interpretation of content, but it did influence their general evaluations of program characters. Moreover, the teaching of older siblings, who were 3 to 6 years older, rarely focused on events that adults would consider essential to comprehension of the plot or to motives and emotions of the characters. Perhaps the older siblings were not fully understanding the material themselves, or they may have been simply reflecting their unique perspective. Thus, children learn to interpret television in a rich interpersonal context, and they can use that understanding of the medium to obtain information about the nontelevision world as well (Wartella, 1986).

In a more recent study (Wilson & Weiss, 1993), researchers gave two versions of a scene to preschoolers. One was a normal scene and one was a dream that included a prologue and epilogue to convey that it was a dream; coviewing produced both positive and negative results. Those preschoolers who were coviewing with an older sibling showed less ability to recognize the special effects and the dream. They also were less aroused emotionally and liked the program more than those viewing alone. Those watching alone, on the other hand, were more likely to recall the dream in later story reconstruction. The authors suggested that coviewing did not appear to improve comprehension, perhaps because older siblings did not interact much or help the younger ones with the dream. The young children also attended less when coviewing than when viewing alone, perhaps because they were distracted by the presence and conversation of their older siblings, making it harder for them to process the story. Coviewing did lead to less fear, perhaps because the distraction may have reduced negative emotions (Wilson & Weiss, 1993), or perhaps because they felt safer than if they had been viewing alone.

FAMILIES AND PERCEIVED REALITY

Other studies have demonstrated the impact of family communication on children's perception of the reality of television content. In one field study of 627 children and 486 of their parents, Austin et al. (1990) studied the effects of the family communication environment and parental mediation of TV content on Grade 3, 6, and 9 children's perceptions of TV realism and its similarity to real life, as well as their identification with characters on TV. Television was a secondary information source, with actual experience and communication with others a more dominant socialization force. Moreover, active communication—especially about TV content—increased parents' effects on their children's TV interpretation.

In another study of over 90 kindergarten and first-grade children and their parents, parental mediation styles were linked with children's comprehension and beliefs regarding the reality of the medium (Desmond, Singer, Singer, Calam, & Colimore, 1985). Family control of television, strong discipline, and low viewing were associated with an increased ability to determine what is real. Not surprisingly, children who were heavy viewers came from homes with heavy viewing parents and low mediation. Desmond et al. (1985) suggested that one of the most important functions of parental mediation may be to increase the amount of mental effort and attention of their children during viewing.

Dorr and her colleagues (1990) studied 460 grade 2, 6, and 10 children to find the relation between a child's viewing of television families and their perception of typical real-life families. The researchers concluded that children between 6 and 16 years old feel that roughly half of all real American families are like television families, especially in the realm of emotions. The way in which television families resolve emotional problems was perceived to be the most realistic of all of the content tested. Therefore, how a program deals with common problems of "growing up" would seem likely to have a strong effect on the viewing audience: Healthy portrayals could positively affect family dynamics and unrealistic portrayals might cause some difficulty (Dorr, Kovaric, & Doubleday, 1990).

In their study of third, sixth, and ninth graders, Austin and his colleagues (1990) found that communication within families helps develop real-world perceptions of families that are then used to assess realism of the television world. There are "several contexts in which children evaluate a television family's reality: against *other* families (perceived realism), against their *own* families (perceived similarity), and as a possible object for aspiration (identification)" (Austin et al., 1990, p. 547). They claimed that:

> Perceived realism predicts perceived similarity, which in turn predicts identification....Once children settle on real-life and television-world perceptions they can compare the two, developing reality constructs based on everything so far experienced—both in real life and vicariously through the media. (pp. 547, 549)

Children's perceptions of the similarity between the real world and the world of TV are influenced by their parents' perceptions of that similarity and by conversations the children have with their parents about television. When there was a mismatch between the two, there was a decrease in perceived realism. The family proved to be a reliable information source about the world, including media, and was a help in developing strategies to analyze the media world (Austin et al., 1990).

Rubin (1986a) found a relation for 5- to 7-year-olds between family control and both children's preferences and television realism. Children's viewing attitudes (e.g., perceived realism and affinity to the medium) and their behaviors (e.g., program preferences) varied as a function of their sense, or perception, of viewing control. Children who had more control of viewing felt that TV was more realistic than did children with little control. Rubin concluded that children's viewing preferences and patterns are influenced by family–child interactions.

FAMILY CHARACTERISTICS AND PARENT CONTROL

Parents also may intervene deliberately to try to control a child's behavioral response to television, such as when they make comments or give advice, or when they try to prevent exposure by reducing excessive viewing. Jason (1987) studied the reduction of children's excessive television viewing in two related studies. The first study was done with two families, one with a 10-year-old and one with a 13-year-old. During the first phase, parents monitored their children's viewing. In the second phase a token-actuated timer was used and children had free access to tokens. In the next (intervention) phase, children could earn tokens for engaging in desired activities. This program effectively reduced excessive viewing time and the gains lasted.

In Jason's (1987) second study with a third family, a similar intervention again was effective. In addition, there were also positive results with siblings whose viewing was not considered a problem by the parents. Jason concluded that children can be prevented from spending too much time with TV, cable, and computers, so that interaction with video images does not replace real-world experiences and interactions. He said his studies show that long-standing viewing patterns can be reversed by shifting a child's sources of reinforcement from TV to more active behavior.

Rothschild and Morgan (1987) found an interaction between family characteristics and television's effects. Less parental control, whether in general or regarding television, was associated with a greater impact of television on adolescents, especially where family cohesion was low. Adolescents who watched with their parents, who discussed programs with them, and whose parents did not set viewing rules seemed most vulnerable to television. Perhaps the fact that the parents also watched, that they set no viewing rules, and that they considered the content worth discussing enhanced the importance of the programs for the adolescents. Perhaps the adolescents in families who used fewer controls but demonstrated cohesion around television programs more often used television as a creditable source of information.

In another study (Cohen, Brown, & Clark, 1981), parents' attitudes toward television and the family's media environment (e.g., access to cable and use of the print media, including the availability of magazines and newspapers) were the best predictors of preschoolers' viewing of public television. The data suggested that parents of children who view public television are more selective media users. Moreover, the perceived educational quality of programs predicted viewing of public television better than the amounts of general viewing.

Rothschild and Morgan (1987) concluded that although television has taken over some of the socializing roles previously held by the local community, it acts with the family to shape adolescents' attitudes about the world.

Not all families are as actively involved in their children's viewing, however, or as selective in their own viewing. A study done in 1991 for the Corporation for Public Broadcasting found that nearly half, 47%, of 6- to 17-year-olds had a TV in their own room, and only 50% of them reported any parental rules about their TV viewing (Abbott, 1995). However when a child has parents who are heavy viewers, who have few other interests, who set few rules about television viewing, and who emphasize TV as a major recreational activity, an atmosphere may be created that results in an increased likelihood that the children will show more restlessness, fearfulness, aggression-proneness, and negative emotional reactions (J. L. Singer & D. G. Singer, 1986).

IMPACT OF VCRS

With the rapid increase in the number of VCRs, questions about their impact on family viewing patterns and family interactions are important as well. Using longitudinal and cross-sectional data from adolescents, Morgan, Alexander, Shanahan, and Harris (1990) found that VCRs primarily augment and extend a family's pattern of viewing and they can be a symptom or a cause of family conflicts. According to Morgan et al., adolescents see VCRs as an essential part of television, so their use of a VCR was usually predicted by the pattern of their use of television. Familial conflicts about television were a good predictor of conflicts about the VCR, especially among siblings, and there was a strong relation between the frequency of adolescents' use of VCRs and the frequency of arguments with parents and siblings, not just over the VCR. The researchers concluded that a VCR can play multiple roles in a household and it can be used to avoid conflict in the family or it can be a source of arguments.

More research findings on VCR use and its impact on children are discussed in chapter 10.

SUMMARY

The context for television viewing is a very significant component in children's television experiences. Those children who receive parental comment, input, and supplementary information and interaction have a very different experience of television viewing than those who view alone or with less involved parents. Such differences in the viewing context play an important role in determining the strength and nature of television's impact. Families differ in their attitudes toward and their use of television, which in turn influence children's understanding and attitudes, perceived reality, conflicts over television and VCR use, and, ultimately, the impact of television on children and adolescents. Coviewing with siblings—the most common context—and with peers also affects children's exposure and response to different kinds of television content.

8

Television's Impact on Exceptional and High-Risk Children

Although the viewing experience of normal children of all ages has been studied extensively, only a small number of studies has been done on exceptional children (Abelman, 1990; Sprafkin et al., 1992). The work that has been done has been consistent in demonstrating that children with learning, behavioral, and emotional disorders have even greater problems than other children in distinguishing fantasy and reality (Gadow, Sprafkin, Kelly, & Ficarrotto, 1988; Sprafkin, et al., 1992; Sprafkin, Gadow, & Dussault, 1986), in understanding TV content, and in linguistic processing of the material (Gadow et al., 1988; Sprafkin et al., 1992; Sprafkin et al., 1986). Moreover, these children are likely to view greater amounts of television, to have poorer social skills and fewer social contacts and experiences that would provide information to counter television's messages, and to have fewer coviewing experiences with parents or other adults (Sprafkin & Gadow, 1986; Sprafkin et al., 1992). For all of these reasons, they are more vulnerable to television's influence in their lives.

VIEWING PATTERNS

Amount of Viewing

Sprafkin and her colleagues (1992) noted that exceptional children are at risk for viewing greater amounts of TV and for being more attracted to and reactive to adult or violent programs. They included gifted children as well, noting that although these children may be intellectually ready for some content, they may not be socially or emotionally ready. Sprafkin et al. wanted to see if the advanced cognitive abilities of gifted children help reduce adverse effects that exist for average children or whether the cognitive, social, and emotional characteristics of gifted children might actually lead to adverse responses to some content.

According to Sprafkin et al. (1992), TV has the unique potential to educate children who have fewer social skills, do not learn well with traditional methods, need frequent repetition to learn, and have attentional problems. For gifted children, TV can also educate by supplementing classroom learning with access to new and exciting topics.

Of all the exceptional groups, Sprafkin and her colleagues (1992) considered mentally retarded (MR), emotionally disturbed (ED), and learning disabled (LD) children to be the most vulnerable, as they are more at risk for heavy viewing and for adverse reactions to some content. The special education group viewed significantly more TV than controls, watched more soaps and sitcoms than controls, watched more crime shows, and were twice as likely to say that they often pretended to be their favorite character. The ED group watched the most, with the LD group second and the MR group next. According to the researchers, special education groups were higher in overall exposure to TV, perhaps because viewing may substitute for real interactions, characters may provide social acceptance (especially for the ED group), caretakers may allow more TV viewing to preserve quiet time, and television viewing is stress free. The LD children performed more poorly on the TV knowledge measure and showed less critical attitudes (Sprafkin et al., 1992).

Gifted children generally view less television than other children except at preschool age and adolescence, when they watch more. Curiosity and enthusiasm may lead them to watch more adult programs as preschoolers, and in adolescence, they watch more than average children, perhaps for social and emotional reasons such as isolation (Sprafkin et al., 1992).

Family Context

Others have found that television use can be an important diagnostic indicator in work with children and their families. Shanahan and Morgan (1989) found family viewing patterns to be related to certain kinds of clinical indicators and suggested that a family's television use could be a helpful indicator of family health. They approached the family, illness, and use of television as reciprocal and interacting aspects of a dynamic system, and looked for relations between television viewing and specific diagnoses, as well as the role television could play in the therapeutic process. For example, they assumed that if problematic behavior occurs around television viewing, that information would be helpful to a therapist and might provide unique clues to the family's patterns of daily life, interaction style, and vicarious experiences of the child being treated. They did not find amount of viewing to be strongly related to specific diagnoses, but it was strongly related to the more general problem of acting out, especially in the absence of parental mediation during viewing. Children who acted out tended to watch more television, as did their parents, but they watched with their parents less frequently. Shanahan and Morgan speculated that the greater amount of parental viewing may both sustain the child's behavior and serve as an escape from it.

Sprafkin et al. (1992) noted that the most efficient way for parents to influence what their children learn from television is through directly mediating their children's television viewing. However, parents offer only modest amounts of such mediation. In a comparison of parental mediation with gifted and traditional children, Abelman (1987a) found that giftedness did not affect the amount of parental mediation, which was modest in both groups, but the nature of the intervention was significantly different between the two groups. Giftedness and the amount of television viewed influenced parents' perception of television's impact and the type of mediation strategy they use but not the level of mediation. According to Abelman, children do not just receive their parents' practices—they help to shape them. Giftedness makes the parents more sensitive to television's possible impact, and they use more explanation and critical modes of mediation, talking to their children more about television, explaining programming, and so on. Parents of normal children were more likely to just react to television and use more unfocused and restrictive kinds of remediation.

Moreover, parents of exceptional children also differ in their perceptions of TV's impact. Sprafkin and her colleagues (1992) found that parents of nonlabeled children see television's effects as largely behavioral, but parents of labeled children do not. Parents of gifted children saw the effects as largely cognitive, whereas parents of LD children saw the effects as affective, cognitive, and behavioral. Gifted children were more responsive to parent disciplinary style regarding television viewing and disabled children less so.

Abelman (1991) also reported that parents' use of inductive communication and interaction, such as reasoning and explanation, as opposed to "less sensitizing" (p. 23) modes, such as physical punishment and deprivation of privileges, affect indirectly what their children observe while watching TV, but gifted children were especially responsive to parents' style of communication.

Uses of Television

The relation between reading time or reading skills and time spent watching television is inconsistent (Ritchie, et al., 1987); and some viewing behavior may be a result of poor academic performance. Not achieving is frustrating and reduces the child's ability to deal with difficult situations; the television viewing may contribute to academic decline (Huesmann & Eron, 1986a).

Children's use of television also may be due in part to frustrating experiences with print specifically, such that poor readers may turn to television for learning more than for entertainment. Such children may use television to obtain information that they cannot get from reading, and hence they process television information with more depth as compensation for their reading failure (Salomon, 1984). For such children, television may be an especially negative intellectual influence because they are precisely the children who need to do a great deal of reading to overcome their problems (Winn, 1985).

Other marked differences between children in regular and special classes regarding behavior, socialization opportunities, and television viewing patterns have also emerged. Exceptional children may substitute television for actual socialization activities and try to solve interpersonal problems with aggressive behavior seen on television or engaged in by favorite characters (Sprafkin & Gadow, 1986). Low IQ exacerbates the effect, because children with lower IQs tend to watch more television and the violent and aggressive solutions they see may seem like easy ones (Huesmann, 1986).

Sprafkin, Gadow, and Grayson (1987) also found a significant interaction of aggression with IQ in children with learning disabilities and children with lower IQs were significantly more physically aggressive after control cartoons compared with aggressive ones. Sprafkin et al. (1987) suggested, however, that the interaction with IQ may have been a spurious finding and was a modest effect that may not be important clinically. Behavior after the aggressive cartoons was the same as in the baseline condition.

TELEVISION VIEWING AND AGGRESSIVE BEHAVIOR

Research consistently has shown an association between maladaptive or undesirable social behavior and viewing of violence, whether it is realistic, fantasy, or cartoon violence. There is also an association between poor adjustment in school and aggressive behavior in heavy viewers (J. L. Singer & D. G. Singer, 1983). In a comparison of the viewing habits of three exceptional groups of children (ED, MR, and LD), Sprafkin and Gadow (1986) found that exceptional children watched more television generally and more programs with aggressive content, such as cartoons and crime dramas, perhaps because those children also are less often involved in sports or with friends. ED children were more attracted to crime and adult content, significantly more often named crime shows as favorites, identified less with nonaggressive characters, and showed higher aggressiveness (Sprafkin & Gadow, 1986; Sprafkin, Watkins, & Gadow, 1990). They also watched cartoons for significantly more hours, unlike older children in regular classes who showed less interest in cartoons than younger ones. Gadow, Sprafkin, and Ficarrotto (1987) found that preschool ED children showed reactivity to both aggressive and control cartoons. Some reacted adversely and some did not, but many kinds of content appeared to have the potential ability to increase antisocial behavior (Gadow, Sprafkin, & Ficarrotto, 1987). Moreover, such children may be more likely to view others' intentions as antisocial and more likely, then, to respond aggressively (Sprafkin et al., 1992).

On the other hand, in other studies (Sprafkin, Gadow, & Grayson, 1987, 1988) researchers found no major differences between conditions in slightly older ED or LD viewers who viewed aggressive and nonaggressive control cartoons. In the study with 6- to 9-year-old ED children (Sprafkin et al., 1988) whose behavior was observed at lunch and at recess before (baseline) and after viewing the two kinds of cartoons, researchers surprisingly found more aggression after control cartoons than after the aggressive cartoons and more than at baseline levels.

In an effort to explain this unexpected finding, Sprafkin et al. (1988) noted other differences in the cartoons as well. The aggressive cartoons were much more aggressive and involved all fantasy characters that behaved aggressively, whereas the control cartoons had more realistic animation about a family. Moreover, the control ones were more suspenseful which may have been more stimulating, although Sprafkin et al. (1988) noted that general arousal does not explain their finding totally because appropriate social interactions did not increase significantly. They speculated that the low interest of the control cartoons may have led to resentment and later antisocial behavior.

According to Sprafkin and her colleagues (1988) aggression-laden cartoons appear to be no worse for children than nonaggressive ones in the short term, and common sense ideas about what is harmful TV for children are not always accurate. In fact, they suggested that "forcing a wholesome television diet on children may be counterproductive" (Sprafkin et al., 1988, p. 97). One cartoon condition did lead to more aggressive behavior, however, which could worsen an ED child's social problems, so there probably should be efforts to reduce the amount of television viewed, to encourage adult coviewing, and to teach critical viewing skills to ED children (Sprafkin et al., 1988).

In Donohue's (1977) study of seriously ED adolescents, boys preferred more violent programs than girls, but both genders saw themselves violently and aggressively about equally. That is, ED girls were as aggressive in orientation as ED boys. Donohue concluded that ED adolescents were more likely to be influenced by favorite TV characters and peers than by adults or authority figures. Because they are already predisposed to violence, TV has a negative effect, especially because other forces in their lives are not reducing the antisocial influences as would happen with normal children (Donohue, 1977). Because children tend to emulate high status models, ED adolescents who identify less with their parents and show fewer appropriate behaviors would be more likely to imitate characters they saw as most like themselves. If favorite characters use violence or antisocial behavior as appropriate and successful problem-solving methods, they are providing antisocial models (Donohue, 1977).

If exceptional children react as much in inappropriate ways to television aggression as research suggests normal children do, however, and if they are exposed to more television violence because of their viewing habits, then those habits should be modified (Sprafkin & Gadow, 1986).

PERCEIVED REALITY

Gadow and his colleagues (1988) suggested that although ED and LD children differ in the nature of their social problems and interactions, they share the misperception of television's reality, and they suggested that this may be due to the fact that both groups are likely to engage in fewer social interactions of a type that would lead to a more realistic view of the world.

Children with learning disabilities are even less able to make a distinction between fantasy and reality, even with control for IQ (Gadow et al., 1988). Using the Perception of Reality on Television measure developed by Sprafkin, Gadow, and Dussault (1986) to test perceptions of reality without reliance on reading ability, Sprafkin et al. (1992) found that ED and LD children were less likely to understand that an actor's role does not continue off the screen. These children saw TV portrayals of unrealistic situations as representative of the real world.

Sprafkin, Gadow, and Dussault (1986) compared school-identified ED children with normal children on a measure of perceived television reality, the Videotest. They found that ED children scored significantly lower on that measure, even when IQ was controlled for, indicating their lesser ability to distinguish between fantasy and reality on television. These children were more likely to consider television programs and commercials to be accurate portrayals of the real world, more like younger children. Sprafkin et al. (1986) suggested further that, given the relation between perceived realism and aggressive behavior and the ED child's more likely perception of aggression as real, ED children might show greater behavioral reaction to TV aggression than their normal counterparts. They might also be expected to want advertised products. Videotest scores correlated highly with achievement and IQ scores. The authors urged consideration of the usefulness of a school-based curriculum to teach such children how to make the distinction between reality and fantasy more easily both in programs and advertising.

In a parallel study with LD children, also using the Stony Brook Videotest, Gadow and his colleagues (1988) obtained similar results. The LD students, who were severely handicapped and in self-contained classes in a special school, were more likely to think that television programming reflected real life. They also were less knowledgeable about the use of special effects and more likely to believe in the veracity of TV commercials. This was true for both genders and for all three age groups (7, 9, and 11 years old), although they did improve with age just as their non-LD counterparts do. The researchers noted further that social skills deficits of many LD children may be compounded by mis-perceptions of television's reality.

Gadow et al. (1988) suggested that the LD children's poorer perform-ance in relation to peers, even when IQ has been controlled, may reflect their more basic information-processing deficits. That is, the same deficits that contribute to their social skills difficulties may also be involved in a more general misperception or poor understanding of reality. These findings, however, pertain to a particular population with very severe learning problems, who may be in even more need of instruction in viewing skills.

Given the importance of perceived realism in television's impact, it follows that LD children might well be more vulnerable to its effects. Sprafkin et al. (1992) suggested that LD children in special classes may be at greater risk because they are not in the mainstream educational situation. Gifted children saw television as least realistic, whereas disabled children lacked the skills necessary to determine whether content is real or not, for example not assessing how plausible a situation is. Therefore, they watch more and tend to see the fiction as real (Sprafkin et al., 1992).

Again, however, one must consider how much of the problem lies in the inability of these children to understand such a distinction and how much is due to their inability to explain it because of their more limited verbal skills. According to Sprafkin et al. (1992), normal children even-tually understand television as their basic intellectual and social skills develop, but there are clear developmental differences among the excep-tional children, especially with complex media presentations.

VIDEO GAMES

Given the demonstrably poorer ability of children with various learning and behavioral problems to separate fantasy and reality and their apparently greater vulnerability to television's influence, the use and content of video games is also a concern. Games now are more realistic and more violent than earlier ones. Funk and Buckman (1996) pointed out that computer and video games offer opportunities for learning just as television does, but their active or interactive dimension may intensify a game's impact, and we should examine the implications of pervasive preferences for violent media as well as whether there are high-risk players or high-risk habits.

Several researchers (Kestenbaum & Weinstein, 1985; McClure & Mears, 1986), on the other hand, have concluded that playing video games is not related to psychopathology. McClure and Mears (1986) found no association between playing games and conduct disorders, neuroticism, or other measures of pathology. Frequent game users did not act out more or show more school-related or drug-related problems than those who played less frequently, but they were more extroverted and less achievement oriented. McClure and Mears concluded that playing games is a fun, escapist activity for most, unrelated to psychopathology. There may even be some positive effects from playing video games. Kestenbaum and Weinstein (1985), for example, suggested that heavy use of video games helps adolescents manage developmental conflicts, especially regarding the expression of aggression and competition, and this does not lead to increased withdrawal, fantasy, or neuroticism, although these individuals did show a lower tolerance for frustration.

Although video games have not been shown to be related directly or causally to psychopathology, however, the fact remains that exceptional children's poorer social skills, usually lower academic achievement, weaker behavioral controls, and poorer discrimination between fantasy and reality make their heavy use of aggressive video games cause for concern. Emotionally disturbed children who play violent video games for hours, for whom the line between fantasy and reality is blurred, who have few alternative and satisfying activities, and who experience little parental mediation or control of their viewing and game-playing activity would appear to be at highest risk for seeing violence as appropriate and realistic and acting out aggressively. Much more research is needed.

INSTRUCTIONAL USE OF TELEVISION

Interestingly, although these groups are the most vulnerable, they also stand to gain the most from instructional use of television, but, little research has been done on the use of the media in teaching exceptional children (Sprafkin et al., 1992).

Hattemer and Showers (1995b) reported a 1982 study that found that prosocial programming could affect children with behavior disorders who normally chose violence and action shows and then acted out what they had seen. After seeing programs that had at least 29 prosocial acts and fewer than 3 aggressive ones per hour, children's concern for others' interests went up, whereas it decreased among those children who watched the action and violent shows. In addition, the children were as attentive to the prosocial programs as the violent ones.

Television certainly can be used to educate others about various disorders and exceptional children's experience of them. For example, Bianculli (1994) described how *The Cosby Show*'s episode on dyslexia informed viewers of some of the difficulties of a LD child and, for some, led to recognition of it in their own family.

Finally, technology can be used in innovative ways to help exceptional children. Irvin et al. (1992), for example, used video and computer technology to develop a videodisc assessment program for measuring children's social skills and for sociometric assessment. They point to it as an example of technology contributing to better assessment of children with handicaps. It allows them to assess children's perceptions and social knowledge directly, without having to rely on others' reports. They can present computer-based video portrayals of various situations and interactions, that do not require high levels of language or reading, and they can sequence items to simulate real life.

HIGH-RISK CHILDREN

Although the data are fairly clear about television's impact on normal children and on children with clear and significant behavioral or emotional difficulties, virtually no work has been done on those children who have not yet been identified clearly as having such problems, but who do appear to be at some risk for developing them: those children who show more behavioral or emotional signals or who stand out for teachers as somewhat problematic in the classroom. Even though they have not been identified specifically as behavioral, learning, or emotionally troubled youngsters, they have weaker behavioral controls, fewer satisfactory social relationships, more inappropriate verbal or motor expressions, and some academic difficulties or underachievement. They are the "gray area" children who are at risk for more serious difficulties; they are also children who might be expected to be more strongly influenced by television in the same direction as those who already have clear problems. They may even be especially vulnerable because they are not in special classes or a treatment program and may be watching more television in unsupervised contexts and with virtually no mediation or intervention involved in their viewing experience.

According to Singer and Singer (1984), the following combination of variables increases a child's risk of problematic behavior by early school age: a home where there is uncontrolled viewing; heavy viewing by preschoolers; heavy viewing of violence; parents who emphasize physical discipline; and parents whose self-descriptions do not emphasize creativity, curiosity, and imagination that might lead to alternatives to the imitation of television behaviors or to reliance on television for entertainment. Children from such backgrounds made less cognitive progress; were more suspicious and fearful; and showed less imagination, more aggression, and poor behavioral adjustment in school (Singer & Singer, 1984). Television may also add to children's restlessness and dysphoria with negative emotional reactions such as anger, fear, and sadness (Singer & Singer, 1986), as well as to peer difficulties, family problems, and lower achievement.

If these children at risk for emotional and behavioral problems react to and interpret television content in the same way as we know LD and ED children react and interpret, important steps could be taken to prevent the undesirable effects that their TV viewing behavior is likely to have. They would be the ones who would benefit most, for example, from critical viewing skills training, reduced viewing time, and greater selectivity in program choices before more serious problems develop.

NEED FOR PREVENTION AND INTERVENTION

There is a need for tailor-made programs for exceptional children (Sprafkin et al., 1992). Sprafkin, Watkins, and Gadow (1990) compared the viewing habits of ED and LD elementary school children, using the Curriculum for Enhancing Social Skills Through Media Awareness (CESSMA; Sprafkin, Watkins, & Gadow, 1986). CESSMA is a viewing skills curriculum that leads to improved perception of reality versus fantasy, knowledge of special effects, and accuracy or truth of advertising. The researchers obtained especially strong results in the area of knowledge of TV, using the Stony Brook Videotest–2 (TV knowledge). Emotionally disturbed children who received the skills curriculum identified less with aggressive characters, but there was no effect of the curriculum on attitudes toward television or habits of viewing, either in amount of viewing or in program choices. Sprafkin et al. (1990) concluded that most studies show that viewing is associated with higher levels of antisocial behavior, regardless of content, so a television literacy curriculum should include lessons on both nonaggressive and aggressive content. Television literacy also can be adapted to be a truly stimulating aspect of education for the gifted (Abelman, 1987b).

As previous research has demonstrated a clear relation between perceived reality and television's impact, one would expect that at-risk children are also more vulnerable to television's influence. Hence important preventive measures should be introduced to prevent further more serious behavioral and emotional difficulties such as modeling of violent or antisocial behavior that they observe frequently in television content or movies. The importance of early intervention lies in its ability to reach high-risk children before television has had as great an impact as it might otherwise have.

Finally, Sprafkin and her colleagues (1992) noted that cable service, VCRs, personal computers, and home video games may open up the market in a way that helps exceptional children, which may lead to more time spent with the media, not just replacing their use of commercial television.

SUMMARY

Research has demonstrated that exceptional children have different viewing patterns and experiences than normal children. Children with learning, behavioral, and emotional disorders tend to view larger amounts of television and to perceive television content as more realistic. They also often have poorer social skills and fewer social contacts and experiences, as well as fewer coviewing experiences with parents and siblings, that would provide information to counter television's messages. For all of these reasons, they are more vulnerable to television's influence in their lives.

In addition, exceptional children may use television viewing to avoid academic or other problems, to get information they cannot get from print, and as a substitute for other social interactions. Because they perceive more television content to be realistic, they also may come to see violence and aggression as realistic solutions to problems.

Critical viewing skills programs can help exceptional children view television more critically and objectively. Nonetheless, their viewing must be monitored carefully to avoid undue influence of television in their already troubled lives. Children at risk for developing problems need attention in these areas as well to prevent more serious behavioral and emotional difficulties.

III

Theoretical Perspectives and Future Directions

9

Theoretical Perspectives

A thorough study of television's influence on children's development requires a close look both at the communication side and at developmental characteristics of the child viewers that influence their experience. Integration of these two major fields of research is essential; emphasizing only one leaves out a whole side of the equation. The wealth of research data on all aspects of children's television experiences has led to the development of various theoretical interpretations and explanations within both the communication literature and the psychological and child development literature. Three theoretical perspectives are discussed in this chapter, and an integrative approach is proposed.

SOCIAL LEARNING THEORY

Basic Assumptions

Social learning theory was one of the first theories to be used to explain television's impact on children. Much of the early work in this area, spearheaded by Bandura's (1967) work in the 1960s, pointed to observational learning and imitation of modeled behavior as the critical components of television's impact. In the classic studies by Bandura, children who viewed violence directed against a Bobo doll were observed in later play sessions. Those who had seen the aggressor punished did not engage in aggressive behavior following the viewing, whereas the others did. In other words, the children imitated the model unless they were deterred through the effects of vicarious learning. Both groups "learned" the aggressive behaviors, but only one group actually imitated them in the later play sessions. The other group inhibited them until the post viewing conditions were changed; then they, too, engaged in more aggressive behavior, thus demonstrating their latent learning of the aggressive response.

Bandura (1967) himself related one of the most graphic and entertaining accounts of modeling:

I remember reading a story reported by Professor Mowrer about a lonesome farmer who decided to get a parrot for company. After acquiring the bird, the farmer spent many long evenings teaching the parrot the phrase, "Say Uncle." Despite the devoted tutorial attention, the parrot proved totally unresponsive and finally, the frustrated farmer got a stick and struck the parrot on the head after each refusal to produce the desired phrase.

But the visceral method proved no more effective than the cerebral one, so the farmer grabbed his feathered friend and tossed him in the chicken house. A short time later the farmer heard a loud commotion in the chicken house and upon investigation found that the parrot was pummeling the startled chickens on the head with a stick and shouting, "Say Uncle! Say Uncle!" (p. 42)

A considerable amount of research done since then on the relation between viewing violent television and increased aggressive behavior has replicated and extended Bandura's findings. Concern about gender-role stereotyping on television stems from our knowledge of imitative behavior and the effects of modeling on children's attitudes and behavior. Similarly, studies that have been done on prosocial behavior have attributed the appearance of desirable behavior to the child's observation and imitation of models who have demonstrated those behaviors and who were reinforced for them.

On the other hand, not all children imitate all of the behavior they see in their many hours of television viewing and the variables affecting their learning and imitation are discussed in the following paragraphs.

Variables Affecting Modeling

Similarities between viewer and model, the credibility of the model, the context of the viewing, and similarities and differences between the televised models and real-life models in the child's environment are important determinants of which behaviors are actually imitated. A child's motivational state, the perceived reality of what is being observed, and the number of other experiences that provide competing models and information are additional significant influences on the imitation of television models that social learning theory predicts.

According to script theory, children do not simply imitate behavior that they view. Rather, they acquire behavioral scripts through observational learning that can then be activated by cues in the environment or activation of memory (Huesmann, 1988). Thus TV viewing affects behavior by activating certain scripts in the viewer, such that the behaviors seen on television are associated in the viewers' minds with other thoughts, events, or conditions.

The determinants of imitation, then, are complex and involve significant cognitive activity, learning, and semantic associations.

Evaluation

Despite the consistency of many findings, there are limitations and problems with using only social learning theory to explain the data. First, not all children imitate what they see. Moreover, as the relation reported often is based on correlational data, causation cannot be demonstrated definitively. For example, although viewing violence on television may lead to imitation of that content and increased aggression, it also is possible that aggressive children may choose to watch more violent programs, and independent factors that lead both to viewing high levels of violence and to increased aggressive behavior need to be investigated further.

It is also important to look at the viewer's perception in the viewing situation. What some individuals find to be very violent may be seen as harmless by others (Gunter, 1985). Young children's greater reliance on perceptually salient cues, for example, and their more concrete approach to material (e.g., reacting to things that look violent), may result in very different perceptions than those of older children. Thus, age and gender differences, as well as personality, experiential, and contextual ones, interact with the television content to affect what is perceived as violent and what the viewer response will be.

Social learning theory has been used most effectively to interpret the short-term effects that have been demonstrated in the many laboratory experiments that have been conducted, rather than the long-term socialization influences that are examined in naturalistic studies (Milavsky et al., 1982; Wackman et al., 1977). The long-term effects of viewing, and the relative influence of many other factors that contribute to the appearance of specific behaviors are not as obvious, however. Clearly the elements of observational learning, modeling, vicarious reinforcement, and imitation are essential components of a child's viewing experience, but they are mediated by a host of other variables.

CULTIVATION THEORY

The cultivation hypothesis as espoused by Gerbner, Gross, Morgan, and Signorielli (1980, 1982, 1986) asserts that for heavy viewers, television cultivates reality perceptions of the world that are consistent with television's portrayals and that lead to homogeneity of perceptions (Cook et al., 1983). The more time spent viewing television, the more likely the viewer is to accept television's version of things, especially in areas where the viewer has little direct experience, such as in the expectation of violence or in getting information about other groups with whom the person does not interact.

Cultivation analysis is "the investigation of the consequences of this ongoing and pervasive system of cultural messages" (Gerbner et al., 1980, p. 14), and of television's contribution to viewer conceptions (Gerbner et al., 1982). Cultivation theory predicts or expects frequent viewers to give more answers consistent with television's portrayal of the world as shown in content analyses, than of the real world as shown by actual statistics (Wright, 1986).

According to a cultivation perspective, the amount of viewing or exposure is a very important variable in television's impact on thought and behavior. According to Gerbner et al. (1982), heavy viewers differ systematically from light viewers in beliefs, values, and assumptions that may relate in consistent ways to the groups' life situations and views. Cultivation theory assumes that heavy viewers are also less selective in their viewing, engage in habitual viewing, and experience a good deal of sameness of content. Moreover, television's impact is greatest when it functions as the only information source and when it is relevant to the person. Light viewers are more likely to have many other sources of information (whether social interaction, reading, or vocational experience) that take up much of their time and displace TV viewing time. They have more diverse sources of information and a greater number of behavioral models; they are also, perhaps, less likely to take television content seriously. Heavy viewers have few other sources of ideas and thus are more likely to report reality perceptions that are consistent with television portrayals (Gerbner et al., 1980).

However, television does not act in a vacuum; nor does it act on everyone in the same way. Not only do heavy viewers at one developmental level have a different experience than heavy viewers at another level; those of a different gender, socioeconomic level, or family background also experience television differently. Any potential cultivation effect must be evaluated against the significance and impact of these other factors on a child's development and experience.

Television also dramatically changes children's access to information about the world. Because of their more limited experience and knowledge base and in the absence of competing information, television may have a particularly potent effect on them. Huston and her colleagues (1992) reported that children who are heavy viewers of television show a high level of concern about getting sick and have higher perceptions of medical relief and over-the-counter remedies. We must look, then, at the developmental differences, over the long run, between children who have been brought up on television—those for whom television has portrayed and defined "reality" to a larger extent—and those whose television experience has been more limited, either to a certain period of their lives, in terms of total amount of viewing, or as an informational source.

Perceived Reality

An important variable in any cultivation effect is perceived reality. If the television content is seen as real, it is more involving and relevant, which should enhance its effect (Hawkins & Pingree, 1980). Moreover, viewers who perceive and believe in television as a source of useful information that can help them to solve problems vicariously and to cope likely also perceive television as fairly realistic (Potter, 1986).

Even the concept of perceived reality itself appears to be more complex than has usually been thought. Potter (1986, 1988), for example, discussed the importance of identity, or "the degree of similarity the viewer perceives between television characters and situations and the people and situations experienced in real life" (Potter, 1986, p. 163). Individuals high on this dimension feel close to television characters, have a strong sense of reality about them, and feel about them the way they feel about real friends. They believe that television characters are similar to individuals they meet in real life, and they are likely to be more susceptible to television's influence.

Finally, Kubey and Csikszentmihalyi (1990) pointed out, however, that television and film are likely to have more of a homogenizing effect than print because people's perception of content on television is more likely similar to others' than is true of print. Viewers know exactly what a character looks like, for example, and do not have to construct an image in their mind.

Mainstreaming and Resonance

According to Gerbner, Gross, Morgan, and Signorielli (1980), there are varying patterns of associations between amounts of viewing and conceptions of reality for different social groups that can be explained in relation to two systematic processes, mainstreaming and resonance.

Mainstreaming refers to an overall effect of television portrayals and it is related more to general norms and images and social reality (Gerbner et al., 1980). In mainstreaming, the viewing may override differences in behavior or perspective that arise from other cultural, social, and demographic influences in "a homogenization of divergent views and a convergence of disparate views" (Gerbner et al., 1986, p. 31), or the cultivation of common outlooks in heavy viewers. That is, heavy viewers, even in high-educational and high-income groups, share a commonality that light viewers do not (Gerbner et al., 1980).

According to cultivation theory, then, television has the power to cultivate mainstreamed perceptions or outlooks (such as fear or mistrust) and to assimilate groups that ordinarily diverge into a mainstream. There is more interpersonal distrust among heavy viewers, an idea that people cannot be trusted or that they will take advantage of others (Signorielli, 1987), "a heightened and unequal sense of danger and risk in a mean and selfish world" (p. 267). Heavy viewers in one study (Shrum, 1996) gave significantly higher estimates of the frequency of real-world crime, particular occupations, and marital discord than light viewers did.

Others have found very different reactions and perceptions among viewers. For example, Rubin and his colleagues (1988) found that respondents felt safe and connected to others regardless of exposure levels, and in fact higher exposure was associated with perceived safety. Moreover, in contrast to what cultivation theory would predict, heavy and ritualistic viewing was not associated with negative effects, which instead depended on specific content (Rubin et al., 1988).

Television interacts with real world and demographic factors as well. Signorielli (1990) noted that the unequal sense of danger and vulnerability or general malaise from "entertainment" evokes aggression, but also repression and exploitation as people who are fearful are more easily controlled and manipulated and are more likely to yield to tough, hard-line positions that are "deceptively simple." (p. 102).

Resonance on the other hand, refers to situations in which television information about specific issues has particular salience, and what is seen is congruent with a person's actual experiences, with reality, or with the individual's perceived reality (Gerbner et al., 1980). That combination then may give added weight to the television message and lead to an increased effect. The "congruence of the television world and real-life circumstances may 'resonate' and lead to markedly amplified cultivation patterns" (Gerbner et al., 1980, p. 15). Thus, resonance occurs when a topic in the television world has special salience or personal relevance for a group (e.g., overvictimization of the elderly) and it is in that situation that correlations with heavy viewing are clearest.

As research cited earlier indicates, young children find television content more realistic and have greater difficulty distinguishing realistic material from unrealistic material, so its impact on them should be stronger. This impact is enhanced even more by the fact that they have fewer alternative or competing sources of information with which to compare television's messages, so in situations in which parents or peers have minimal input or influence, television is more likely to have an effect. Thus, personal interaction and affiliation reduce cultivation, presumably by providing alternate sources of information (Gerbner et al., 1986).

New Technologies and the Cultivation Effect

According to Perse and her colleagues (Perse, Ferguson, & McLeod, 1994), new technology may change how television viewing could cultivate beliefs about social reality because of the diversity of programming and increased viewer control and selectivity. Perse et al. (1994) found more interpersonal distrust with higher exposure to broadcast-type channels, but less mistrust and less fear of crime with greater exposure to more specialized cable channels. Cable had the greatest impact on television's mainstreaming effect, but these researchers also found an inverse relation between fear of crime and ownership of VCRs.

Perse et al. (1994) suggested that cable may pull away from dominant themes of networks, or may offer other themes that are reassuring or that increase perceptions of self-efficacy. Cable may weaken a mainstreaming impact over time; that is, new technologies change the homogenization of heavy viewing, but heavy viewers are less likely to own a VCR and may use cable for "more of the same." These researchers urged more study of the impact of new technology on traditional ideas about media effects.

Evaluation

Not everyone agrees with the validity of this conceptualization, however, and cultivation analysis has been criticized on methodological grounds. Rubin and his colleagues (1988) concluded that factors such as response bias may explain cultivation effects that had previously been seen as a function of levels of exposure to television. Moreover, cultivation studies also have omitted attention to antecedent and intervening variables, and factors like program choice or perceived reality may override television content in structuring one's perceptions (Rubin et al., 1988). In addition, as it is basically a correlational analysis, causal direction is not easily established. Although heavy viewers may develop a certain perception of the world, their perception of the world also may determine their viewing habits and program choices. Moreover, heavy and light viewers also differ in other ways and some subgroups seem to show an effect, whereas others do not (Dominick, 1987).

Other variables such as age, socioeconomic level, gender, and perceived realism predicted faith in others better than television exposure, and there is a need for further study of the impact of viewer choice and individual differences on perception, especially with the greater diversity of communication alternatives (Rubin et al., 1988).

Other serious criticisms have been leveled against Gerbner's cultivation theories (Wober, 1978; Wober & Gunter, 1988). Wober and Gunter (1988), for example, claimed that those theories have not been verified empirically, that other research has shown the conclusions to rest on small correlations without other related variables being partialed out, and the hypothesis did not hold for Blacks. In a survey commissioned by the Independent Broadcasting Authority in Great Britain involving over 1,000 adults, Wober (Wober & Gunter, 1988) asked questions based on items from Gerbner's work. She found no systematic tendency toward feelings of less security among heavy viewers than among light viewers, which should have occurred if the claimed effects were robust.

After reviewing studies that questioned Gerbner's findings, Wober and Gunter (1988) offered the following possible explanations for the discrepancies between U.S. and British findings:

1. Cultivation effects may be specific to U.S. audiences.
2. The nature of the questions in Gerbner's work.
3. Levels of real violence in viewers' worlds were not taken into account but could affect perceived threat and amount of viewing (e.g., staying in to watch television).
4. Regarding giving "TV answers" for opinions about various events, "substantially different patterns of association between viewing and social beliefs can emerge for different social groups" (p. 39).
5. Not everyone watches the same programs, so the content that is viewed and the information obtained vary depending on a viewer's choice of what to watch.

Shrum (1995) applied social cognitive theory to cultivation research and found that heuristic processing strategies are more likely to be used when involvement in a judgment task is low or when one feels pressure to make a judgment quickly. This, according to Shrum, has implications for cultivation effects because both of those conditions exist in the usual survey research used in much of the cultivation research that has been published. Shrum suggested that passive viewers are more likely to show a cultivation effect (when measured by first-order judgments such as prevalence estimates of people or behaviors or objects) because of heuristic processing, so viewer involvement is important. Virtually all people overestimate such things as violent crime and prevalence of certain occupations, such as police. This may not have anything to do with television viewing, however; the important difference is the one between the estimates of heavy and light viewers (Shrum, 1995).

Amount of viewing alone, however, does not appear to be the most important cause of a cultivation effect, according to Potter (1986). More recent research suggests that any cultivation effect that is observed is a function of more complex variables than simple level of viewing. For example, Potter found a cultivation effect only in the high school students who were high on the Magic Window dimension; and, in fact, a reverse effect was observed on some measures in the group that was low on that dimension. Levels of identification with television characters and levels of perceived reality also need to be taken into account (Potter, 1986), as do developmental factors. Four-year-old heavy viewers do not receive and respond to the same information as 14-year-old viewers or 40-year-old viewers. Their needs and their motivations for viewing differ widely, their ability to comprehend and retain television information is very different, and their experience and the scripts by which they interpret television material are widely disparate.

Cultivation results cannot be explained away via situational or attitudinal variables, however; and perhaps they could be accounted for by some third variable, or a competing information source (Hawkins & Pingree, 1980). Interactions among such variables as cognitive maturity, attention, experience with television, viewing context, family attitudes, and other social and emotional variables need to be addressed in any effort to understand whether and how a phenomenon, such as a cultivation effect, occurs in children's television viewing experience. Other possible explanations and interpretations are discussed later in this chapter.

USES AND GRATIFICATIONS THEORY

Whereas cultivation theory emphasizes the impact of television content on heavy viewers, other theoretical perspectives place more emphasis on viewer characteristics and motivations and on the processes and interactions involved in the viewing experience. For example, social learning theory focuses on both the content and the viewer and on the modeling, vicarious reinforcement, and other processes that determine viewers' imitation of observed behavior. A uses and gratifications model deals with the actual motivations of viewers, the uses they make of television, and the actual needs they have that are satisfied by the media. It looks at what people do with the media rather than what the media do to them (Wright, 1986).

Further, a uses and gratifications model addresses the functional alternatives to one's use of the media, the social and psychological environments of viewers, and their communication behavior and its consequences (Rubin, 1986b).

Basic Assumptions

The various uses and gratifications that can be derived from the television experience fall into four major categories, summarized by Dominick (1987):

1. Cognition, to obtain information or knowledge.
2. Diversion, for stimulation, relaxation, or emotional release.
3. Social integration, utility, to strengthen contact with others, to overcome loneliness, to allow parasocial relationships with TV characters and so on.
4. Withdrawal, for example, to provide a barrier or avoid chores.

Television also can help in the resolution of developmental tasks or life-stage issues, such as adolescent crises, by providing direct learning and information, stimulating fantasies, or stimulating interpersonal discussion of options (Faber, Brown, & McLeod, 1986).

Motivation for Viewing

A uses and gratifications approach assumes that individuals interact actively with the media based on their needs and motivations, and that the media compete with other sources of satisfaction. The motives for viewing may vary with television content and among viewers (Rubin, 1984), but children and adolescents, as well as adults, use media content to satisfy personal needs or wants (Rubin, 1985). It is further assumed that the audience selects and uses content that will best meet their needs and that the same program may gratify different needs in different audience members (Fiske, 1982).

Personality differences among viewers affect not only what they watch and why they watch but also how they react emotionally to the content. A large segment of the television audience may seek out viewing as a simple, effortless, and mildly involving activity that is rewarding in itself, regardless of content (Tannenbaum, 1985; Winn, 1985).

Johnston (1995), for example, used a uses and gratifications model to study adolescents' motivations for viewing graphic horror. She found that their motivations for viewing slasher films differed and mediated the relation between violent content and affective and cognitive responses to it. She also found that the motivations were related to different preferences, ideas about positive attributes of those movies, patterns of affect before and after viewing, character identification, and different personality profiles. The four motivations she discussed reflected very different affective and cognitive experiences in the viewers' response to violence. The motives (gore watching, thrill watching, independent watching, and problem watching) were each associated with varying levels of empathy, positive and negative affect, adventure seeking, substance abuse, and identification with victim or killer. It seems clear that such distinctions among viewers of violence would shed considerable light on the differential effects of television violence on child and adolescent viewers.

Important differences also exist between heavy viewers and nonviewers in motivation toward or away from television. Foss and Alexander (1996) found that heavy viewers generally attribute their reason for viewing to external circumstances (e.g. being ill, having time, having nothing better to do). Both groups felt that television viewing could have negative consequences, such as addiction, but heavy viewers felt immune because they viewed television just for escape and relaxation. Nonviewers chose not to watch so that they would not succumb to addictive effects or become passive or noncritical thinkers. Heavy viewers saw television as unimportant and simply a means to relax; nonviewers also saw television as unimportant, but chose to spend their time doing other things. Therefore, even agreement on these basic themes of motivation, consequences, and importance, and on the addiction metaphor, still led to very different behavior in the two groups.

Selective Exposure

Zillmann and Bryant (1985b) suggested that viewers are sensitive to the effects of various program characteristics and that they use that knowledge to choose messages that are most capable of achieving desirable results. That is, they emphasize and focus on exposure to content involving comforting messages and tend to minimize exposure to programs with disquieting information; they use or select messages for their therapeutic value (Zillmann & Bryant, 1985a). Individuals who are in a bad mood or want to extend a good one are more likely to choose humor and comedy, for example (Zillmann, 1985). Such selective exposure occurs under, or as a function of, all kinds of conditions and moods, including fear, stress, and boredom (Zillmann & Bryant, 1985a).

The therapeutic value of television entertainment lies in its power to improve one's mood, to calm one down, to reduce boredom, or in other ways to provide psychological benefits from viewing it (Zillmann & Bryant, 1986). Even children as young as 4 or 5 years old were found to use television to improve their moods, although results were clearer for boys than for girls (Zillmann, 1985).

Kubey (1986) stressed the importance of examining the actual experience of individuals in a wide range of activities—of which television viewing is one—to try to discern correlates and causal directions. Studying moods should help establish when and why individuals view television. The Experience-Sampling Method (ESM) can be used to get data, in naturalistic settings, on the frequency and patterns of various daily activities and interactions, on psychological states and on thought patterns; and evidence for its validity exists in the correlations with physiological measures, psychological tests, and behavioral indices (Csikszentmihalyi & Larson, 1987). ESM data are based on self-reports of individuals at random points through their waking hours, measuring variability within people over time (Kubey & Csikszentmihalyi, 1990).

Kubey and Csikszentmihalyi (1990) employed three dimensions: location (where participants were when they were beeped), activity (what they were doing when they were beeped), and companionship (whether they were alone or with someone and, if so, with whom when they were beeped). They found a relation between amount of viewing and discomfort during solitary and unstructured time, especially for those with marital disruption or breakup and for less affluent and less educated viewers. Such viewers are more likely to continue viewing to avoid time alone with feelings and thoughts and turn to TV when they feel bad and others are not around (Kubey, 1986).

Anderson, Collins, Schmitt, and Jacobvitz (1996) also suggested that viewers use media to displace thoughts that might lead to dysphoric moods and choose content that will lead to positive moods. However, they warned that if TV is used chronically to avoid thinking about problems and how to solve them, it will interfere with the development of more effective coping strategies. Nonetheless, television viewing may be a good way to reduce stress and anxiety temporarily, especially when the viewer has little control over the stress, and perhaps viewers who feel especially stressed use TV for this purpose (Anderson et al., 1996). Children also use television viewing to reduce stress, especially because they have even less control over many stressful events in their lives.

Finally, some cultural differences have been reported as well. Zohoori (1988), for example, reported that foreign children, compared with U.S. children, were more likely to use television to learn about themselves and others, although they all used television for escape in equal numbers.

Instrumental and Ritualistic Viewing

In a further analysis of audience motives, Rubin (1984, 1986b, Rubin & Perse, 1987) distinguished between an active audience that selects specific programs and views purposefully, and one in which viewers watch nonselectively and ritualistically. Such a distinction between instrumental and ritualized types of viewing also provides information about amount of viewing and content preferences.

Instrumental viewing, for example, refers to a goal-directed use of the media, such as for information. It is selective, purposeful, and infrequent, and it does not show high regard for television as a medium (Rubin, 1984). Viewing is more selective and intentional or purposeful, and there is greater involvement. Ritualized viewing, on the other hand, is a more habitualized, frequent, and nonselective use of television such as for diversion, or to relax or pass time, and television is valued as a medium (Rubin, 1984). Thus, the activity of the audience may vary by degree and kind.

All audiences are not active for the same reason or in the same way. Audience activity is a variable concept and individuals might view television instrumentally or ritualistically depending on time, background, and situation (Rubin, 1984). Finally, with new technological developments, viewers have many more alternatives and paths by which they can gratify their needs (Williams, Phillips, & Lum, 1985).

Developmental Variables

Developmental level is an important variable in a uses and gratifications approach, and developmental changes in the use of television as a medium have emerged in many studies. Filling time was the most common one across ages, and there was a general decline in all motivations with age (Rubin, 1977). Moreover, the use of television for excitement decreases between age 9 and 17 (Rubin, 1985). Rubin's (1977) findings suggest that motivation for purposeful viewing changes with age, whereas for nonpurposeful viewing it does not. One would expect less reliance on television with increasing age because of the greater likelihood of other sources of information. Young children watch more both because they lack other information and experience and because they more often see it as realistic and therefore more relevant. Age is also important because an age cohort is an indicator of what role individual and social factors play at different developmental levels (Rubin, 1985).

Evaluation

Uses and gratifications theory also has come under serious criticism in more recent work, however. Kubey and Csikszentmihalyi (1990), for example, noted that the assumptions underlying a uses and gratifications approach assume voluntary use of the media to satisfy needs and do not take into account that users do not always have choice about what is viewed. Family members may view a program because that is what other family members are watching. In addition, insufficient consideration is given to the fact that viewers have many needs at the same time, and they might be satisfied by a wide range of programs. However, the strongest concern is that uses and gratifications thought sees gratifications and effects as separate, when, according to Kubey and Csikszentmihalyi, gratifications *are* effects. They also claimed that uses and gratifications theory ignores the fact that many people are affected in similar ways and there are general media effects that hold the greatest potential for studies of mass communication.

AN OVERVIEW AND INTEGRATION

Each of the various theoretical perspectives discussed in the previous sections has a very different focus or emphasis. Cultivation approaches stress the media content and its power to cultivate attitudes among heavy viewers. Discussions about information-processing abilities, perceived reality, and social learning processes focus on the viewer's cognitive processes as intervening variables between the medium and behavioral effects. Studies of family influence and mediation point to the environment in which children watch television and place television within a socialization context. Finally, a uses and gratifications approach emphasizes the interaction between the television message and viewer characteristics, needs, and motives. Looking at the television viewing experience from only one of these perspectives leads to an incomplete understanding and, perhaps, misinterpretation of many research data. What is needed is a means by which these various theoretical perspectives and emphases can be integrated into a consistent and coherent conceptualization of what actually happens during and as a result of a child's television viewing, and how those events are caused, mediated, facilitated, or impeded.

If one takes into account the diverse theoretical views and empirical data described throughout this book, two rather distinct viewing patterns emerge that help to integrate many of the research findings. These patterns consist of viewing variables that tend to cluster together and reflect very different viewing experiences.

In the first one, television is viewed seriously in an effort to derive information and knowledge from what is being viewed. A considerable amount of mental effort is invested, and logical and critical skills are brought to bear in goal-directed viewing. Such viewers have more intense and focused attention and stronger motivation to extract relevant information from the television content. Under those conditions, television would be expected to have maximum impact *in that content area*; it is being taken seriously. Whether that influence was positive or negative would depend on the content being viewed. Moreover, if they engage in heavy viewing, and hence displace opportunities for comparing television information with that from other sources, one would expect those viewers to be particularly vulnerable to television's influence and to the cultivation of attitudes and outlooks by the television portrayals.

This interpretation is entirely consistent with script theory in that individuals with little information in an area would have only a limited script (little alternate information) and would depend more heavily on the television experience for information to develop a script for a given area or topic. If the television portrayal is the only, or the major model for a child (or for viewers who are disadvantaged, in minority groups, poorly educated, or lower functioning), or if it is the only or major source of information for a script, that viewer will be more likely to take it seriously, to emulate the television model, or to internalize the television script.

On the other hand, if viewers already have a rich variety of informational sources and are viewing television simply for diversion or entertainment, not for information, they are more likely to experience the television content in a more emotional and less critical way, to exert less mental effort, and to take it less seriously. They would seem to be less susceptible to television's influence or to cultivation of attitudes by its content. Even if they engage in heavy viewing, its impact might be less than if they were using television as a serious and primary source of information, although subtle messages are still conveyed.

The considerable significance of developmental level must be taken into account, however. In the absence of other informational sources, and without extensive experience, as is the case with young children, viewing large amounts of television for entertainment might also serve an important informational function. Young children may use entertainment to gain information they need. If they have few other avenues to learn about a content area, heavy viewing, even for entertainment, would likely provide them with information and would increase television's impact on them.

One way to interpret the data, then, is to underscore the complex interaction that appears to exist between cultivation and uses and gratifications approaches, an interaction that is made more complex by developmental differences among viewers. When television is used differently—to satisfy specific needs—other aspects of the viewing experience also differ significantly. In addition, perceived reality mediates whether the portrayals viewed actually have an impact, particularly if there are few competing views from other informational sources. Even in the case of light viewers, then, when television is being used for information, and when the content is perceived to be very realistic, one would expect it to have more effect than if it is being used for diversion and/or if it is perceived as less realistic. These complex interactions are illustrated in Fig. 9.1.

Thus, the use made of television and the seriousness of one's involvement in it may be more important than sheer level of exposure. Cultivation theory suggests that heavy viewers are most influenced by television's messages. Perhaps the amount of viewing is secondary to the motivation for viewing, at least for older children who have other experiences and sources of information to counter television's messages. Viewers who demonstrate a cultivation effect are likely the ones who take television seriously and who rely on it for information. Indeed, recent data have confirmed this expectation. Perse (1986), for example, contrary to cultivation hypothesis assumptions, found that the limited

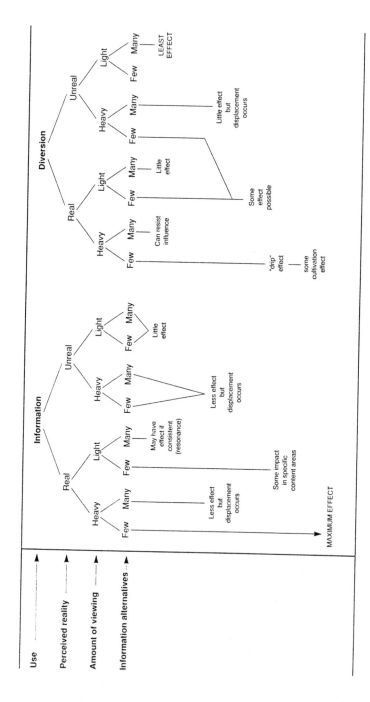

FIG. 9.1. Interactions among use and amount of viewing with perceived reality and information alternatives. Developmental level, socioeconomic level, race, gender, and other factors determine use made of television, reality perceived, amount viewed, and informational alternatives.

cultivation effect that she found was related to instrumental viewing motives, as well as to higher levels of perceived reality and affinity. The instrumental motives, however, included a search for exciting entertainment as well as for information. The key component, then, in the limited cultivation effect observed appeared to be the goal-directedness of the viewing.

The cultivation effect often associated with heavy viewing, then, may be greater in some viewer groups, not only because they watch more television, but also because they are members of groups (e.g., ethnic minorities, disadvantaged individuals, young children, elderly, poorly educated) who use television very differently. They more often rely on television as a source of information, and they have fewer, or less diverse alternative sources. Even if those heavy viewers use television primarily for entertainment, if they perceive it to be realistic, and if they have little competing information, they are still likely more vulnerable to its influence.

Because individuals view specific programs for various reasons and at different times, they may use television for one purpose on one occasion, or for a given program or time period, and use it for another reason at another time.

With increasing maturity, then, and the greater likelihood of having alternative sources of information, television may have less impact. One would expect television to be taken less seriously with age, to be perceived as less realistic, and to be used more often for diversion, entertainment, and escape, although SES, gender, content, and format variables also affect its influence. For children who have reasonable educational and interpersonal opportunities, television should play a less central role in their lives and socialization as they mature, and as their range of experiences expands.

For those older children and adults who do not have other sources of information, however, or who have not developed skills to obtain it, television would be expected to continue to be a primary source of information and to exert a stronger influence. For children from disadvantaged homes, children with reading problems, or children whose parents are not involved in their viewing and are not thereby providing alternative information (i.e., for children who watch a considerable amount of television in order to get the information that they need), the potential for influence and cultivation of attitudes is much greater.

Such a distinction also helps to clarify seemingly conflicting views among researchers who claim that children do not take television seriously, such as Cullingsford (1984), and those who claim that children are very much affected by it, such as those who explain its effect through social learning and modeling (e.g., Bandura, 1967; Winett & Kramer, 1989) or script theories (e.g., Berkowitz & Rogers, 1986; Durkin, 1985; Eron, 1982; Huesmann, 1988).

When one studies viewers who are using television as a serious source of information, all of the characteristics, intervening variables, and processes discussed in earlier chapters on information processing of television material are very relevant and important and they further complicate the issue. The effects of formal features on attention, for example, the varying levels of comprehension, the factors that influence retention, the importance of verbal encoding and rehearsal, the effects of age and previous experience on a child's interpretation of television content, and many other variables interact to determine the level and accuracy of the information that the child derives from the viewing experience. Therefore, even when a child is using television seriously to obtain information, many developmental and experiential factors influence the actual quality of the information obtained. Two children viewing the same program for the same purpose (e.g., for information) still might well get very different input from the experience, depending on their age, gender, socioeconomic level, cognitive maturity, general experience, and family background. The study of television's impact on children, then, is clearly an extraordinarily complex and challenging task.

Cultivation theory has been criticized as relying too heavily on correlational findings in its claim that heavy viewers are more likely to develop attitudes consistent with television portrayals, when in fact it is perhaps those attitudes that lead to heavy television viewing. An emphasis on the purpose of the viewing, however, provides an intervening variable to help explain the relation between amount of viewing and attitudes. Whether heavy viewing leads to the development of a cultivated perception of the world or whether one's perception leads to heavy viewing, why one views television, the use made of television, and the seriousness with which it is taken, as well as other sources of competing information, are important considerations in predicting the extent of its influence.

Viewing preferences are also important, because if one is seeking information, the content selected may be rather different than if one is watching for entertainment or diversion, although individual viewers vary in their judgments about which content is informational and which is entertaining. Hence patterns of viewer preference also affect the influence that television has, not necessarily directly through the content perhaps, as much as through the purpose for which the viewer watches that content.

Television content itself can be seen as varying along informational and entertainment dimensions, but its interpretation and the use made of it also can vary depending on the motivation of the viewer. On the surface, one might assume, for example, that shows such as news shows and documentaries would appeal primarily to individuals seeking information and shows such as situation comedies would appeal primarily to those looking for diversion. However, young and inexperienced children, socially inhibited children, or shy adults (i.e., those with limited alternative information and strategies) might rely on situation comedies for information as well, as a model for social interaction, or as a source of strategies in their own interpersonal relationships.

Such television portrayals, then, in the face of less competing information, and especially if viewed alone without input from others about the relative effectiveness of those interactions, should exert a far greater impact than is ordinarily associated with them. Conversely, some viewers are likely to watch documentaries solely for diversion or entertainment rather than to obtain information. There may also be a kind of blending of the two as "infotainment" (Morgenstern, 1989), in which information is presented entertainingly. Morgenstern (1989) pointed out that most Americans connect with reality through television rather than through newspapers, and that the television medium is "where relentless sensationalism is now blurring the line between information and entertainment" (p. 28).

The fact that empirical data do not consistently support cultivation theory (Berkowitz & Rogers, 1986) may be because the purpose of viewing or the use made of television and developmental differences among viewers were not taken into account at the same time. Identical content viewed for different reasons by viewers with very different levels of information and experience should have quite different effects. Moreover, the importance of other variables that have been found in a considerable amount of research, such as age, viewing context, SES, and minority status, may well lie, at least in part, in their impact or influence on the use that is made of specific television content at any given point in time. Conceptualizing the research data in this way allows for integration of many seemingly contradictory findings into a more consistent explanatory picture of television's impact.

SUMMARY

Various theoretical perspectives and models for explaining and interpreting the complex interaction of variables and events that influence children's television experience have been put forward over the years. The earliest of these in the psychological literature was a social learning perspective, which emphasized observational learning and modeling of behaviors viewed on television.

Research in the communication field has emphasized television's potential for the cultivation of attitudes and behavior change in viewers. It also has stressed the needs of viewers, the context of viewing, the use that is made of television viewing, and the gratifications that viewers obtain from their television experiences. Perceived reality of the content and the availability of and access to alternative and competing sources of information, as well as the purpose for viewing, are critically important variables in the assessment of television's impact. Knowledge of the interactions among media components and content; viewer variables, perceptions, and motivations; and characteristics of the viewing context are essential factors in our efforts to understand children's television experiences.

10

New Technologies

New technological developments can influence the impact of media on children in both direct and indirect ways. They already have changed the nature of programming content and, more importantly, children's access to that content. Technological changes in the communication field and changes in viewer behavior have occurred with breathtaking rapidity over the past decade. According to Mayer (1994), by the early 1990s, 70% of households had VCRs and remote control devices for their televisions, 60% had cable, 45% had answering machines, and 20% to 30% had personal computers and compact disc players. Some put these figures even higher, with 75% of homes having VCRs and 80% having cable (Wartella, Heintz, Aidman, & Mazzarella, 1990). Mayer (1994) contended that as the percentages of ownership increase, the devices are used less frequently and less innovatively. For example, with an increase from 2% to 73% of homes with VCRs, there is now evidence that owners tape fewer shows, rent fewer movies, and are less likely to skip commercials when taping something (Mayer, 1994).

Even the sizes have changed. Dorr and Kunkel (1990) noted that the size of TVs has decreased so that in 1989, a viewer could get a videocassette system with a self-supporting VCR system, functional screen, and full-length movie in a product that would fit in a shirt pocket. Of course, TV screens have also grown in the opposite direction as well, making giant TV screens for home use much more available, including 35-inch conventional sets and 40 inch to 65 inch rear projection models (Marshall, 1997). In any case, television technology is always available and caters to our needs like a good mother (Nelson, 1987).

THE "NEW MEDIA"

Mayer (1994) reminded us that the phrase *new media* is relative—even the printing press was a new medium once—but the term usually includes VCR, computers, cellular phones, CDs, fax and answering machines, e-mail, satellite dishes, cable TV, and interactive television, all of which are used for the development, storage, and transmission of information and have transformed traditional media.

153

The new media refer to technologies in which distribution is virtually unlimited in channel capacity (e.g., cable TV, VCRs), and programming has more diversity. The old media are traditional network distribution systems with a smaller number of channels and a fixed timetable (Webster, 1989b). One of the most important aspects of the new technological developments is the increase in the alternatives available, both for access to stimuli and for interaction with them (Williams et al., 1985). They also make distance all but irrelevant and free television from the restrictions of broadcast schedules (Williams et al., 1985).

VCRS AND CABLE

The new technologies mean access to more channels and more kinds of programs on cable, some considered to be positive (e.g., educational), and some negative (e.g., graphic violence). Others, such as video games and VCRs, also limit the user more than a computer, but allow more choice than television, and cable and satellite dishes, although similar in interactivity to broadcast television, offer more choice (Dorr & Kunkel, 1990).

Some warn, however, that choice in itself does not guarantee quality. As one writer put it:

> Television choice is sold to us with surprisingly little reference to what is to be chosen. There is far more talk about 500 channel television sets and direct broadcast satellites than there is about the actual choices they will offer. It is assumed that choice itself is a sufficient guarantee of quality. (Feldman, 1994, p. 29)

Feldman (1994) went on to note that many of the channels offer significant amounts of repetition and commercialism. Having a greater sense of increased control and participation via remote controls, telethons, home videos on television, on-air shopping and, especially phone-in talk shows, however, increased the appeal of choice, interactivity, and direct involvement.

Morgan and Shanahan (1991) noted that VCR and television exposure interact with each other, and they argued that VCR effects depend on previous viewing patterns. They said that society looks at media diversity in terms of number of channels rather than content, and that technological changes may bring superficial changes in how people use media but are not likely to decrease the central role of television: "All this suggests that traditional messages can be transmitted in nontraditional ways with decidedly traditional results" (Morgan & Shanahan, 1991, p. 134).

Wartella and her colleagues (1990) found that although cable provides significantly greater program choices, VCRs and broadcast television provide little diversity in content for children. For example, most weekday programs were cartoons, two thirds of which were toy-related, and on weekends, only 3 of 28 commercial programs for children were not cartoons. Public television offered alternatives and was almost the only source of educational content, as fewer than 5% of cable programs and none of the commercial programs were rated as educational. Fifty-nine per cent of the younger viewers' favorite programs were educational programs on public television. Cable, although still half cartoons, offered much more diversity. Of videocassette rental tapes, 50% to 70% were animated, most toy-related, and most represented products that began on television, such as Saturday morning television (Wartella et al., 1990).

Without access to cable, then, children experience less diversity and variety, and VCR rentals appear to present just more of what is on television and cable: little educational and much toy-related content. In addition, according to parents, television still dominated and VCR use did not increase or decrease television viewing time (Wartella et al., 1990).

Others have suggested that VCRs and specialty channels have, in fact, contributed to decreasing amounts of viewing time by children and adolescents. A senior vice president of an advertising company was cited as reporting a 6% drop in children's overall viewing of TV on Saturday morning programs and weekday afternoons and attributed the drop to the fact that children were watching videos or playing computer games instead (Stead, 1997).

With remote control devices now found in most homes and many more viewing alternatives available, a new viewing behavior—grazing—has developed, in which viewers skim through options or follow several programs simultaneously.

Children who do have access are exposed to content on cable and via VCRs that is not available on commercial television, including mature themes, violence, and graphic sexual content. MTV, for example, has at least one violent occurrence in over half of its videos, a much higher rate than commercial programs (Donnerstein et al., 1994).

Dorr and Kunkel (1990) noted that there is increased interaction to be sure, but also much continuity despite changes in the media, and VCR use tends to follow or be similar to one's TV use. For example, Dobrow (1990) found that all viewers used their VCRs for greater selectivity and control, but heavy viewers tended to watch more of the same via the VCR, whereas light viewers used the VCR more to view content that they liked. That is, heavy viewers concentrated on their favorite programs and did not really use the greater diversity. Morgan and Shanahan (1991) also found that overall, VCR use tends to strengthen television's effects and cultivation, because although there is more diversity, it is not necessarily incorporated by all viewers. They also found that heavy viewers were more exposed to consistent messages, whereas light viewers were more selective and their VCR use took them further from network TV's messages.

Morgan, Shanahan, and Harris (1990) noted that the similarities between television and other technologies are greater than the differences, and new ones may absorb roles of the old ones in maintaining media effects. If adolescents watch less TV and it has less effect, perhaps VCRs make up the difference, and cultivation should be considered regarding the 'teaching potential,' regardless of the medium.

According to Einsiedel and Green (1988), two aspects of VCRs that are significant for their cultural impact are that they are stand-alone or independent devices and they are user controlled. Viewers can shift program times and, with fast forward, they can even control the tempo of viewing (Lull, 1988a). In fact, VCRs are used most frequently for movies and second most frequently for time shifting, especially during prime time (Einsiedel & Green, 1988). Moreover, because VCRs allow viewers to watch a video or programs repeatedly, they make video more like other art forms such as books, records, or paintings that can be enjoyed over and over (Lull, 1988a).

Lindlof and Shatzer (1990) pointed out that the VCR has had the greatest impact on viewing patterns because it freed television use from dependence on broadcast fare and times, and camcorders allow families to develop their own presentations as well.

AUDIENCE CHANGES

Many of the technological developments also allow increases in targeting of smaller audiences through more specialty programming of the type that was offered traditionally by public television with its emphasis on programs high in excellence, cultural value, and responsiveness to viewer needs (Agostino, 1980). The new media also result in fragmented audiences who have not all seen the same thing at the same time (Heeter, 1989; Webster, 1989b).

Although there is not a mass audience in the same way as before, however, viewers in the smaller audiences have more in common with others in those audiences who avail themselves of the same content (Heeter, 1989). Moreover, audiences with interests in common may be very far-flung geographically; or households in close proximity may be experiencing very diverse media content and environments (Webster, 1989a). Although having increased numbers of channels available does not guarantee diverse programs, greater heterogeneity of content has begun to emerge, perhaps most importantly in more programs catering to ethnic and racial minorities (Webster, 1989b).

VCRs can be used more instrumentally by allowing viewers to actively choose programming that has utility for them and to view those selections at convenient times (Rubin & Bantz, 1989). In other words, according to Rubin and Bantz (1989), the use of VCRs is more goal directed; it requires intentional and selective viewing and program choices and decisions by viewers. Moreover, Rubin and Bantz found that the use of VCRs for different purposes was related to the age, gender, and socioeconomic characteristics of viewer groups, and it complements and mediates other communication behavior.

VCRs also allow for changes in who controls a child's viewing and they enhance viewer selectivity. The steady increase in the use of VCRs gives parents less control over their older children's viewing choices and patterns, but it can actually allow parents of younger children greater control. Parents of young children can determine which programs will be viewed and through videotaping they also can control when and for how long the child watches television. Moreover, Bianculli (1994) cited Peggy Charren on the value of repetition in reading, and noted that with a VCR, children can go over things or skip things and thus exercise some control over the content they view.

Finally, the purchase of a VCR not only increases entertainment choices; it also forces families to develop new viewing patterns, and it makes family interpersonal dynamics even more complex (Lull, 1988a). Lindlof and Shatzer (1990), however, found that VCRs appear to make little difference in parental mediation, and VCR use in the family is likely to be part of a much broader and more complex context of parental values and competence, characteristics of the children, and activity patterns in the home. They concluded that the VCR has some impact on viewing times and viewing frequencies, but generally its impact on families' more basic functioning and well-being is modest or small.

Cohen, Levy, and Golden (1988) used uses and gratifications theory to try to determine what position VCRs have in children's media environments. Their results suggested considerable "gratificational interchangeability among the three media" (p. 778). Cohen et al. concluded that although children use them, VCRs are not part of a revolution in how children communicate; they have no special priority or identity; and they blend with movies, records, and tapes.

VIDEO GAMES

The earliest video games originated in the early 1960s, and microcomputer games became popular during the 1980s, which led to home computers becoming largely game machines (Haddon, 1993). Then in the early 1990s, with the growth of CD technology, CD-ROM games and other software appeared on the market as well. Funk and Buckman

(1996) recalled that the first games were introduced in the 1970s, and studies on their impact on health, school achievement, personality, and other variables began in the 1980s. Preliminary results at an Atari-sponsored conference in 1983 seemed to show many positive aspects, but as Funk and Buckman pointed out, current games are more realistic and more violent than earlier ones. They noted the need for more research on age-related changes in habits and preferences in game playing, the need to address developmental issues, and the need to see what the implications are of pervasive preferences for violent media and whether there are high-risk players or high-risk habits. Reasons for playing also vary among users and must be taken into account. Some of the reasons for playing that Harris and Williams (1985) found among children included something to do, excitement, friends played, to cheer themselves up, and being good at it.

As video games allow significant interactivity and many are extremely vivid and graphic they may be more problematic for subgroups of children who are more vulnerable for any number of reasons discussed in other contexts.

Gender Differences

According to Haddon (1993), games in arcades became a collective leisure activity for boys, but not for girls. Girls tended to play them at home or with friends but their use of them was not the same as that of boys, who also talked about them and exchanged them. Girls tended to play whatever was available, which was often determined by boys.

Others (Schutte, Malouff, Post-Gorden, & Rodasta, 1988) found that 5 to 7-year-olds imitated characters from both aggressive and nonaggressive video games, and Grade 5 girls were more aggressive after exposure to video games whether playing or observing (Cooper & Mackie, 1986). Moreover, girls' activity decreased and their quiet activity increased after they played a low-aggressive video game. Neither group gave significantly more rewards or punishment after playing the games. Funk and Buckman (1996) found significant gender differences in game habits and in self-perceptions. Boys spent more time playing and preferred more violent games. For girls, more time with games was associated with lower self-esteem. Funk and Buckman suggested it may be more socially acceptable for boys and lack of attention to gender may have obscured differences in some past studies.

Other researchers (Kubey & Larson, 1990) have found gender differences in the use of video entertainment, including music videos, video games, and video cassettes. For boys, use of these media was related to higher reported arousal and more positive affect than there was with reading, watching television or listening to popular music. Girls showed lower arousal and affect, relative to boys, especially for music videos and video games. The researchers used the ESM which elicits not only time spent but more information regarding viewers' subjective experience of various activities and thus can help to evaluate the assumptions of uses and gratifications theory and assess whether viewers are active or passive.

Kubey and Larson (1990) found that with the new media, children showed higher than average arousal, whereas they showed lower than average arousal with traditional media. Boys responded more favorably to new media than girls, perhaps partly because of the way the genders are portrayed. That is, the 'male-oriented' music videos and video games are perhaps less pleasant and more threatening for girls (Kubey & Larson, 1990). Griffiths (1991) also suggested that the gender differences that emerge may be due to the content of the games.

Video Games and Aggression

In many violent games, the user is obliterated if they have failed to choose a correct and predetermined strategy. There are no compromises, there are sexual stereotypes, and there is little portrayal of any realistic consequences of violence (Funk and Buckman, 1996). The authors said there is no strong research yet regarding causal statements about the impact of playing these violent games, although important variables include gender of the person playing, amount of time spent playing, and location (whether at home or in an arcade).

Dominick (1984) found a positive correlation among grade 10 and 11 boys and girls between time spent playing games in arcades and both time spent watching violent television and engaging in aggressive behavior. All of these behaviors, however, could be due to other factors (e.g., school problems or poor parental supervision) and as always, correlation cannot be used as evidence of causation. However, frequent exposure to violent games may have subtle long-term negative effects and may lead to disinhibition of aggressive responses (Comstock & Strasburger, 1993).

Griffiths (1991) reported short-term aggressive effects, especially in young children, after either playing or observing someone playing violent video games, but he raised some questions about the measures used and noted that studies on the effects of long-term exposure are still lacking. Indirect support for the arousal hypothesis comes from a study by Silvern and Williamson (1987) of the effects of violent video games on aggression. They hypothesized that exposing 4 and 6-year-olds to violent video games would lead to increased aggression. They found no difference in results between the video game and television conditions. The children were more aggressive after exposure to violent video games, whether the child was playing or observing, which is similar to findings about behavior that follows viewing of violent cartoons on TV.

Video Games and Television Viewing

According to Funk and Buckman (1996), research on electronic games typically uses similar strategies to those evaluating TV's effects, such as modeling effects. As with TV, computer and video games offer opportunities for observational learning, but they add an active or interactive dimension that may intensify a game's impact.

Selnow (1984) noted that earlier research showed that heavy users of TV also tend to be heavy users of arcade video games. He suggested that many of the same needs are served as with TV except, in addition, there is active involvement. Selnow suggested that players may see a game as a surrogate friend or companion and thus see the interaction with it as social. Thus, their experience with games would teach them lessons about people. In fact, heavy users may use games instead of real people—who may be less available or less fun—to satisfy their need for companionship or may use them for escape and solitude.

Children's experiences of video games and videocassettes are different from that of television in the greater arousal and more choice. There also is more viewer activity and selectivity with video games and VCRs (Kubey & Larson, 1990). Kubey and Larson (1990) also found that music videos evoked similar subjective ratings as viewing television with somewhat higher arousal and choice for the music videos. Watching a movie in a theater was more cognitively involving than viewing one on a VCR.

Some researchers also have reported game-playing effects on prosocial behavior. Chambers and Ascione (1987) studied children in Grades 3 to 4 and 7 to 8 and exposed them to four conditions—playing alone or cooperatively with another child and playing aggressive or prosocial video games—after which donating and helping behavior levels were measured. They found that the older children donated more than the younger ones, and children who played aggressive games donated significantly less than children who played prosocial games alone. There were no significant differences in helping behavior. Although playing prosocial games did not lead to more prosocial behavior, playing the aggressive game led to less prosocial behavior. Chambers and Ascione speculated that the failure to improve prosocial behavior after prosocial games may have been due to the brief responses or the particular game used and they suggested that longer exposure may have greater effects.

Kubey and Larson's (1990) cross-media comparisons showed that despite media changes, children still spend most of their media time with broadcast television. The researchers found a generally low frequency of use in this group of children and young adolescents 9 to 15 years old who spent more time reading than watching videocassettes, watching music videos, or playing video games. To explain this variance from previous studies, Kubey and Larson suggested that participants may overestimate the time spent when that is the main focus of study, and perhaps other studies focused on older participants. They also found that time spent alone with the media increases with age, providing more exploratory opportunities for adolescents and increased independence. Kubey and Larson concluded that the overall television experience has improved in homes with VCRs.

Conclusions

In general, the research does not seem to offer evidence to fuel parental concerns about video game playing. Kestenbaum and Weinstein (1985), for example, suggested that playing games can even have positive results; it can help adolescents manage developmental conflicts around expression of aggression and competition and does not lead to greater withdrawal, fantasy, or neuroticism.

According to Griffiths (1991), game players have little uniformity of personality and there has been little research into whether playing these games is a social or a nonsocial activity. Nonetheless, playing video games can use up a lot of time and it is clear that some individuals do show a dependency on them. Furthermore, users may spend inordinate amounts of time there because of poor peer or parental relationships and may feel rewarded through the decision making required and the interactivity with the screen.

VIRTUAL REALITY

The key to a definition of virtual reality is the strong sense of actually being present in an environment or at a destination (Biocca, 1994; Steuer, 1992). Steuer (1992) used the term *telepresence* to refer to a person's experience of being in a mediated rather than a physical environment: "Telepresence is defined as the experience of presence in an environment by means of a communication medium" (p. 76). It makes use of systems other than the auditory and visual, such as the tactile system.

Entering virtual reality means going into a computer-generated world where objects exist in a three-dimensional space. Pryor and Scott (1993) explained that there is not only input and output with a computer, but also information into and out of the individual who is in the virtual reality setting, such as what the person is seeing, hearing, and feeling. The user moves through it with hand and head movements, not actually with legs, and the person is represented by an arrow cursor.

Biocca (1994) described virtual reality as a medium designed to extend our senses. According to Biocca, in virtual reality, a person's perception is so immersed in the simulation that they feel a sense of actually being there. It uses the way we ordinarily interact with the physical world, except that intuitive actions and unconscious or conscious movements become commands or potential input. Even the sound is interactive and changes as the user's head moves: "The goal is a computer interface that is fully responsive to actions of the user" (Biocca, 1994, p. 28). Moreover, future head-mounted displays may be much smaller and lighter, more like regular glasses. Virtual reality includes tactile images as well (Biocca, 1994; Steuer, 1992), which enhances the idea of presence and can communicate subtle information. Some simulate body movement through a large space, like walking around or being transported by a car, and one can even 'talk' with the computer—type in a command and the computer responds (Biocca, 1994).

Pryor and Scott (1993) raised the additional question of the effect of that technology (e.g. strong magnetic fields) on our bodies and the fact that the information that is exchanged is disembodied. They also raised questions about the future implications of virtual reality and its use: "Virtual Reality is located at a major point of intersection between Humans and Computers; it makes disturbingly intimate symbioses possible" (pp. 177–178).

Other research adds weight to the basis for concern. In one study (Calvert & Tan, 1994), participants in an aggressive virtual reality game showed higher physiological arousal (e.g., heart rate) and more aggressive thoughts than did observers, but this was not true of hostile feelings. Calvert and Tan (1994) interpreted this as support for arousal theory because although both control and virtual reality groups moved, the latter showed more arousal.

Of more concern in the Calvert and Tan (1994) study was their finding that violent virtual reality interactions overrode personal characteristics like pregame hostility or gender, resulting in similar aggressive levels or effects for all players. They explained that shifts in technologies from observational to interactional allow linking of emotions, thought, and behavior, and societal and personal aggression may increase when participants become actively involved in such violence-filled entertainment (Calvert & Tan, 1994).

Shapiro and McDonald (1992) also considered some of the ramifications of virtual reality on users. First, they noted that people are likely to be influenced most when they do not have other experiences to help them evaluate the information. Although they may know fiction from reality, virtual reality has additional sensory experiences and feelings of being immersed in an environment that might have greater emotional and physiological effects.

For one thing, the detail in virtual reality makes memories more vivid and thus more likely to affect reconstruction over time. Unreal items can seem as real or more real than actual ones, and although it may be easier for healthy individuals to make judgments about virtual reality than it is for mentally ill people or those under stress, with more and more realistic media technology, such judgments become harder (Shapiro & McDonald, 1992).

As Feldman (1994) said, "The better virtual reality gets, the more the viewer's sensory apparatus surrenders to an entirely artificial construct. As the session progresses, there is no memory of perception outside the perfectly enclosed televised world" (p. 29). According to Shapiro and McDonald (1992), virtual reality also may blur the distinction between watching and participating, and people might have to make internal or external checks to see if something is real or virtual reality (e.g., did I turn on the machine?). They warned that spending too much time in a virtual reality environment could be harmful to those who need to confront reality rather than escape from it, and could be especially damaging to children and adolescents. Shapiro and McDonald also foresaw its potential use in advertising, as for example, in having a virtual reality ad that allowed children to play with a toy.

Virtual reality games as home-based products are still some time away, but software producers continue to make games, including multimedia games, more of a mainstream entertainment and various developments make them seem more realistic (Haddon, 1993). There are continued efforts to give them a higher profile, according to Haddon (1993), who cited *Cyberzone* on children's television, on which participants compete in a computer-generated environment where they have to make physical movement to get virtual movement (walk on a pad with sensors), which introduces elements of virtual reality.

COMPUTERS

Computers in Learning

Lepper and Gurtner (1989) pictured us moving toward a world where computers will be the dominant delivery system for education at all ages and in most subject areas:

> Consider first the "dream" toward which adherents of the computer aspire. Imagine a 21st-century school in which each student is provided a portable computer comparable to current state-of-the-art machines in artificial intelligence. Imagine, as well, that these machines are linked to laser-disk devices, each capable of randomly accessing 56,000 "pgs" of text on a single disk and networked to one another. This entire system, moreover, is tied into a telecommunications network that permits classroom computers to communicate with students' homes, national data files, and other schools thousands of miles away. What opportunities for learning and motivation might such a truly technology-rich classroom provide? (p. 170)

Lepper and Gurtner went on to describe the uses or purposes that could be made of computers: tutor, medium for experiential learning (e.g., learning skills not usually taught in the regular curriculum and complex simulations), multipurpose tool for creative work and expression (e.g., spell check, editing, writing skills), and motivator, making learning more enjoyable and facilitating cooperative work.

Some who are less enthusiastic about computers worry that they will result in a homogenization of classroom experiences, more regimentation, less social interaction with peers and guidance from teachers, undue influence in shaping the curriculum, and perhaps insufficient transfer of learning to other areas where basic skills will not be strong enough to deal with complex problems in the future (Santrock & Yussen, 1992). In a study of some of the correlates of children's use of computers and video games, Lin and Lepper (1987) found that computer use was positively related with teacher ratings of impulsivity, it was negatively related to academic achievement, and it was independent of sociability.

According to Dorr and Kunkel (1990), computers have brought the most significant change in children's media environments, and the overall media environment now is less homogenous across homes than before. Computers mean users can interactively create the media environment they are going to use. Dorr and Kunkel noted further that computer use requires initiative and much input from a user, whereas broadcast television is less responsive and provides a more limited range that can only be used as presented.

According to Salomon (1990), the qualities of computer use that may affect children's cognitive functioning include: (a) interactivity, which involves a very different quality to a child's engagement; (b) intellectual guidance and dynamic feedback, what Salomon called an "intellectual partner"; (c) multiplicity of symbol systems for presentation and manipulation of information; and (d) the supplanting of users' memories where viewers do not have to remember so much to carry out a task.

Salomon (1990) raised the question of whether effects with the technology are short lived, only occurring when an individual is using the technology, or whether they can turn into lasting effects. He suggested that there is a "cognitive residual" only when a program has led to a redefinition of an activity or stretches the child's skills, and he felt that computers actually may provide opportunities that human interaction does not.

The Internet

A Nielsen Media Research study in 1995 revealed that there were 37 million individuals over age 16 in the United States who had access to the Internet (nearly 13% of the population), 24 million actually used it

(11%), and 17.6 million were using the World Wide Web (Vivian, 1997). Parks and Floyd (1996) cited Hahn and Stout (1994) who said there are 5,000 Internet discussion groups. Others say counting the hundreds of thousands of information sources is impossible: "Call it the death of the Renaissance ideal: there is simply too much information to consume for anyone to be truly knowledgeable" (Chiose, 1996, p. C1)

Even people with no opportunity to access the Internet are affected by it because they read about it (Morris & Ogan, 1996). Vivian (1997) noted that most Web users are fairly affluent, with an average annual household income over $80,000. Advertising is big business on the Web, too. In 1995, America Online charged American Express $300,000 for a year's messages, and some companies spend over $500,000 a year on elaborate Web sites (Vivian, 1997).

Children who are growing up with computers and who use them with ease have become familiar with the offerings on the Internet. Description of one child's use of this medium is very telling:

> [She] swoops in and out of her family's computer files. The mouse seemingly one with her hand, she glides through applications and directories looking for a functioning Internet launcher. See her take on the computer in a quick chess match. Check her Sailor Moon scrapbook. The 12-year old Montrealer has put together a thick annotated and carefully organized binder on the animated TV adventure series, filled with drawings and texts she downloaded from cyberspace…[and] friends she was meeting…before her parents canceled the online service that was costing them a fortune but had opened up safe "chat" rooms for her. "It's like talking on the phone, except with three or 10 people," says the bubbly girl. Meet the Net-Generation. (Binder, 1996).

According to Morris and Ogan (1996), until recently most researchers have stuck with broadcast and print media and overlooked the entire field of communication via computer. If that continues, they contend, communication theories will become less useful. The new technology means that research will have to reexamine old definitions of mass audience, communication media, and mediation of messages (Morris & Ogan, 1996).

Internet communication is highly varied and includes e-mail, news groups, Web pages—which can be viewed somewhat like a small town newspaper—special interest messages, and specialized TV stations. Each alone does not reach a mass audience, but together they constitute mass media (Morris & Ogan, 1996). According to Morris and Ogan (1996), as of September 1995, searches revealed over 120 different U.S. news services and 1,300 magazine services that had their own Web sites. In addition to abbreviated versions of well-known magazines, there also are whole electronic magazines, or e-zines, that can be read on the Internet. They have a huge distribution advantage over print, although to date much of the writing is poor, and the articles are often overloaded with catchy visual material (Everett-Green, 1997).

Now several electronics and computer giants are making Web-TV hybrids that allow access to the Web via a television set. These new Web TVs offer a future in which TV viewing is combined with basic Web access features such as e-mail, running CD-ROMs, and even game playing with others over a network (Sternbergh, 1996). This is especially attractive to the approximately 68% of individuals who have a television set but not a computer. According to Sternbergh (1996), some of these devices are computers that look like television sets; others are television sets that act like a computer. There are also systems available that combine full multimedia computers with a regular large-screen television set, so that you can surf the Net, play games, play CD-ROM software, or watch TV all with the same receiver (Brockhouse, 1996).

So what impact does Internet communication have? Morris and Ogan (1996) suggested that uses and gratifications and information seeking are important here, but as the Internet sometimes is used for entertainment, too, we need to ask whether it is similar to other entertainment media, whether there are negative effects on the audience, and whether addictions develop. According to Morris and Ogan, credibility is more of a problem with the Internet, even whether 'contributors' are who they say they are. They predicted that more emphasis will fall to users to judge the credibility of given sources.

Parents today are justifiably concerned about their children's use of the Internet. Although they recognize its huge informational advantage, they also realize that it is used for entertainment as well, and it can take up many hours, most of which are spent in isolation from other family members. Parents are also concerned about the discussion groups their children use, pornographic content available to them, and relationships they may form with strangers, especially when they lead to face-to-face meetings.

Parks and Floyd (1996) noted that there is much variation among participants and little control and the line becomes blurred between interpersonal communication and mass media communication.

Parks and Floyd (1996) noted that online personal relationships are fairly common (60% in this sample) and that was true across the board, not just in certain news groups. They said there is very little information yet about who develops online relationships, although women are more likely to and age does not matter. The more involved someone was in news groups, the more likely they were to develop relationships, and it seems more a matter of experience than of personal or demographic variables. This finding is especially important regarding children and adolescents who lack experience and as mentioned earlier, there is growing parental concern that relationships children might form on the Internet can turn dangerous if carried over into real life (e.g., meeting someone they met on the Net). Parks and Floyd claimed that often, perhaps two thirds of the time, these relationships are expanded from computer-mediated communication to other kinds of contact, such as phone, mail, or face-to-face communication, so the relationships that start online rarely stay there.

Other concerns have arisen about the graphic and violent or pornographic material available to children on the Internet. Kapica (1997) described one of the scariest examples, called the Virtual Voodoo Doll, which is a small rag doll that can be stabbed with pins from a pincushion that is supplied, burned with a candle, or cut with a knife. Each time it is hurt, the doll sends out a series of screams. Worse, the doll then can be sent via e-mail to others who then see a rerun of all the stabbings or cuts along with the sounds, plus whatever message the sender composes to go with it. The true sender may or may not be apparent to the recipient, all of which suggests that it could be used to terrify or harass other children and adolescents.

According to Morris and Ogan (1996), uses and gratifications may be a useful way to start work on the Internet and the nature of audience activity with the Internet, such as whether it is ritualized or instrumental, also needs to be studied. According to Morris and Ogan, old ideas about senders of messages and receivers are not adequate to study the Internet, and researchers need to look at the interactivity and interchangeability involved. Finally, there are ethical questions regarding the study of this communication without the participants' permission (Morris & Ogan, 1996).

TECHNOLOGY'S INFLUENCE ON CHILDREN

So how do all of these changes in technology affect children? What influences do technological advances have on children's developmental processes? How has the nature of the information to which they are exposed actually changed? How do families with access to the proliferating choices differ from those without such access? For example, VCR owners tend to be younger and to have families; and three quarters of them subscribe to cable, compared with two thirds of the total population (Einsiedel & Green, 1988). Moreover, studies have shown that the viewing habits of cable subscribers differ from those who watch conventional television in that the former watch more, are generally younger, and have higher incomes (Dominick, 1987).

Goal-Directed Viewing

The proliferation of new stations, cable programs, videotapes, VCRs, and other broadcast formats has expanded viewer choices and has weakened network control over the television medium and over the viewing audience. VCRs can be used more instrumentally by allowing viewers to actively choose programming that has utility for them and to view those selections at convenient times (Rubin & Bantz, 1989). In other words, according to Rubin and Bantz (1989) the use of VCRs is more goal directed; it requires intentional and selective viewing and program choices and decisions by viewers. Moreover, Rubin and Bantz found that the use of VCRs for different purposes was related to the age, gender, and socioeconomic characteristics of viewer groups, and that it complements and mediates other communication behavior.

Dorr and Kunkel (1990) also pointed out that several different delivery systems (e.g., cable, satellite, VCRs, broadcast television) all operate through the television set, which has implications for trying to regulate, as there may be less violence on broadcast television, for example, but violence is still available through other systems: "Each technology has its own particular characteristics and associated symbol systems and communication forms" (p. 18), but the content that the technologies deliver is still the most significant aspect.

Feldman (1994) worried that with increasingly complex games, more extensive menus for entertainment and sports, access to data banks, and other technological advances, "knowledge and power per se will become increasingly defined as highly individual experiences" (p. 29) and electronic activity will replace real-life experience to a much greater degree.

> Family life has evolved into watching sitcom families. Public life is something that happens on the other side of the glass. The talk show has replaced the neighbors we no longer see because we are at home watching talk shows. (p. 29)

Two of the major aspects of the new technologies that are important from a developmental point of view are the greater access allowed and the interactivity that is possible.

Access to Information

For many children, VCRs, cable, and home videos have significantly increased their access to adult information. With the flick of a switch, at least in the absence of direct parental control, children can open a window onto everything from old movies to sexually explicit and pornographic material. They have significantly greater access to programs intended for an adult audience. Moreover, they have access to information unavailable even to many adults not so long ago. As Postman (1982) said, television is "forcing the entire culture to come out of the closet...[and] the subject matter of the psychiatrist's couch and the Confessional Box [to] come...into the public domain" (p. 82). This public domain is now available to children as well.

Because of this increased access, children are privy at a much younger age, to many adult behaviors that were unknown to previous generations of children at that age. Their access to adult information, however, does not bring with it, necessarily, a complete or "adult" understanding of that information. Their ability to process and react to what they see is still constrained by many of the developmental factors discussed throughout the preceding chapters, by what they bring to the viewing situation in terms of developmental level, gender, range of experiences, socioeconomic level, perceived reality, and motivation for viewing.

Children who are watching material intended for adults may still be having considerable difficulty sorting out real information from fantasy material; they may not be cognizant of some of the formal features of television and hence they may find flashbacks, dream sequences, and other dramatic techniques confusing and incomprehensible. They may still be unable to grasp subtle messages or "morals to the story" and hence they may overreact to salient but irrelevant or inappropriate aspects of a program. The accessibility of adult information to child viewers, then, clearly has important developmental and behavioral implications. Questions about the mental operations necessary to comprehend content, as well as degrees of control and functions served need to be asked of the new technologies just as they were of television (Murray & Salomon, 1984).

Technology also can be used to help parents monitor and control their children's TV viewing. An example is the V-chip, described earlier, that works with a rating system to assist parents in screening out programs they do not want their children to watch, by screening out those above the parents' rating along 4 categories: nudity and sexuality, language, violence, and age of intended audience.

Such technology, or others such as electronic locks on the television to preset available times and channels (Centerwall, 1995) can help parents. Centerwall (1995) pointed out, however, that such technology would exclude poor families unless made widely available, as was done for 24 million hearing-impaired individuals. Sprafkin et al. (1992) were also concerned about the impact of the new media on parent mediation, which is infrequent as it is.

Interactivity

Two-way interactive television and computers provide yet another whole area of technological experience for children and have implications for their learning styles and developing feelings of mastery. Computer-generated images are controlled by the user even though they are programmed by others (Schwartz, 1984). Salomon and Murray (1984) urged further study of this control and of the effects that active involvement and interaction have on the child's learning, the results of which would further researchers' understanding of how they master television as well. These new technologies lie somewhere between the extremes of programming one's own computer and consumption of the mass media (Heeter, 1989).

The interactive component of the new technology is also important from the point of view of the child as a learner. Much psychological research tells us clearly that children's learning is facilitated significantly by active involvement; seeing, trying out, actually "doing" (i.e., active learning is the most effective type).

Although home computer games have some features in common with television (Silvern & Williamson, 1987), even video games require a response including eye–hand coordination and various cognitive decisions that make them different from other TV viewing (Doerken, 1983).

DIFFERENTIAL ACCESS

Although the expanding choice is likely to continue and even to increase, some writers worry about the differential access of various population groups to these choices. Sprafkin et al. (1992), for example, also noted the problem with access and the unavailability of the new technologies to lower SES families. And, according to Sprafkin et al., disabled children are likely to have less access, and gifted children are likely to have more, which may well create inequities and greater distances among the various populations. Cantor (1980) suggested, for example, that this increasing diversity and greater choice may be only for the affluent and well-educated. Although they provide alternative program distribution, each of the new forms requires direct payment in some form by consumers (Pepper, 1984). The old media traditional network television programming, on the other hand, was equally available to all who owned a TV set (Webster, 1989b).

Furthermore, as Webster (1989b) pointed out, differential availability depends on geographic as well as economic variables. Thus, homes in sparsely populated areas might not be able to gain access to cable and, hence, to many channels available to viewers in other areas. In examining the social impact of the new communication technology, Wright (1986) noted that new technology may be a way to get around controls or to add variety, but it is also significant for audience composition in that only a relatively few can afford things like antennae and computers. These technological changes will almost certainly continue to affect the nature and quality of interpersonal relationships as well (Cathcart & Gumpert, 1986).

Unequal access to or different uses of, the new technology by different population segments raises the possibility of serious social ramifications and of a division between information-rich and information-poor individuals (Wright, 1986). Imagine the huge advantage of a child working on a school assignment at home, with a computer, CD-ROM, encyclopedia on disk, and access to the Internet, compared with another child who has the same assignment but no computer and access only to school texts, a few resources at home, and the public library.

Dorr and Kunkel (1990) pointed out, however, that despite changes, considerable constancy or continuity exists, the overall patterns of media use have changed less than expected, and media environments do not affect media use as much as expected. Moreover, differences by age, socioeconomic level, gender, and race continue or are still apparent in interactions with old and newer media, such as time spent, preferences, and coviewing patterns, presumably because of fairly constant differences in needs, perspectives, and interests across generations (Dorr & Kunkel, 1990).

Clearly, the impact on children of recent technological advances, as well as those sure to come, is an important area of investigation. Issues of access to information, selectivity, and interactivity all touch on significant developmental concerns. Greater access will alter children's knowledge base and perhaps even the tempo of their development. Such increases in information and interactivity with technological devices also affect children's developing sense of mastery and their means of coping with their expanding world. There is a pressing need to study the effects of all of these technological changes on children's developmental processes and on their family interactions.

SUMMARY

The impact of new technologies on children's use and experience of television is an important area of investigation. There is some indication that any decreases in television viewing are likely associated with increased time spent with video games, computers, and VCR use, which displace television time. Although they may offer educational content, often they do not.

The proliferation of cable channels, VCRs, computers, and other technological advances has changed the kinds of programming and the number of viewer choices available, as well as the level of control and interactivity for viewers, which also affect the nature and quality of a child's learning and mastery. Moreover, more sophisticated and realistic video games and developing virtual reality technology make the fantasy–reality distinction ever more elusive. The difficulty making this separation, coupled with children's significantly increased access to adult information, has very important developmental, social, interpersonal, and psychological implications.

11

Critical Viewing Skills and Intervention Strategies

The act of watching television need not require much of viewers. Without ever leaving their easy chairs, viewers can be stimulated, entertained, educated, horrified, or intrigued by a never-ending smorgasbord of material. They need not respond or interact with the material; they do not have to analyze it or criticize it; they do not have to remember it; they do not even have to attend to it continuously, and they frequently engage in other activities simultaneously. The television set simply provides continuous stimuli until someone turns it off. On the other hand, viewers can interact with, attend to, remember, analyze, and criticize what they see. Several authors have underscored the need to help children to develop critical viewing skills, what might be called metamedia, to help children to derive greater benefits from their television experience.

Programs to improve children's viewing skills generally aim to help them learn how to watch and how to understand the television medium, to distinguish fantasy from reality, to learn about advertising and special effects, and to see how television can have an influence (J. L. Singer & D. G. Singer, 1983). As there are concerns in many areas—including purchase-influencing requests, aggressive behavior, race and gender-role attitudes, impact on reading and ability to concentrate and think critically—such curricula set out to teach them to understand television "and to use their interest in it in conjunction with reading, writing, and discussion skills" (Singer, Zuckerman, Singer, 1980, p. 86).

Kubey and Csikszentmihalyi (1990) considered it essential to teach children formally about television, as most will spend 1,000 hours of each of their childhood and adult years watching television. They pointed out that no one doubts the benefits of teaching children how to read essays or novels or poems, but they will spend far less time reading those than viewing television.

AIMS OF TELEVISION LITERACY CURRICULA

Most media literacy programs aim to teach students about television's grammar and syntax and how they are expressed in different forms; to increase their understanding of types of programs and how they are created, and about the technical aspect of television and special effects; to help students analyze the use of types of advertising and the persuasive appeals used and how they are related to buying behavior; to help them compare media, and to increase their tendency to compare television information with that from other sources; to compare television's values with their own and those of the community; to teach about the role of television violence and aggression; to see television's effects on behavior, feelings, self-concept, and other characteristics; to distinguish television information and reality; to use rules of logic and to be able to devise counterarguments; to identify major components of dramatic productions; to teach about television's multiple roles and purposes in society; to help them evaluate content and describe and evaluate news stories; and to devise strategies for time spent viewing or for program selection (Anderson, 1983; Anderson & Collins, 1988; Dorr, Graves, & Phelps, 1980; Singer et al., 1980).

Dorr et al. (1980) found that even young children could learn a television literacy curriculum and could discuss it, but that did not seem to mediate television's influence on social attitudes. As television content is unlikely to be altered dramatically any time soon, another tack is to try to modify its effects, to help children become more critical in their evaluation of content. Dorr et al. (1980) found that even the young kindergartners and second and third graders they studied could learn a lot about television and other sources of information in as little as 6 hours and then could apply it when asked to reason about television content. That is, they were able to understand and evaluate television content more effectively.

SPECIFIC VIEWING SKILLS PROGRAMS

There are many examples of specific programs that have been carried out, some of which are described in the following paragraphs. Evaluation of their effectiveness is discussed at the end of the chapter.

A program by Singer et al. (1980) was designed to teach children about television techniques and to help teach vocabulary, writing, critical thinking skills, and math. They urged the inclusion of television as a subject in the regular educational curriculum. They sought to provide their critical viewing skills within a language arts framework so that language skills such as grammar, critical thinking, verbal expression, and reading could be practiced. They used videotape equipment so that the children they worked with could tape each other "disappearing" and could learn the mechanics of television as well as engaging in discussion about stereotypes, aggression, and advertising.

One way to capitalize on student interest in television has been to use actual television scripts for network programs in order to motivate children to read (Lee, 1980). Students, after first reading old scripts and then watching replays of them, showed considerable improvement in reading performance.

Another project, the Television Literacy Project, was designed to look at skills involved in "reading" television to see if those skills were equally applicable to different kinds of programming, such as news and drama. Researchers found that a classroom course on television programming and production techniques led to significant improvements in critical viewing (Kelley, Gunter, & Buckle, 1987).

One curriculum was designed specifically for adolescents who view less television than other age groups, because of school, social life, and interest in other media. They are less likely to believe that television is "real" although many think television is similar to "real" (Lloyd-Kolkin, Wheeler, & Strand, 1980). The authors defined four critical viewing variables for adolescents: to evaluate one's own viewing behavior, to question the reality of television, to recognize television's persuasive messages and be able to refute them, and to recognize television's effects in one's own life. A fifth skill that they hoped to develop was the ability to use television to enhance family communication. They also developed textbooks and teachers' guides, with an emphasis on creative thought and writing. Their package reinforced the first four skills in the classroom but also included a "family guide" so that families could complete forms and then compare and discuss viewing behavior and other issues.

Doerken (1983) tried to help children increase their media literacy by having them keep a log of their viewing. Those data then were used in class discussions on such questions as what role television played, how much time was spent viewing, what was learned from it as compared with what was learned from family and friends, and other topics. Doerken (1983) also developed units on content analysis, analyzed advertising content, analyzed news presentations, and discussed various aspects of television, such as entertainment, education, and broadcasting.

Gadow, Sprafkin, and Watkins (1987) used the critical viewing skills curriculum that they developed for exceptional children (CESSMA) with typical elementary school classes of kindergartners and second graders and they found that increased knowledge about television did not lead to changes in attitudes or kindergartners' beliefs in the reality of the characters or the aggression. They seemed to think the television aggression was real, that victims were really hurt, and that the aggression that they saw happens frequently in real life.

Second graders recognized and understood the fantasy portrayals, and even without instruction they could interpret aggressive scenes more accurately. Interestingly, both groups had difficulty understanding animation and attributed real-life characteristics, like having a home and money, to cartoon characters. Testing of sixth graders revealed that they had acquired most of the CESSMA information on their own.

Most of the programs, then, have been designed for use in the classroom and have been integrated into the educational curriculum. Kubey and Csikszentmihalyi (1990) pointed out that children can be taught to view television more critically both through formal educational channels or in less formal ones. In school, for example, students can be taught about many aspects of television such as techniques of persuasion, character development, advertising, and economics, and can be taught to think about how television reflects society and why it does so in certain ways. They also suggested that parents can help children view television more critically also, but it should be done in a relaxed way; not to develop "right" answers, but to help them learn various ways to perceive and evaluate television.

Even television shows can be used to increase children's media awareness. *Street Cents*, for example, is a program of the Canadian Broadcasting Corporation on which children examine advertising and criticize ads and other television messages (Saunders, 1996).

Other critical viewing skills programs, which have been used with exceptional children, are described in chapter 8.

TELEVISION AS AN EDUCATIONAL TOOL

Some researchers have stressed the need to make better use of television's educational potential. Palmer (1984), for example, urged the use of television as a major and very cost-effective educational supplement. Providing even an hour a weekday, 260 hours a year, equals about one fifth of students' total time in school and one fifth of their total time with television. If well-filled, that would amount to a very significant educational enrichment. Palmer emphasized that what is wanted is not more television, but better alternatives to the adult-oriented diet that is available now. Among the advantages of television are that it is ubiquitous and nonthreatening, it can organize and present material clearly, it can depict live models, and it does not depend on reading skill or ability (Palmer, 1984). Finally, at school, unlike at home, an adult is always available and using television in classroom discussion might reduce the differences between advantaged and disadvantaged children (Greenfield, 1984b).

Television's video presentation is uniquely suited to enhancing social competence promotion programs in the schools, and could be especially useful for training children with behavior problems and social skills deficits (Harwood & Weissberg, 1987). It can use powerful models and present situations graphically, making it easier to discuss difficult topics. It is especially good regarding social interaction because of the visual way it can reproduce a nonlinguistic context and nonverbal communication (Harwood & Weissberg, 1987).

Television can be brought into the school curriculum in various positive ways to help children become more discriminating viewers (Hodge & Tripp, 1986). For example, Doerken (1983) suggested several techniques for helping children increase their media literacy and put television in perspective with other communication forms. These should not involve simply more viewing of television; rather, the aim is to have children watch less eventually, but to do it more selectively and critically (Doerken, 1983).

Critical viewing skills also should include metacognitive skills and awareness of the effort involved so that children learn not only about television content, but also about television's role as a displacer of other activities that offer other advantages (Williams, 1986). The differences and benefits of perusing information from a wide range of sources, including print, should also be a part of such critical viewing skills, according to Williams (1986), so that the importance of such mental activities as elaboration and reflection can be underscored.

EVALUATION AND FOLLOW-UP

The evaluation and follow-up to such literacy and critical viewing programs reveals rather mixed results. For example, Dorr and her colleagues (1980) found that their curriculum seemed to affect the selectivity of their young children but not their attitude testing. In Johnston and Ettema's (1986) Freestyle program, mere viewing in the classroom did not achieve the series goals, although there were no negative effects, and class discussion was generally much more effective than viewing alone. Their findings suggested the possibility of being able to communicate some messages without classroom mediation, although effects were smaller in the home-viewing study and limited to only the heaviest viewers, likely, they thought, because viewing at home is less attentive.

About two thirds of Lee's (1980) participants indicated that using television scripts to enhance reading actually facilitated their comprehension of television content and thus added to their enjoyment. They reported that they usually were not able to follow everything on television but studying it beforehand helped them to understand characters and story meaning in more depth and allowed them to go over details again. Moreover, discussion of the programs in class, after reading and viewing them, led to attitude changes such as more acceptance of an epileptic child and greater interest in the elderly. Lee concluded that television can be a strong impetus for discussion of attitudes and values. Students also enjoyed acting out the scripts, and minority students were very enthused and most positive. Parents who were willing to participate responded to questionnaires, and 85% of them mentioned benefits to their relationship with their children in improved parent–child interaction (Lee, 1980).

Roberts, Christenson, Gibson, Mooser, and Goldberg (1980) found *Six Billion $$$ Sell* to be effective but only with fourth graders, not with sixth or eighth graders, whose scores were high to begin with. They were already skeptical by age 12. Roberts et al. concluded that children can be taught to be more critical of commercials by viewing films that describe how commercials try to persuade. These films were most effective among children who had shown the greatest susceptibility initially to the appeals. That is, younger children who were vulnerable because of their immaturity showed the greatest increase in skepticism after the films, and we need to ask whether this would be true of other relatively naive or vulnerable viewers such as socially and educationally disadvantaged ones (Roberts et al., 1980).

Roberts et al. (1980) also found heavy viewers to be more trusting and less skeptical in the control group but not so in the experimental groups. Films had a greater impact on heavy viewers perhaps because they had less consumer socialization from others, perhaps because they had more examples to apply when they were exposed to the instructional films, or maybe because they were less critical in their thought until critical strategies were pointed out.

The third-, fourth-, and fifth-grade children in the Singer et al. (1980) study were able to learn to understand and criticize television programs and commercials, but their parents' viewing habits and attitudes toward television remained a significant influence on the children's behavior. In another study, Singer and Singer (1984) also found that the results after trying to help parents control their children's viewing were not encouraging. They were more optimistic, however, about intervention through the schools to develop critical viewing skills that produced at least short-term gains. Their sessions to encourage parents to reduce preschool viewing were not very successful, and they suggested that the lack of success was likely because the tendency to use television as a babysitter is very strong in the middle and lower SES families. Helping parents to train imaginative and cognitive skills in their children, however, led to a decrease in television viewing, some increase in spontaneous language ability, and improved social behavior (Singer & Singer, 1984).

Parent training in an effort to decrease time spent watching television, then, especially violent shows, has not been highly effective (Eron, 1986). More promising are cognitive and behavioral interventions that include observation of prosocial behavior, along with other training such as thinking before acting, considering alternatives, and role playing in efforts to change children's attitudes about the acceptability of aggression and about the unreality of television portrayals. These procedures were helpful even for heavy viewers (Eron, 1986).

Providing additional and alternate information to the television content, then, can work against undue influence of the television information. Anderson and Collins (1988) concluded that although critical viewing skills can help children to learn about television, there have not been studies of the long-term impact of such programs either on children's viewing patterns or on the way they process the television content.

In any case, such programs are very expensive, and more responsible programming, along with more viewing control by parents, are still needed as essential concomitants to curricular work (Dorr et al., 1980).

SUMMARY

Many have urged the introduction of a television curriculum into the schools in an effort to encourage and develop children's critical viewing skills and television literacy. Many media literacy and critical viewing skills programs have been developed. They appear to be effective in increasing children's awareness of many aspects of television, but their long-term influence has not been demonstrated. It is hoped that such programs will enable children to enjoy television and to benefit from its many positive aspects, at the same time minimizing its potential negative influence and manipulation.

12

Summary and Conclusions

Children's active involvement with television to some degree for an average of 4 hours a day has important implications for their cognitive, social, emotional, and behavioral development. New trends in research are based on recognition of the significant complexity of the viewing experience. Dozens of variables and, more importantly, their interactions, need systematic study if we are to further our understanding of television's influence on children's development. This book's aim was to bridge communication and psychological fields of inquiry to achieve the most thorough, accurate, and up-to-date picture of all of that influence. It drew heavily on research literature from both areas in order to provide as comprehensive and balanced a picture as possible of children's television viewing experience and its interaction with their other life experiences and developmental processes.

Children's experience of television is the result of very complex interactions among formal features of television, children's expectations and past experience, family attitudes and practices, level of cognitive maturity, motivation for viewing, format characteristics and content of the television programming, and the context for viewing. Previous views of children's comprehension may have been significant underestimates; they appear to understand the "basics" of television at an earlier age, although at times their limited verbal skills may prevent them from communicating their comprehension. At other times, methodological problems may lead to inaccurate or inappropriate conclusions. Nonetheless, their interpretation of television content becomes more accurate with age and experience, and young children's understanding of much of what they see is distorted and incomplete.

Children are not just passive viewers who absorb information; they actively process it and their strategies for doing so become more efficient as their general cognitive skills mature and as they acquire more experience with television. They increasingly use verbal encoding of television material, which enhances their comprehension and retention; conversely, television can also enhance their language development. Children vary developmentally in their reliance on salience to guide their television experience. Young children's attention is largely to salient stimuli. As they mature, conceptual information and information seeking become more important than perceptual salience. They can distinguish more efficiently between relevant and irrelevant material. Older children also develop a sounder awareness of the difference between "apparent" and "real."

Specific aspects of television's input, such as an emphasis on language-based or holistic stimuli, are important components that warrant further attention. A careful look at the interaction of such characteristics with differences in processing requirements and styles may provide us with more avenues for interpretation of research findings and for understanding television's effects on development.

Children appear to be most affected by television events that are perceived to be realistic or plausible and that involve characters with whom they identify. At the same time, television also helps to shape their expectations. Heavy viewers, particularly those who are using television as an important source of information, may be more likely to accept television's version of reality and may become more fearful, more biased, or less tolerant.

As television competes with other activities and experiences in a child's life, parents' role in providing alternatives is crucial. Moreover, their own attitudes and beliefs, both about television and about life in general, are important determinants of children's response to television. Television may be a socialization force, but it interacts in complex ways with all of the other forces in a child's life to determine the patterns of socialization for that child.

Television's role in the perpetuation of aggressive tendencies, or of ethnic, racial, age, gender, or occupational stereotypes, should not be underestimated. Although television's causal role in these areas has not been established definitively, and debate continues over the relation between violence and real-life aggression and violence, television's relentless depiction of violence, as well as its unrealistic and stereotypic portrayals of women, minorities, and the elderly can exacerbate aggressive and biased attitudes and behaviors in viewers. It is essential that we discover which specific aspects of the viewing situation lead to increased negative behavioral influences and which ones mitigate against such undesirable effects. Television programmers also need to seek more appealing and salient ways to present socially desirable and harmonious behaviors and to facilitate positive interpersonal relationships.

Much of television's power and influence over adults as well as children lies in its capacity to strike deep emotional chords in viewers—to increase their identification with characters, to arouse an emotional response, and, in general, to deepen their involvement in the television experience. Such involvement leads to stronger responses to television's messages. Moreover, the ability to persuade viewers to see needs where they had none, or to feel dissatisfaction when they had previously been content, lies at the heart of successful advertising. However, it also affects the influence that other television content has on viewers.

A considerable body of research suggests that when viewers use television seriously, to obtain information they need, especially when they perceive it as realistic and when they have few alternate sources of information, television's potential impact is great. Its influence is less significant when viewers use television primarily for diversion, view less frequently, do not take it so seriously, and have other sources of information and knowledge. However, these patterns are mitigated by developmental, gender, contextual, and family variables and by the amount of viewing engaged in by children.

As most children spend more time engaged in television viewing than in any other single activity besides school, television's impact on their cognitive, social, and affective development cannot be over-emphasized. Discerning the critical components and determinants of that impact can facilitate both our understanding of how children process television information and our understanding of the extent to which television programming actually affects children of diverse age, gender, and background groups. Such knowledge should help us to devise ways of helping children to resist such negative aspects of television as stereotypic portrayals of minority groups or the manipulative tactics of advertising and to enhance the positive and constructive learning and enjoyment that can be derived from the viewing experience.

The newer technologies raise some of the same concerns as television, but they have unique features that lead to other concerns. They generally are more interactive and make the fantasy reality distinction more difficult for some children and more arousing. They increase the diversity of children's media opportunities and their access to information, which can have either a positive or negative influence.

A conceptualization that integrates cultivation and uses and gratifications theories from the communication field and social learning and other developmental theories from psychology, can be very useful in explaining many of the attitudinal and behavioral differences among child viewers that abound in the literature:

The message is clear. Media messages do not affect all of the people all of the time, but some of the messages affect some of the people some of the time. As we move into an age of ever-expanding technological options in the mass media, we need to recognize that the process is as complex on the human side as it is on the technological side. (Heath & Gilbert, 1996, p. 385)

The integration of communication and psychological literature, then, provides a broader framework within which all of the issues can be considered. Developmental, gender, and other child variables clearly are critical, but they cannot be studied or evaluated independently of communication factors, including television's content and formal features, as well as the use of other technological media.

References

Abbott, W. S. (1995). Increased government regulation of media violence is necessary. In C. Wekesser (Ed.), *Violence in the media* (pp. 110–116). San Diego, CA: Greenhaven Press.

Abelman, R. (1987a). Child giftedness and its role in the parental mediation of television viewing. *Roeper Review, 9*(4), 217–220, 246.

Abelman, R. (1987b). Television literacy for gifted children. *Roeper Review, 9*(3), 166–168.

Abelman, R. (1990). Determinants of parental mediation of children's television viewing. In J. Bryant (Ed.), *Television and the American family* (pp. 311-326). Hillsdale, NJ: Lawrence Erlbaum Associates.

Abelman, R. (1991). Parental communication style and its influence on exceptional children's television viewing. *Roeper Review, 14*(1), 23–27.

Adler, R. P., Friedlander, B. Z., Lesser, G. S., Meringoff, L., Robertson, T. S., Rossiter, J. R., Ward, S. (1979). *Research on the effects of television advertising on children.* Washington, DC: National Science Foundation.

Adler, T. (1991, October). By age 4, most kids see what's real. APA Monitor.

Adventures in Learning. (1992). Toronto: Discis Knowledge Research.

Agostino, D. (1980). New technologies: Problem or solution? *Journal of Communication, 30*(3), 198–206.

Alvarez, M. M., Huston, A. C., Wright, J. C., & Kerkman, D. D.(1988). Gender differences in visual attention to television form and content. *Journal of Applied Developmental Psychology, 9*(4), 459–475.

Ambrose, M. (1991, June 20). Cross current. *The Globe and Mail*, p. C1.

American Psychological Association. (1995, December). Violence is sowing the seeds for educational, emotional setbacks. *APA Monitor*, pp. 6–7.

Anderson, D. R., & Collins, P. A. (1988). *The impact on children's education: Television's influence on cognitive development* (Working paper No. 2). Washington, DC: U.S. Department of Education, Office of Educational Research and Improvement.

Anderson, D. R., Collins, P. A., Schmitt, K. L., & Jacobvitz, R. S. (1996) Stressful life events and television viewing. *Communication Research, 23*(3), 243–260.

Anderson, D. R., Field, D. E., Collins, P. A., Lorch, E. P., & Nathan, J. G. (1985). Estimates of young children's time with television: A methodological comparison of parent reports with time-lapse video home observation. *Child Development, 56*, 1345–1357.

Anderson, D. R., & Levin, S. R. (1976). Young children's attention to "Sesame Street." *Child Development, 47*, 806–811.

Anderson, D. R., & Lorch, E. P. (1983). Looking at television: Action or reaction? In J. Bryant & D. R. Anderson (Eds.), *Children's understanding of television* (pp. 1–33). New York: Academic Press.

Anderson, D. R., Lorch, E. P., Field, D. E., Collins, P. A., & Nathan, J. G. (1986). Television viewing at home: Age trends in visual attention and time with TV. *Child Development, 57*(4), 1024–1033.

Anderson, D. R., & Smith, R. (1984). Young children's tv viewing: the problem of cognitive continuity. In F. J. Morrison, C. Lord, & D. P. Keating (Eds.), *Applied developmental psychology* (Vol. 1; pp. 116–163). Orlando, FL: Academic Press.

Anderson, J. A. (1983). Television literacy and the critical viewer. In J. Bryant & D. R. Anderson (Eds.), *Children's understanding of television* (pp. 297–330). New York: Academic Press.

Argenta, D. M., Stoneman, Z., & Brody, G. H. (1986). The effects of three different television programs on young children's peer interactions and toy play. *Journal of Applied Developmental Psychology. 7*, 355–371.

Atkin, C., Hocking, J., & Block, M. (1984). Teenage drinking: Does advertising make a difference? *Journal of Communication, 34*, 157–167.

Atkin, C. K. (1981). Communication and political socialization. In D. D. Nimmo, & K. R. Sanders (Eds.), *Handbook of political communication* (pp. 299–328). Beverly Hills, CA: Sage.

Atkinson, B. (1996, Fall). The man behind the V-chip. *University of Waterloo Magazine,* 12–14.

Austin, E. W., Roberts, D. F., & Nass, C. I. (1990). Influences of family communication on children's television-interpretation processes. *Communication research, 17*(4), 545–564.

Babrow, A. S., O'Keefe, B. J., Swanson, D. L., Meyers, R. A., & Murphy, M. A. (1988). Person perception and children's impressions of television and real peers. *Communication research, 15(6), 680–698.*

Ball, S., Palmer, P., & Millward, E. (1986). Television and its educational impact: A reconsideration. In J. Bryant & D. Zillmann (Eds.), *Perspectives on media effects* (pp. 129–142). Hillsdale, NJ: Lawrence Erlbaum Associates.

Bandura, A. (1967). The role of modelling processes in personality development. In W. W. Hartup & N. L. Smothergill (Eds.), *The young child: Reviews of research* (pp. 42–58). Washington, DC: National Association for the Education of Young Children.

Barcus, F. E. (1980). The nature of television advertising to children. In E. L. Palmer & A. Dorr (Eds.), *Children and the faces of television* (pp. 273–285). New York: Academic Press.

Baron, J. N., & Reiss, P. C. (1985). Same time, next year: Aggregate analyses of the mass media and violent behavior. *American Sociological Review, 50*, 347–363.

Beagles-Roos, J., & Gat, I. (1983). Specific impact of radio and television on children's story comprehension. *Journal of Educational Psychology, 75*(1), 128–137.

Beentjes, J. W., & Van der Voort, T. H. (1988). Television's impact on children's reading skills: A review of research. *Reading Research Quarterly, 23*(4), 389–413.

Beentjes, J. W. J. & van der Voort, T. H. A. (1993). Television viewing vs. reading: Mental effort, retention, and inferential learning. *Communication Education, 42*, 191–205.

Berkowitz, L. (1986). Situational influences on reactions to observed violence. *Journal of Social Issues, 42*(3), 93–106.

Berkowitz, L. (1988). Frustrations, appraisals, and aversively stimulated aggression. *Aggressive Behavior, 14*, 3–11.

Berkowitz, L., & Rogers, K. H. (1986). A priming effect analysis of media influences. In J. Bryant & D. Zillmann (Eds.), *Perspectives on media effects* (pp. 57–81). Hillsdale, NJ: Lawrence Erlbaum Associates.

Bianculli, D. (1994). *Teleliteracy: Taking television seriously.* New York: Touchstone.

Binder, S. (1996, December 9). Cyber-savvy Net Generation abandoning TV. *Kitchener-Waterloo Record,* p. C1.

Biocca, F. (1994). Virtual reality technology: A tutorial. *Journal of Communication, 42*(4), 23–72.

Blosser, B. J., & Roberts, D. F. (1985). Age differences in children's perceptions of message intent. *Communication Research, 12*(4), 455–484.

Brockhouse, G. (1996, December). A computer for couch potatoes. *Home Computing,* pp. 38–39.

Brown, D., & Bryant, J. (1990). Effects of television on family values and selected attitudes and behaviors. In J. Bryant (Ed.), *Television and the American family* (pp. 253–274). Hillsdale, NJ: Lawrence Erlbaum Associates.

Brown, J. D., Childers, K. W., Bauman, K. E., & Koch, G. G. (1990). The influence of new media and family structure on young adolescents' television and radio use. *Communication Research, 17*(1), 65–82.

Brucks, M., Armstrong, G. M., & Goldberg, M. E. (1988). Children's use of cognitive defenses against television advertising: A cognitive response approach. *Journal of Consumer Research, 14*(4), 471–482.

Burton, S. G. , Calonico, J. M., & McSeveney, D. R. (1979). Effects of preschool television watching on first-grade children. *Journal of Communication, 29*(3), 164–170.

California Assessment Program. (1980). *Television and student achievement.* Sacramento: California State Department of Education.

California Assessment Program. (1982). *Survey of sixth grade school achievement and television viewing habits.* Sacramento: California State Department of Education.

California Assessment Program. (1988). *Annual report, 1985–1986.* Sacramento: California State Department of Education.

Calvert, S. L. (1988). Television production feature effects on children's comprehension of time. *Journal of Applied Developmental Psychology, 9*(3), 263–273.

Calvert, S. L., & Gersh, T. L. (1987). The selective use of sound effects and visual inserts for children's television story comprehension. *Journal of Applied Developmental Psychology, 8*(4), 363–374.

Calvert, S. L., Huston, A. C., Watkins, B. A., & Wright, J. C. (1982). The relation between selective attention to television forms and children's comprehension of content. *Child Development, 53,* 601–610.

Calvert, S. L., Huston, A. C., & Wright, J. C. (1987). Effects of television preplay formats on children's attention and story comprehension. *Journal of Applied Developmental Psychology, 8*(3), 329–342.

Calvert, S. L., & Tan, S. L. (1994). Impact of virtual reality on young adults' physiological arousal and aggressive thoughts: Interaction vs. observation. *Journal of Applied Developmental Psychology, 15*(1), 125–139.

Campbell, T. A., Wright, J. C., & Huston, A. C. (1987). Form cues and content difficulty as determinants of children's cognitive processing of televised educational messages. *Journal of Experimental Child Psychology, 43*(3), 311–327.

Canadian Advertising Foundation. (1987). *Sex-role stereotyping guidelines.* Ottawa, Canada: Author.

Canadian Association of Broadcasters. (1985). *Broadcast advertising and children.* Ottawa, Canada: Author.

Cannon, C. M. (1995). Media violence increases violence in society. In C. Wekesser (Ed.), *Violence in the media* (pp. 17–24). San Diego, CA: Greenhaven Press.

Cantor, J., & Sparks, G. G. (1984). Children's fear responses to mass media: Testing some Piagetian predictions. *Journal of Communication, 34,* 90–103.

Cantor, M. G. (1980). *Prime-time television: Content and control.* Beverly Hills, CA: Sage.

Carpenter, E. (1986). The new languages. In G. Gumpert & R. Cathcart (Eds.), *Inter / media: Interpersonal communication in a media world* (3rd ed., pp. 353–367). New York: Oxford University Press.

Cathcart, R., & Gumpert, G. (1986). The person–computer interaction: A unique source. In G. Gumpert & R. Cathcart (Eds.), *Inter / media: Interpersonal communication in a media world* (3rd ed., pp. 323–332). New York: Oxford University Press.

Caughey, J. L. (1986). Social relations with media figures. In G. Gumpert & R. Cathcart (Eds.), *Inter / media: Interpersonal communication in a media world* (3rd ed., pp. 219–252). New York: Oxford University Press.

Celebrating television. (1989, Summer). *People Extra*, p. 6.

Centerwall, B. S. (1995). Television and violent crime. In R. L. DelCampo & D. S. DelCampo (Eds.), *Taking sides: Clashing views on controversial issues in childhood and society* (pp. 180–187). Guilford, CT.: Dushkin.

Chambers, J. H., & Ascione, F. R. (1987). The effects of prosocial and aggressive videogames on children's donating and helping. *Journal of Genetic Psychology, 148*(4), 499–505.

Cheney, G. A. (1983). *Television in American society*. New York: F. Watts.

Chiose, S. (1996, December 14). Bombarded by culture. *The Globe and Mail*, p. C1.

Christenson, P. G., & Roberts, D. F. (1983). The role of television in the formation of children's social attitudes. In M. J. A. Howe (Ed.), *Learning from television* (pp. 79–99). New York: Academic Press.

Clifford, B. R., Gunter, B., & McAleer, J. (1995). *Television and children: Program evaluation, comprehension, and impact*. Hillsdale, NJ: Lawrence Erlbaum Associates.

Cohen, A. A., Levy, M. R., & Golden, K. (1988). Children's uses and gratifications of home VCRs. *Communication Research, 15*(6), 772–780.

Cohen, A. A., & Salomon, G. (1979). Children's literate television viewing: surprises and possible explanations. *Journal of Communication, 29*(3), 156–163.

Cohen, M. E., Brown, J. D., & Clark, S. (1981). Canadian public television and preschool children: Predictors of viewers and nonviewers. *Communication Research, 8*(2), 205–231.

Collins, W. A., Sobol, B. L., & Westby, S. (1981). Effects of adult commentary on children's comprehension and inferences about a televised aggressive portrayal. *Child Development, 52*, 158–163.

Comstock, G., & Paik, H. (1991). *Television and the American child*. San Diego, CA: Academic Press.

Comstock, G., & Strasburger, V. C. (1993). Deceptive appearances: Television violence and aggressive behavior. *Journal of Adolescent Health Care, 11*, 31–44.

Cook, T. D., Kendzierski, D. A., & Thomas, S. V. (1983). The implicit assumptions of television research: An analysis of the 1982 NIMH report on television and behavior. *Public Opinion Quarterly, 47*, 161–201.

Cooke, P. (1995). Media violence may not harm children. In C. Wekesser (Ed.), *Violence in the media* (pp. 49–50). San Diego, CA: Greenhaven Press.

Cooper, J., & Mackie, D. (1986). Video games and aggression in children. *Journal of Applied Social Psychology, 16*, 726–744.

Corder-Bolz, C. R. (1980). Mediation: The role of significant others. *Journal of Communication, 30* (3), 106–118.

Corteen, R. S., & Williams, T. M. (1986). Television and reading skills. In T. M. Williams (Ed.), *The impact of television* (pp. 39–86). Orlando, FL: Academic Press.

Csikszentmihalyi, M., & Larson, R. (1987). Validity and reliability of the Experience-Sampling Method. *Journal of Nervous and Mental Disease, 175*(9), 526–536.

Cuff, J. H. (1995, January). Television: The real victims of constant viewing. *The Globe and Mail*, p. D1.

Cullingsford, C. (1984). *Children and television*. Aldershot, England: Gower.

de Groot, G. (1994, June). Psychologists explain "Barney's" power. *APA Monitor*, p. 4.

Desmond, R. J., Hirsch, B., Singer, D., & Singer, J. (1987). Gender differences, mediation and disciplinary styles in children's responses to television. *Sex Roles, 16* (7–8), 375–389.

Desmond, R. J., Singer, J. L., & Singer, D. G. (1990). Family mediation: Parental communication patterns and the influences of television on children. In J. Bryant (Ed.),

Television and the American Family (pp. 293–309), Hillsdale, NJ: Lawrence Erlbaum Associates.

Desmond, R. J., Singer, J. L., Singer, D. G., Calam, R., & Colimore, K. (1985). Family mediation patterns and television viewing: Young children's use and grasp of the medium. *Human Communication Research, 11*(4), 461–480.

Dietz, W. H., Jr., & Gortmaker, S. L. (1985). Do we fatten our children at the television set? Obesity and television viewing in children and adolescents. *Pediatrics, 75,* 807–812.

Disney, A. (1995). Media violence should be treated as a public health problem. In C. Wekesser (Ed.), *Violence in the media* (pp. 130–131). San Diego, CA: Greenhaven Press.

Dobrow, J. R. (1990). Patterns of viewing and VCR use: Implications for cultivation analysis. In N. Signorielli & M. Morgan (Eds.), *Cultivation analysis: New directions in media effects research* (pp. 71–83). Newbury Park, CA: Sage.

Doerken M. (1983). *Classroom combat: Teaching and television.* Englewood Cliffs, NJ: Educational Technology Publications.

Dominick, J. R. (1984). Videogames, television violence, and aggression in teenagers. *Journal of Communication, 34,* 136–147.

Dominick, J. R. (1987). *The dynamics of mass communication.* New York: Random House.

Donnerstein, E., Slaby, R. G., & Eron, L. D. (1994). The mass media and youth aggression. In L. D. Eron, J. H. Gentry, & P. Schlegel (Eds.), *Reason to hope: A psychosocial perspective on violence and youth* (pp. 219–250). Washington, DC: American Psychological Association.

Donohue, T. R. (1977). Favorite TV characters as behavioral models for the emotionally disturbed. *Journal of Broadcasting, 21,* 333–354.

Dorr, A. (1980). When I was a child, I thought as a child. In S. B. Withey & R. P. Abeles (Eds.), *Television and social behavior: Beyond violence and children* (pp. 191–230). Hillsdale, NJ: Lawrence Erlbaum Associates.

Dorr, A. (1983). No shortcuts to judging reality. In J. Bryant & D. R. Anderson (Eds.), *Children's understanding of television* (pp. 199–220). New York: Academic Press.

Dorr, A. (1986). *Television and children: A special medium for a special audience.* Beverly Hills, CA: Sage.

Dorr, A., Graves, S. B., & Phelps, E. (1980). Television literacy for younger children. *Journal of Communication, 30*(3), 71–83.

Dorr, A., Kovaric, P., & Doubleday, C. (1989). Parent–child coviewing of television. *Journal of Broadcasting and Electronic Media, 33*(1), 35–51.

Dorr, A., Kovaric, P., & Doubleday, C. (1990). Age and content influences on children's perceptions of the realism of television families. *Journal of Broadcasting and Electronic Media, 34*(4), 377–397.

Dorr, A., & Kunkel, D. (1990). Children and the media environment: Change and constancy amid change. *Communication Research, 17*(1), 5–25.

Douglas, W. (1996). The fall from grace? The modern family on television. *Communication Research, 23*(6), 675–702.

Douglas, W., & Olson, B. M. (1996). Subversion of the American family? An examination of children and parents in television families. *Communication Research, 23*(1), 73–99.

Drabman, R. S., & Thomas, M. H. (1975). Does TV violence breed indifference? *Journal of Communication, 25*(4), 86–89.

Durkin, K. (1984). Children's accounts of sex-role stereotypes in television. *Communication Research, 11*(3), 341–362.

Durkin, K. (1985). *Television, sex roles and children: A developmental social psychological account.* Philadelphia: Open University Press.

Dworetzky, J. P. (1993). *Introduction to child development* (5th ed.). St. Paul, MN: West.

Eaman, R. A. (1987). *The media society: Basic issues and controversies.* Toronto: Butterworths.

Edell, J. A. (1988). Nonverbal effects in advertisements: A review and synthesis. In S. Hecker & D. W. Stewart (Eds.), *Nonverbal communication in advertising* (pp. 11–28). Lexington, MA: Heath.

Einsiedel, E. F., & Green, S. (1988). VCRs in Canada: usage patterns and policy implications. *Canadian Journal of Communication, 13*(1), 27–37.

Engelhardt, T. (1987). The Shortcake strategy. In T Gitlin (Ed.), *Watching television: A pantheon guide to popular culture* (pp. 68–110). New York: Pantheon.

Eron, L. D. (1980). Prescription for reduction of aggression. *American Psychologist, 35*(3), 244–252.

Eron, L. D. (1982). Parent–child interaction, television violence, and aggression of children. *American Psychologist, 37*(2), 197–211.

Eron, L. D. (1986). Interventions to mitigate the psychological effects of media violence on aggressive behavior. *Journal of Social Issues, 42*(3), 155–169.

Everett-Green, R. (1997, January 28). E-zines explore uncharted Internet territory. *The Globe and Mail*, p. C1.

Faber, R. J., Brown, J. D., & McLeod, J. M. (1986). Coming of age in the global village: Television and adolescence. In G. Gumpert & R. Cathcart (Eds.), *Inter / media: Interpersonal communication in a media world* (pp. 550–572). N.Y.: Oxford University Press.

Farrington, D. P. (1991). Childhood aggression and adult violence: Early precursors and later life outcomes. In D. J. Pepler & K. H. Rubin (Eds.), *The development and treatment of childhood aggression* (pp. 5–29) Hillsdale, NJ: Lawrence Erlbaum Associates.

Feldman, S. (1994, November 15). Chameleon in a box: Where TV is taking us. *The Globe and Mail*, p. 29.

Fetler, M. (1984). Television viewing and school achievement. *Journal of Communication, 34*(2), 104–118.

Fiske, J. (1982). *Introduction to communication studies*. London: Methuen.

Flavell, J. H., Flavell, E. R., & Green, F. L. (1987). Young children's knowledge about the apparent–real and pretend–real distinctions. *Developmental Psychology, 23*(6), 816–822.

Forge, K. L. S., & Phemister, S. (1987). The effect of prosocial cartoons on preschool children. *Child Study Journal, 17*(2), 83–88.

Foss, K. A., & Alexander, A. F. (1996). Exploring the margins of viewing. *Communication Reports, 9*(1), 61–67.

Fowles, J. (1992). *Why viewers watch: A reappraisal of television's effects*. Newbury Park, CA: Sage.

Freedman, J. L. (1984). Effect of television violence on aggressiveness. *Psychological Bulletin, 96*(2), 227–246.

Freedman, J. L. (1986). Television violence and aggression: A rejoinder. *Psychological Bulletin, 100*(3), 372–378.

Friedrich-Cofer, L., & Huston, A. C. (1986). Television violence and aggression: The debate continues. *Psychological Bulletin, 100*(3), 364–371.

Full of sound and fury (1994, Spring). *Tennessee Alumnus*, pp. 1–4.

Funk, J. B., & Buckman, D. D. (1996). Playing violent video and computer games and adolescent self-concept. *Journal of Communication, 46*(2), 19–32.

Gadow, K. D., Sprafkin, J., & Ficarrotto, T. J. (1987). Effects of viewing aggression-laden cartoons on preschool-aged emotionally disturbed children. *Child Psychiatry and Human Development, 17*(4), 257–274.

Gadow, K. D., Sprafkin, J., Kelly, E., & Ficarrotto, T. (1988). Reality perceptions of television: a comparison of school-labeled learning-disabled and nonhandicapped children. *Journal of Clinical Child Psychology, 17*(1), 25–33.

Gadow, K. D., Sprafkin, J., & Watkins, T. L. (1987). Effects of a critical viewing skills curriculum on elementary school children's knowledge and attitudes about television. *The Journal of Educational Research, 81*(1), 165–170.

Gardner, H. (1983). *Frames of mind.* New York: Basic Books.

Gardner, H., & Krasny Brown, L. (1984). Symbolic capabilities and children's television. In J. P. Murray & G. Salomon (Eds.), *The future of children's television* (pp. 45–51). Boys Town, NE: Father Flanagan's Boys Home.

Geen, R. (1994, October). Psychologists explore the origins of violence. *APA Monitor.*

Geen, R. G., & Thomas, S. L. (1986). The immediate effects of media violence on behavior. *Journal of Social Issues, 42*(3), 7–27.

Gerbner, G., Gross, L., Morgan, M., & Signorielli, N. (1980). The "mainstreaming" of America: Violence profile no. 11. *Journal of Communication, 30*(3), 10–29.

Gerbner, G., Gross, L., Morgan, M., & Signorielli, N. (1982). Charting the mainstream: Television's contributions to political orientation. *Journal of Communication, 32*(2), 100–127.

Gerbner, G., Gross, L., Morgan, M., & Signorielli, N. (1986). Living with television: The dynamics of the cultivation process. In J. Bryant & D. Zillmann (Eds.), *Perspectives on media effects* (pp. 17–40). Hillsdale, NJ: Lawrence Erlbaum Associates.

Gibbons, J., Anderson, D. R., Smith, R., Field, D. E., & Fischer, C. (1986). Young children's recall and reconstruction of audio and audiovisual narratives. *Child Development, 57*(4), 1014–1023.

Gilbert, D. A. (1988). *Compendium of American public opinion.* New York: Facts on File.

Goldberg, M. E., & Gorn, G. J. (1983). Researching the effects of television advertising on children: A methodological critique. In M. J. A. Howe (Ed.), *Learning from television* (pp. 125–151). New York: Academic Press.

Gow, J. (1996). Reconsidering gender roles on MTV: Depictions in the most popular music videos of the 1990's. *Communication Reports, 9*(2), 151–161.

Greenberg, B. S. (1986). Minorities and the mass media. In J. Bryant & D. Zillmann (Eds.), *Perspectives on media effects* (pp. 165–188). Hillsdale, NJ: Lawrence Erlbaum Associates.

Greenfield, P. M. (1984a). *Mind and media.* Cambridge, MA: Harvard University Press.

Greenfield, P. M. (1984b). Using television to overcome educational disadvantage. In J. P. Murray & G. Salomon (Eds.), *The future of children's television* (pp. 81–86). Boys Town, NE: Father Flanagan's Boys Home.

Greenfield, P., & Beagles-Roos, J. (1988). Radio vs. television: Their cognitive impact on children of different socioeconomic and ethnic groups. *Journal of Communication, 38*(2), 71–92.

Greenfield, P. M., Bruzzone, L., & Koyamatsu, K. (1987). What is rock music doing to the minds of our youth? A first experimental look at the effects of rock music lyrics and music videos. *Journal of Early Adolescence, 7*(3), 315–329.

Greenfield, P., Farrar, D., & Beagles-Roos, J. (1986). Is the medium the message? An experimental comparison of the effects of radio and television on imagination. *Journal of Applied Developmental Psychology, 7,* 202–218.

Greer, D., Potts, R., Wright, J. C., & Huston, A. C. (1982). The effects of television commercial form and commercial placement on children's social behavior and attention. *Child Development, 53,* 611–619.

Griffiths, M. D. (1991). Amusement machine playing in childhood and adolescence: A comparative analysis of video games and fruit machines. *Journal of Adolescence, 14*(1), 53–73.

Griffiths, M. D., & Shuckford, G. L. J. (1989). Desensitization to television violence: A new model. *New Ideas in Psychology, 7*(1), 85–89.

Gunter, B. (1985). *Dimensions of television violence.* Aldershot, England: Gower.

Gunter, B., McAleer, J., & Clifford, B. (1991). *Children's views about television.* Aldershot, England: Avebury.

Haddon, L. (1993). Interactive games. In P. Hayward & T. Wollen (Eds.), *Future visions. New technologies of the screen* (pp. 123–147). London: British Film Institute.

Haefner, M. J., & Wartella, E. A. (1987). Effects of sibling coviewing on children's interpretation of television programs. *Journal of Broadcasting and Electronic Media, 31*(2), 153–168.

Hahn, H. & Stout, R. (1994). *The Internet complete reference.* Berkeley, CA: Osborne McGraw Hill.

Harris, M. B., & Williams, R. (1985). Videogames and school performance. *Education, 105,* 306–309.

Harrison, L., & Williams, T. (1986). Television and cognitive development. In T. M. Williams (Ed.), *The impact of television: A natural experiment in three communities* (pp. 87–142). New York: Academic Press.

Harwood, R. L., & Weissberg, R. P. (1987) The potential of video in the promotion of social competence in children and adolescents. *Journal of Early Adolescence, 7*(3), 345–363.

Hattemer, B., & Showers, R. (1995a). Heavy metal rock and gangsta rap music promote violence. In C. Wekesser (Ed.), *Violence in the media* (pp. 150–158). San Diego, CA: Greenhaven Press.

Hattemer, B., & Showers, R. (1995b). Prosocial programming by the media can be effective. In C. Wekesser (Ed.), *Violence in the media* (pp. 86–93). San Diego, CA: Greenhaven Press.

Hawkins, R. P., & Daly, J. (1988). Cognition and communication. In R. P. Hawkins, J. M. Wiemann, & S. Pingree (Eds.), *Advancing communication science: Merging mass and interpersonal processes* (pp. 191–223). Newbury Park, CA: Sage.

Hawkins, R. P., Kim, Y., & Pingree, S. (1991). The ups and downs of attention to television. *Communication Research, 18*(1), 53–76.

Hawkins, R. P., & Pingree, S. (1980). Some processes in the cultivation effect. *Communication Research, 7*(2), 193–226.

Hawkins, R. P., & Pingree, S. (1986). Activity in the effects of television on children. In J. Bryant & D. Zillmann (Eds.), *Perspectives on media effects* (pp. 233–250). Hillsdale, NJ: Lawrence Erlbaum Associates.

Hayes, D. S., & Birnbaum, D. W. (1980). Preschoolers' retention of televised events: Is a picture worth a thousand words? *Developmental Psychology, 16*(5), 410-416.

Hayes, D. S., & Casey, D. M. (1992). Young children and television: The retention of emotional reactions. *Child Development, 63*(6), 1423–1436.

Hayes, D. S., & Kelly, S. B. (1984). Young children's processing of television: Modality differences in the retention of temporal relations. *Journal of Experimental Child Psychology, 38,* 505–514.

Hayes, D. S., & Kelly, S. B. (1985). Sticking to syntax: The reflection of story grammar in children's and adults' recall of radio and television shows. *Merrill-Palmer Quarterly, 31*(4), 345–360.

Hayes, D. S., & Schulze, S. A. (1977). Visual encoding in preschoolers' serial retention. *Child Development, 48,* 1066–1070.

Hearold, S. (1986). A synthesis of 1043 effects of television on social behavior. In G. Comstock (Ed.), *Public communication and behavior* (Vol. 1, pp. 65–133). Orlando, FL: Academic Press.

Heath, L., & Gilbert, K. (1996). Mass media and fear of crime. *American Behavioral Scientist, 39*(4), 379–386.

Heeter, C. (1989). Implications of new interactive technologies for conceptualizing communication. In J. L. Salvaggio & J. Bryant (Eds.), *Media use in the information age:*

Emerging patterns of adoption and consumer use (pp. 217–235). Hillsdale, NJ: Lawrence Erlbaum Associates.

Hess, H. (1995, June 17). TV violence tied to aggression. *The Globe and Mail*, p. A4.

Himmelstein, H. (1984). *Television myth and the American mind*. New York: Praeger.

Himmelweit, H. T., Swift, B., & Jaeger, M. E. (1980). The audience as critic: A conceptual analysis of television entertainment. In P. H. Tannenbaum (Ed.), *The entertainment functions of television* (pp. 67–106). Hillsdale, NJ: Lawrence Erlbaum Associates.

Hirsch, B. Z., & Kulberg, J. M. (1987). Television and temporal development. *Journal of Early Adolescence, 7*(3), 331–334.

Hodge, R., & Tripp, D. (1986). *Children and television*. Cambridge, England: Polity Press.

Hodges, C. (1996). *Beyond the computer*. New York: Random House/Broderbund.

Hoffner, C. (1995). Adolescents' coping with frightening mass media. *Communication Research, 22*(3), 325–346.

Hoffner, C., & Cantor, C. (1985). Developmental differences in responses to a television character appearance and behavior. *Developmental Psychology, 21*(6), 1065–1074.

Hoffner, C., Cantor, J., & Thorson, E. (1988). Children's understanding of a televised narrative. *Communication Research, 15*(3), 227–245.

Hollenbeck, A. R., & Slaby, R. G. (1979). Infant visual and vocal responses to television. *Child Development, 50*, 41–45.

Holtzman, J. M., & Akiyama, H. (1985). What children see: The aged on television in Japan and the United States. *The Gerontologist, 25*(1), 62–68.

Hoy, M. G., Young, C. E., & Mowen, J. C. (1986). Animated host-selling advertisements: Their impact on young children's recognition, attitudes, and behavior. *Journal of Public Policy and Marketing, 5*, 171–184.

Huesmann, L. R. (1986). Psychological processes promoting the relation between exposure to media violence and aggressive behavior by the viewer. *Journal of Social Issues, 42*(3), 125–139.

Huesmann, L. R. (1988). An information processing model for the development of aggression. *Aggressive Behavior, 14*, 13–24.

Huesmann, L. R., & Eron, L. D. (1986). The development of aggression in American children as a consequence of television violence viewing. In L. R. Huesmann & L. D. Eron (Eds.), *Television and the aggressive child: A cross-national comparison* (pp. 45–80). Hillsdale, NJ: Lawrence Erlbaum Associates.

Huesmann, L. R., Eron, L. D., Klein, R., Brice, P., & Fischer, P. (1983). Mitigating the imitation of aggressive behaviors by changing children's attitudes. *Journal of Personality and Social Psychology, 44*, 899–910.

Huesmann, L. R., Eron, L. D., Lefkowitz, M. M., & Walder, L. O. (1984). Stability of aggression over time and generation. *Developmental Psychology, 20*(6), 1120–1134.

Huesmann, L. R., Eron, L. D., & Yarmel, P. W. (1987). Intellectual functioning and aggression. *Journal of Personal and Social Psychology, 52*, 232–240.

Huesmann, L. R., Lagerspetz, K., & Eron, L. D. (1984). Intervening variables in the TV violence–aggression relation: Evidence from two countries. *Developmental Psychology, 20*(5), 746–775.

Huston, A. C., & Alvarez, M. M. (1990). The socialization context of gender role development in early adolescence. In R. Montemayor, G. R. Adams, & T. P. Gullotta (Eds.), *From childhood to adolescence: A transitional period?* (pp. 156–181). Newbury Park, CA: Sage.

Huston, A. C., Donnerstein, E., Fairchild, H., Feshbach, N. D., Katz, P. A., Murray, J. P., Rubinstein, E. A., Wilcox, B. L., & Zuckerman, D. (1992). *Big world, small screen. The role of television in American society*. Lincoln: University of Nebraska Press.

Huston, A. C., Greer, D., Wright, J. C., Welch, R., & Ross, R. (1984). Children's comprehension of televised formal features with masculine and feminine connotations. *Developmental Psychology, 20*(4), 707–716.

Huston, A. C., Watkins, B. Q., & Kunkel, D. (1989). Public policy and children's television. *American Psychologist, 44,* 424–433.

Huston, A. C., & Wright, J. C. (1983). Children's processing of television: The informative functions of formal features. In J. Bryant & D. R. Anderson (Eds.), *Children's understanding of television* (pp. 35–68). New York: Academic Press.

Huston, A. C., Wright, J. C., Rice, M. L., Kerkman, D., & St. Peters, M. (1990). Development of television viewing patterns in early childhood: A longitudinal investigation. *Developmental Psychology, 26,* 409–420.

Huston-Stein, A., Fox, S., Green, D., Watkins, B. A., & Whitaker, J. (1981). The effects of TV action and violence on children's social behavior. *Journal of General Psychology, 138,* 183–191.

Huston-Stein, A., & Friedrich, L. K. (1975). Impact of television on children and youth. In E. M. Hetherington, J. W. Hagen, R. Kron, & A. Huston-Stein (Eds.), *Review of child development research* (Vol. 5, pp. 183–256). Chicago: University of Chicago Press.

Irvin, L. K., Walker, H. M., Noell, J., Singer, G. H. S., Irvine, A. B., Marquez, K., & Britz, B. (1992). Measuring children's social skills using microcomputer-based videodisc assessment. *Behavior Modification, 16*(4), 475–503.

Isler, L., Popper, E. T., & Ward, S. (1987). Children's purchase requests and parental responses: Results from a diary study. *Journal of Advertising Research, 27*(5), 28–39.

Jacobvitz, R. S., Wood, M. R., & Albin, K. (1991). Cognitive skills and young children's comprehension of television. *Journal of Applied Developmental Psychology, 12*(2), 219–235.

Jason, L. A. (1987). Reducing children's excessive television viewing and assessing secondary changes. *Journal of Clinical Child Psychology, 16*(3), 245–250.

Jeffrey, D. B., McLellarn, R. W., & Fox, D. T. (1982). The development of children's eating habits: The role of television commercials. *Health Education Quarterly, 9*(2–3), 78–93.

Jensen, E., & Graham, E. (1995). Addressing media violence: An overview. In C. Wekesser (Ed.), Violence in the media (pp. 106–109). San Diego, CA: Greenhaven Press.

Johnston, D. D. (1995). Adolescents' motivations for viewing graphic horror. *Human Communication Research, 21*(4), 522–552.

Johnston, J., & Ettema, J. S. (1986). Using television to best advantage: Research for prosocial television. In J. Bryant & D. Zillmann (Eds.), *Perspectives on media effects* (pp. 143–164). Hillsdale, NJ: Lawrence Erlbaum Associates.

Jollimore, M. (1993, April 26). One TV ad exception to sexist rule. The Globe and Mail, p. D7.

Josephson, W. L. (1987). Television violence and children's aggression: Testing the priming, social script and disinhibition predictions. *Journal of Personality and Social Psychology, 53*(5), 882–892.

Joy, L. A., Kimball, M. M., & Zabrack, M. L. (1986). Television and children's aggressive behavior. In T. M. Williams (Ed.), *The impact of television* (pp. 303–360). Orlando, FL: Academic Press.

Kapica, J. (1997, January 10). Terror on the net. *The Globe and Mail,* p. A6.

Kellermann, K. (1985). Memory processes in media effects. *Communication Research, 12*(1), 83–131.

Kelley, P., Gunter, B., & Buckle, L. (1987). "Reading" television in the classroom: More results from the Television Literacy Project. *Journal of Educational Television, 13*(1), 7–20.

Kelly, A. E., & Spear, P. S. (1991). Intraprogram synopses for children's comprehension of television content. *Journal of Experimental Child Psychology, 52*(1), 87–98.

Kestenbaum, G. I., & Weinstein, L. (1985). Personality, psychopathology, and developmental issues in male adolescents' video game use. *Journal of American Academy of Child Psychiatry, 24*(3), 329–333.

Kimball, M. M. (1986). Television and sex-role attitudes. In T. M. Williams (Ed.), *The impact of television* (pp. 265–301). Orlando, FL: Academic Press.

King, A. (1995, October 13). Beware the temptation to classify violent TV shows. *The Globe and Mail*, p. A19.

Kolata, G. B. (1986). Obese children: A growing problem. *Science, 225*, 302–303.

Koolstra, C. M., & Van der Voort, T. H. A. (1996). Longitudinal effects of television on children's leisure-time reading. A test of three explanatory models. *Human Communication Research, 23*(1), 4–35.

Kubey, R. W. (1986). Television use in everyday life: Coping with unstructured time. *Journal of Communication, 36*, 108–123.

Kubey, R. (1990). Television and family harmony among children, adolescents, and adults: Results from the Experience Sampling Method. In J. Bryant (Ed.), *Television and the American family* (pp. 73–88). Hillsdale, NJ: Lawrence Erlbaum Associates.

Kubey, R., & Csikszentmihalyi, M. (1990). *Television and the quality of life. How viewing shapes everyday experience.* Hillsdale, NJ: Lawrence Erlbaum Associates.

Kubey, R., & Larson, R. (1990). The use and experience of the new video media among children and young adolescents. *Communication Research, 17*(1), 107–130.

Kunkel, D. (1988). From a raised eyebrow to a turned back: The FCC and children's product-related programming. *Journal of Communication, 38*(4), 61–90.

Kunkel, D. (1992). Children's television advertising in the multichannel environment. *Journal of Communication, 42*(3), 134–152.

Kunkel, D., & Murray, J. (1991). Television, children, and social policy: Issues and resources for child advocates. *Journal of Clinical Child Psychology, 20*(1), 88–93.

Lacey, L. (1993, February 4). What is going on? *The Globe and Mail*, p. C1.

Lamson, S. R. (1995). Media violence has increased the murder rate. In C. Wekesser (Ed.), *Violence in the media* (pp. 25–27). San Diego, CA: Greenhaven Press.

Landsberg, M. (1985). *Women and children first.* Markham, Ontario: Penguin.

Lawrence, F., & Wozniak, P. H. (1989). Children's television viewing with family members. *Psychological Reports, 65*(2), 395–400.

Lee, B. (1980). Prime time in the classroom. *Journal of Communication, 30*(1), 175–180.

Lefrancois, G. R. (1995). *Of children* (8th ed.). Belmont, CA: Wadsworth.

Leifer, A. D., Gordon, N. J., & Graves, S. B. (1974). Children's television more than mere entertainment. *Harvard Educational Review, 44*(2), 213–245.

Lemish, D. (1987). Viewers in diapers: The early development of television viewing. In T. R. Lindlof (Ed.), *Natural audiences: Qualitative research of media uses and effects* (pp. 33–57). Norwood, NJ: Ablex.

Lemish, D., & Rice, M. L. (1986). Television as a talking picture book: A prop for language acquisition. *Journal of Child Language, 13*, 251–274.

Leonard, J. (1995). The negative impact of media violence on society is exaggerated. In C. Wekesser (Ed.), *Violence in the media* (pp. 31–37). San Diego, CA: Greenhaven Press.

Lepper, M. R., & Gurtner, J. (1989). Children and computers: Approaching the twenty-first century. *American Psychologist, 44*, 170–178.

Levin, S. R., Petros, T. V., & Petrella, F. W. (1982). Preschoolers' awareness of television advertising. *Child Development, 53*, 933–937.

Levine, S. B. (1995). A variety of measures could combat media violence. In C. Wekesser (Ed.), *Violence in the media* (pp. 142–147). San Diego, CA: Greenhaven Press.

Liebert, D. E., Sprafkin, J. N., Liebert, R. M., & Rubinstein, E. A. (1977). Effects of television commercial disclaimers on the product expectations of children. *Journal of Communication, 27*(1), 118–124.

Liebert, R. M., & Sprafkin, J. (1988). *The early window* (3rd ed.). New York: Pergamon.

Liebert, R. M., Sprafkin, J. N., & Davidson, E. S. (1982). *The early window* (2nd ed.). New York: Pergamon.

Lin, S., & Lepper, M. R. (1987). Correlates of children's usage of videogames and computers. *Journal of Applied Social Psychology, 4*(1), 72–93.

Lindlof, T. R., & Shatzer, M. J. (1990). VCR usage in the American family. In J. Bryant (Ed.), *Television and the American family* (pp. 89–109). Hillsdale, NJ: Lawrence Erlbaum Associates.

Linz, D., Donnerstein, E., & Penrod, S. (1984). The effects of multiple exposures to filmed violence against women. *Journal of Communication, 34*(3), 130–147.

List, J. A., Collins, W. A., & Westby, S. D. (1983). Comprehension and inferences from traditional and nontraditional sex-role portrayals on television. *Child Development, 54,* 1579–1587.

Lloyd-Kolkin, D., Wheeler, P., & Strand, T. (1980). Developing a curriculum for teenagers. *Journal of Communication, 30*(3), 119–125.

Lorch, E. P., Anderson, D. R., & Levin, S. R. (1979). The relationship of visual attention to children's comprehension of television. *Child Development, 50,* 722–727.

Lorch, E. P., Bellack, D. R., & Augsback, L. H. (1987). Young children's memory for televised stories: Effects of importance. *Child Development, 58*(2), 453–463.

Lull, J. (1980). Family communication patterns and the social uses of television. *Communication Research, 7*(3), 319–334.

Lull, J. (1988a). Constructing rituals of extension through family television viewing. In J. Lull (Ed.), *World families watch television* (pp. 237–259). Newbury Park, CA: Sage.

Lull, J. (1988b). The family and television in world cultures. In J. Lull (Ed.), *World families watch television* (pp. 9–21). Newbury Park, CA: Sage.

Lynn, R., Hampson, S., & Agahi, E. (1989). Television violence and aggression: A genotype-environment, correlation and interaction theory. *Social Behavior and Personality, 17*(2), 143–164.

Macklin, M. C. (1988). The relationship between music in advertising and children's responses: An experimental investigation. In S. Hecker & D. W. Stewart (Eds.), *Nonverbal communication in advertising* (pp. 225–244). Lexington, MA: Heath.

Marshall, J. (1997, February 22). Wall units make big-screen comeback. *The Globe and Mail,* p. C21.

Mayer, W. G. (1994). Trends: The rise of the new media. *Public Opinion Quarterly, 58*(1), 124–146.

McClure, R. F., & Mears, F. G. (1986). Videogame playing and psychopathology. *Psychological Reports, 59*(1), 59–62.

McIlwraith, R. D. (1987). Community mental health and the mass media in Canada. *Canada's Mental Health, 35*(3), 11–17.

Meadowcroft, J. M., & Reeves, B. (1989). Influence of story schema development on children's attention to television. *Communication Research, 16*(3), 352–374.

Medrich, E. A. (1979). Constant television: A background to daily life. *Journal of Communication, 29*(3), 171–176.

Meringoff, L. K. (1980). Influence of the medium on children's story apprehension. *Journal of Educational Psychology, 72,* 240–249.

Meringoff, L. K., & Lesser, G. S. (1980). Children's ability to distinguish television commercials from program material. In R. P. Adler, G. S. Lesser, L. K. Meringoff, T. S. Robertson, J. R. Rossiter, & S. Ward (Eds.), *The effects of television advertising on children* (pp. 29–42). Lexington, MA: Lexington Books.

Meringoff, L. K., Vibbert, M. M., Char, C. A., Fernie, D. E., Banker, G. S., & Gardner, H. (1983). How is children's learning from television distinctive? Exploiting the medium methodologically. In J. Bryant & D. R. Anderson (Eds.), *Children's understanding of television* (pp. 151–179). New York: Academic Press.

Messaris, P. (1986). Parents, children, and television. In G. Gumpert & R. Cathcart (Eds.), *Inter / media: Interpersonal communication in a media world* (3rd ed., pp. 519–536). New York: Oxford University Press.

Messaris, P., & Kerr, D. (1983). Mothers' comments about TV: Relation to family communication patterns. *Communication Research, 10*(2), 175–194.

Messaris, P., & Thomas, S. (1986). *Social-class differences in mothers' comments about television.* Unpublished report.

Meyrowitz, J. (1985). *No sense of place: The impact of electronic media on social behavior.* New York: Oxford University Press.

Milavsky, J. R., Kessler, R. C., Stipp, H. H., & Rubena, W. S. (1982). *Television and aggression: A panel study.* New York: Academic Press.

Miller, M. C. (1987). Deride and conquer. In T. Gitlin (Ed.), *Watching television: A pantheon guide to popular culture* (pp. 183-228). New York: Pantheon.

Morgan, M. (1987) Television, sex-role attitudes, and sex-role behavior. *Journal of Early Adolescence, 7*(3), 269-282.

Morgan, M., Alexander, A., Shanahan, J., & Harris, C. (1990). Adolescents, VCRs, and the family environment. *Communication Research, 17*(1), 83–106.

Morgan, M., & Shanahan, J. (1991). Do VCRs change the TV picture? VCRs and the cultivation process. *American Behavioral Scientist, 35*(2), 122–135.

Morgan, M., Shanahan, J., & Harris, C. (1990). VCRs and the effects of television: New diversity or more of the same? In J. R. Dobrow (Ed.), *Social and cultural aspects of VCR use* (pp. 107–123). Hillsdale, NJ: Lawrence Erlbaum Associates.

Morgenstern, J. (1989, January 1) TV's big turnoff. Can "USA Today" be saved? *The New York Times Magazine*, Section 6, pp. 13–15, 26–28.

Morris, M., & Ogan, C. (1996). The Internet as mass medium. *Journal of Communication, 46*(1), 39–50.

Murray, J. (1984). Children and television violence. In J. P. Murray & G. Salomon (Eds.), *The future of children's television* (pp. 37–43). Boys Town, NE: Father Flanagan's Boys Home.

Murray, J. P., & Salomon, G. (1984). The future of children's television is ...? In J. P. Murray & G. Salomon (Eds.), *The future of children's television* (pp. 13–20). Boys Town, NE: Father Flanagan's Boys Home.

Mutz, D. C., Roberts, D. F., & van Vuuren, D. P. (1993). Reconsidering the displacement hypothesis. Television's influence on children's time use. *Communication Research, 20*(1), 51–75.

Nelson, J. (1987). *The perfect machine: Television in the nuclear age.* Toronto: Between the Lines.

Neuman, S. B. (1986). Television, reading, and the home environment. *Reading Research and Instruction, 25*(3), 173–183.

Neuman, S. B. (1988). The displacement effect: Assessing the relation between television viewing and reading performance. *Reading Research Quarterly, 23*(4), 414–440.

New York Times Service and Staff (1997, January 2). U.S. TV networks launch ratings system. *The Globe and Mail*, p. C3.

Nickerson, R. S. (1995). Can technology help teach for understanding? In D. N. Perkins, J. L. Schwartz, M. M. West, & M. S. Wiske (Eds.), *Software goes to school. Teaching for understanding with new technologies* (pp. 7–22). New York: Oxford University Press.

Odom, R. D. (1972). Effects of perceptual salience on the recall of relevant and incidental dimensional values: A developmental study. *Journal of Experimental Psychology, 92*(2), 285–291.

O'Keefe, G. J., & Reid-Nash, K. (1987). Crime news and real-world blues: The effects of the media on social reality. *Communication Research, 14*(2), 147–163.

Oyen, A., & Bebko, J. M. (1996). The effects of computer games and lesson contexts on children's mnemonic strategies. *Journal of Experimental Child Psychology, 62*, 173–189.

Paik, H., & Comstock, G. (1994). The effects of television violence on antisocial behavior: A meta-analysis. *Communication Research, 21*(4), S516–546.

Palmer, E. L. (1984). Providing quality television for America's children. In J. P. Murray & G. Salomon (Eds.), *The future of children's television* (pp. 103–122). Boys Town, NE: Father Flanagan's Boys' Home.

Parks, M. R., & Floyd, K. (1996). Making friends in cyberspace. *Journal of Communication, 46*(1), 80–97.

Pepler, D. J., & Slaby, R. G. (1994). Theoretical and developmental perspectives on youth and violence. In L. D. Eron, J. H. Gentry, & P. Schlegel (Eds.), *Reason to hope: A psychosocial perspective on violence and youth* (pp. 27–58). Washington, DC: American Psychological Association.

Pepper, R. (1984). Cable and the future of children's television. In J. P. Murray & G. Salomon (Eds.), *The future of children's television* (pp. 135–147). Boys Town, NE: Father Flanagan's Boys Home.

Perlmutter, M., & Myers, N. A. (1975). Young children's coding and storage of visual and verbal material. *Child Development, 46*, 215–219.

Perse, E. M. (1986). Soap opera viewing patterns of college students and cultivation. *Journal of Broadcasting and Electronic Media, 30*(2), 175–193.

Perse, E. M., Ferguson, D. A., & McLeod, D. M. (1994), Cultivation in the newer media environment. *Communication Research, 21*(1), 79–104.

Peterson, L., & Lewis, K. E. (1988). Preventive intervention to improve children's discrimination of the persuasive tactics in televised advertising. *Journal of Pediatric Psychology, 13*(2), 163–170.

Peterson, P. E., Jeffrey, D. B., Bridgwater, C. A., & Dawson, B. (1984). How pronutrition television programming affects children's dietary habits. *Developmental Psychology, 20*(1), 55–63.

Pezdek, K., & Hartman, E. F. (1983). Children's television viewing: Attention and comprehension of auditory versus visual information. *Child Development, 54*, 1015–1023.

Pingree, S. (1986). Children's activity and television comprehensibility. *Communication Research, 13*(2), 239–256.

Pingree, S., Hawkins, R. P., Rouner, D., Burns, J., Gikonyo, W., & Neuwirth, C. (1984). Another look at children's comprehension of television. *Communication Research, 11*(4), 477–496.

Pinon, M. F., Huston, A. C., & Wright, J. C. (1989). Family ecology and child characteristics that predict young children's educational television viewing. *Child Development, 60*(4), 846–856.

Postman, N. (1982). *The disappearance of childhood.* New York: Delacorte.

Postman, N. (1985). *Amusing ourselves to death.* New York: Penguin.

Potter, W. J. (1986). Perceived reality and the cultivation hypothesis. *Journal of Broadcasting and Electronic Media, 30*(2), 159–174.

Potter, W. J. (1988). Perceived reality in television effects research. *Journal of Broadcasting and Electronic Media, 32*(1), 23–41.

Potts, R., Huston, A. C., & Wright, J. C. (1986). The effects of television form and violent content on boys' attention and social behavior. *Journal of Experimental Child Psychology, 41*, 1–17.

Prawat, R. S., Anderson, A. H., & Hapkeiwicz, W. (1989). Are dolls real? Developmental changes in the child's definition of reality. *Journal of Genetic Psychology, 150*(4), 359–374.

Pryor, S., & Scott, J. (1993). Virtual reality: Beyond Cartesian space. In P. Hayward & T. Wollen (Eds.), *Future visions: New technologies of the screen* (pp. 166–179). London: British Film Institute.

Reeves, B., & Thorson, E. (1986). Watching television. Experiments on the viewing process. *Communication Research, 13*(3), 343–361.

Reid, L. N., & Frazer, C. F. (1980). Television at play. *Journal of Communication, 30*(4), 66–73.

Reinking, D., & Wu, J. (1990). Reexamining the research on television and reading. *Reading Research and Instruction, 29*(2), 30–43.

Rice, M. (1983). The role of television in language acquisition. *Developmental Review, 3*, 211–224.

Rice, M. L. (1984). Television language and child language. In J. P. Murray & G. Salomon (Eds.), *The future of children's television* (pp. 53–58). Boys Town, NE: Father Flanagan's Boys Home.

Rice, M. L., Huston, A. C., Truglio, R., & Wright, J. C. (1990). Words from "Sesame Street": Learning vocabulary while viewing. *Developmental Psychology, 26*(3), 421–428.

Rice, M. L., Huston, A. C., & Wright, J. C. (1986). Replays as repetitions: Young children's interpretation of television forms. *Journal of Applied Developmental Psychology, 7*(1), 61-76.

Rice, M. L., & Woodsmall, L. (1988). Lessons from television: Children's word learning when viewing. *Child Development, 59*(2), 420–429.

Ridley-Johnson, R., Surdy, T., & O'Laughlin, E. (1991). Parent survey on television violence viewing: Fear, aggression, and sex differences. *Journal of Applied Developmental Psychology, 12*, 63–71.

Ritchie, D., Price, V., & Roberts, D. F. (1987). Television, reading, and reading achievement. *Communication Research, 14*(3), 292–315.

Roberts, D. F., Bachen, C. M., Hornby, M. C., & Hernandez-Ramos, P. (1984). Reading and television: predictors of reading achievement at different age levels. *Communication Research, 11* (1), 9–49.

Roberts, D. F., Christenson, P., Gibson, W. A., Mooser, L., & Goldberg, M. E. (1980). Developing discriminating consumers. *Journal of Communication, 30*(3), 94–105.

Robertson, T. S., & Rossiter, J. R. (1974). Children and commercial persuasion: An attribution analysis. *Journal of Consumer Research, 1*, 13–20.

Robertson, T. S., Ward, S., Gatignon, H., & Klees, D. M. (1989). Advertising and children: A cross-cultural study. *Communication Research, 16*(4), 459–485.

Robinson, J. P. (1990). Television's effects on families' use of time. In J. Bryant (Ed.), *Television and the American family* (pp. 195–209). Hillsdale, NJ: Lawrence Erlbaum Associates.

Roedder, D. L. (1981). Age differences in children's responses to television advertising: An information-processing approach. *Journal of Consumer Research, 8*(2), 144–153.

Rolandelli, D. R., Wright, J. C., Huston, A. C., & Eakins, D. (1991). Children's auditory and visual processing of narrated and nonnarrated television programming. *Journal of Experimental Child Psychology, 51*(1), 90–122.

Rosengren, K. E., & Windahl, S. (1989). *Media matter: TV use in childhood and adolescence.* Norwood, NJ: Ablex.

Rosenkoetter, L. I., Huston, A. C., & Wright, J. C. (1990). Television and the moral judgment of the young child. *Journal of Applied Developmental Psychology, 11*, 123–137.

Roser, C. (1990). Involvement, attention, and perceptions of message relevance in the response to persuasive appeal. *Communication Research, 17*(5), 571–600.

Ross, R. P., Campbell, T., Wright, J. C., Huston, A. C., Rice, M. L., & Turk, P. (1984). When celebrities talk, children listen: An experimental analysis of children's responses to TV ads with celebrity endorsement. *Journal of Applied Developmental Psychology, 5,* 185–202.

Rossiter, J. R. (1980). The effects of volume and repetition of television commercials. In R. P. Adler, G. S. Lesser, L. K. Meringoff, T. S. Robertson, J. R. Rossiter, & S. Ward. (Eds), *The effects of television advertising on children* (pp. 153–183). Lexington, MA: Lexington Books.

Rothschild, N., & Morgan, M. (1987) Cohesion and control: adolescents' relationships with parents as mediators of television. *Journal of Early Adolescence, 7*(30), 299–314.

Rubin, A. M. (1976). Television in children's political socialization. *Journal of Broadcasting, 20,* 51–60.

Rubin, A. M. (1977). Television usage, attitudes and viewing behaviors of children and adolescents. *Journal of Broadcasting, 21,* 355–369.

Rubin, A. M. (1984). Ritualized and instrumental television viewing. *Journal of Communication, 34*(3), 67–77.

Rubin, A. M. (1985). Media gratifications through the life cycle. In K. E. Rosengren, L. A. Wenner, & P. Palmgreen (Eds.), *Media gratifications research. Current perspectives* (pp. 195–208). Beverly Hills, CA: Sage.

Rubin, A. M. (1986a). Age and family control influences on children's television viewing. *The Southern Speech Communication Journal, 52*(1), 35–51.

Rubin, A. M. (1986b). Uses, gratifications, and media effects research. In J. Bryant & D. Zillmann (Eds.), *Perspectives on media effects* (pp. 281–301). Hillsdale, NJ: Lawrence Erlbaum Associates.

Rubin, A. M., & Bantz, C. R. (1989). Uses and gratifications of videocassette recorders. In J. L. Salvaggio & J. Bryant (Eds.), *Media use in the information age: Emerging patterns of adoption and consumer use* (pp. 181–195). Hillsdale, NJ: Lawrence Erlbaum Associates.

Rubin, A. M., & Perse, E. M. (1987). Audience activity and television news gratifications. *Communication Research, 14*(1), 58–84.

Rubin, A. M., Perse, E. M., & Taylor, D. S. (1988). A methodological examination of cultivation. *Communication Research, 15*(2), 107–134.

Ruble, D. N., Balaban, T., & Cooper, J. (1981). Gender constancy and the effects of sex-typed televised toy commercials. *Child Development, 52*(2), 667–673.

Rule, B. G., & Ferguson, T. J. (1986). The effects of media violence on attitudes, emotions, and cognitions. *Journal of Social Issues, 42*(3), 29–50.

Rushton, J. P. (1988). Television as a socializer. In M. Courage (Ed.), *Readings in developmental psychology* (pp. 437-456). Peterborough, Ontario: Broadview Press.

Rutherford, P. (1988). The culture of advertising. *Canadian Journal of Communication, 13*(3–4), 102–113.

Rutherford, P. (1994). *The new icons?: The art of television advertising.* Toronto: University of Toronto Press.

Sadowski, R. P. (1972). Immediate recall of TV commercial elements—Revisited. *Journal of Broadcasting, 16*(3), 277–287.

Salomon, G. (1979). *Interaction of media, cognition, and learning.* San Francisco: Jossey-Bass.

Salomon, G. (1981a). *Communication and education: Social and psychological interactions.* Beverly Hills, CA: Sage.

Salomon, G. (1981b). Introducing AIME: The assessment of children's mental involvement with television. In H. Kelly & H. Gardner (Eds.), *Viewing children through television* (pp. 89–102). San Francisco: Jossey-Bass.

Salomon, G. (1983). Television watching and mental effort: A social psychological view. In J. Bryant & D. R. Anderson (Eds.), *Children's understanding of television* (pp. 181–198). New York: Academic Press.

Salomon, G. (1984). Investing effort in television viewing. In J. P. Murray & G. Salomon (Eds.), *The future of children's television* (pp. 59–64). Boys Town, NE: Father Flanagan's Boys Home.

Salomon, G. (1990). Cognitive effects with and of computer technology. *Communication Research, 17*(1), 26–44.

Salomon, G., & Leigh, T. (1984). Predispositions about learning from print and television. *Journal of Communication, 34*, 119–135.

Salomon, G., & Murray, J. P. (1984). Researching children's television and the new techologies. In J. P. Murray & G. Salomon (Eds.), *The future of children's television* (pp. 125–133). Boys Town, NE: Father Flanagan's Boys Home.

Santrock, J. W., & Yussen, S. R. (1992). *Child development* (5th ed.), Dubuque, IA: Brown.

Saunders, D. (1996, December 7). Babes in TVland. *The Globe and Mail*, p. C1, C7.

Sawin, D. B. (1990). Aggressive behavior among children in small playgroup settings with violent television. In K. D. Gadow (Ed.), *Advances in learning and behavioral disabilities* (Vol. 6, pp. 157–177). Greenwich, CT: JAI.

Scheer, R. (1995). Media violence should not be censored. In C. Wekesser (Ed.), *Violence in the media* (pp. 62–66). San Diego, CA: Greenhaven Press.

Schneider, C. (1989). *Children's television.* Lincolnwood, IL., NTC Business.

Schutte, N. S., Malouff, J. M., Post-Gorden, J. C., & Rodasta, A. L. (1988). Effects of playing videogames on children's aggression and other behaviors. *Journal of Applied Social Psychology, 18*(5), 454–460.

Schwartz, J. L. (1984). Video, computers, and the new technologies. In J. P. Murray & G. Salomon (Eds.), *The future of children's television* (pp. 149–157). Boys Town, NE: Father Flanagan's Boys Home.

Selnow, G. W. (1984). Playing video games: The electronic friend. *Journal of Communication, 34*(2), 148–156.

Selnow, G. W. (1986). Television viewing and the learning of expectations for problem resolutions. *Educational Studies, 12*(2), 137–145.

Selnow, G. W., & Bettinghaus, E. P. (1982). Television exposure and language level. *Journal of Broadcasting, 26*(2), 469–479.

Shanahan, J. & Morgan, M. (1989, Fall), Television as a diagnostic indicator in child therapy: an exploratory study. *Child and Adolescent Social Work, 6*(3), 175–191.

Shapiro, M. A., & McDonald, D. G. (1992). I'm not a real doctor, but I play one in virtual reality: Implications of virtual reality for judgments about reality. *Journal of Communication, 42*(4), 94–114.

Shrum, L. J. (1995). Assessing the social influence of television: A social cognition perspective on cultivation effects. *Communication Research, 22*(4), 402–429.

Shrum, L. J. (1996). Psychological processes underlying cultivation effects. Further tests of construct accessibility. *Human Communication Research, 22*(4), 482–509.

Signorielli, N. (1987) Children and adolescents on television: A consistent pattern of devaluation. *Journal of Early Adolescence, 7*(3), 255–268.

Signorielli, N. (1989). Television and conceptions about sex roles: Maintaining conventionality and the status quo. *Sex roles, 21*(5–6), 341–360.

Signorielli, N. (1990). Television's mean and dangerous world: A continuation of the cultural indicators perspective. In N. Signorielli & M. Morgan (Eds.), *Cultivation analysis: New directions in media effects* (pp. 85–106). Newbury Park, CA: Sage.

Silvern, S. B., & Williamson, P. A. (1987). The effects of video game play on young children's aggression, fantasy, and prosocial behavior. *Journal of Applied Developmental Psychology, 8*(4), 453–462.

Singer, D. G., & Singer, J. L. (1983). Learning how to be intelligent consumers of television. In M. J. A. Howe (Ed.), *Learning from television* (pp. 203–222). New York: Academic Press.

Singer, D. G., Zuckerman, D. M., & Singer, J. L. (1980). Helping elementary school children learn about TV. *Journal of Communication, 30*(3), 84–93.

Singer, J. L. (1980). The power and limitations of television: A cognitive-affective analysis. In P. H. Tannenbaum (Ed.), *The entertainment functions of television* (pp. 31–65). Hillsdale, NJ: Lawrence Erlbaum Associates.

Singer, J. L., & Singer, D. G. (1976). Can T.V. stimulate imaginative play? *Journal of Communication, 26*(3) 74–80.

Singer, J. L., & Singer, D. G. (1983). Implications of childhood television viewing for cognition, imagination, and emotion. In J. Bryant & D. R. Anderson (Eds.), *Children's understanding of television* (pp. 265–295). New York: Academic Press.

Singer, J. L., & Singer, D. G. (1984). Intervention strategies for children's television. In J. P. Murray & G. Salomon (Eds.), *The future of children's television* (pp. 93–102). Boys Town, NE: Father Flanagan's Boys Home.

Singer, J. L., & Singer, D. G. (1986). Family experiences and television viewing as predictors of children's imagination, restlessness, and aggression. *Journal of Social Issues, 42*(3), 107–124.

Singer, J. L., Singer, D. G., & Rapacynski, W. S. (1984). Family patterns and television viewing as predictors of children's beliefs and aggression. *Journal of Communication, 34*(2), 73–89.

Singer, R. S. (1982). Childhood, aggression, and television. *Television and Children, 5,* 57–63.

Slaby, R. G., Barham, J. E., Eron, L. D., & Wilcox, B. L. (1994). Policy recommendations: Prevention and treatment of youth violence. In L. D. Eron, J. H. Gentry, and P. Schlegel (Eds.), *Reason to hope: A psychosocial perspective on violence and youth* (pp. 447–461). Washington, DC: American Psychological Association.

Smith, J. D., & Kemler Nelson, D. G. (1988). Is the more impulsive child a more holistic processor? A reconsideration. *Child Development, 59*(3), 719–727.

Sohn, D. (1982). David Sohn interviews Jerzy Kosinski. A nation of videots. In H. Newcomb (Ed.), *Television: The critical view* (3rd ed., pp. 351–366). New York: Oxford University Press.

Spicer, K. (1995, October 3). TV can have a positive influence on children. *Kitchener-Waterloo Record,* p. A9.

Sprafkin, J., & Gadow, K. D. (1986). Television viewing habits of emotionally-disturbed, learning disabled, and mentally retarded children. *Journal of Applied Developmental Psychology, 7*(1), 45–59.

Sprafkin, J., Gadow, K. D., & Abelman, R. (1992). *Television and the exceptional child: A forgotten audience.* Hillsdale, NJ: Lawrence Erlbaum Associates.

Sprafkin, J., Gadow, K. D., & Dussault, M. (1986). Reality perceptions of television: a preliminary comparison of emotionally disturbed and nonhandicapped children. *American Journal of Orthopsychiatry, 56*(1), 147–152.

Sprafkin, J., Gadow, K. D., & Grayson, P. (1987). Effects of viewing aggressive cartoons on the behavior of learning disabled children. *Journal of Child Psychology and Psychiatry, 28*(3), 387–398.

Sprafkin, J., Gadow, K. D., & Grayson, P. (1988). Effects of cartoons on emotionally disturbed children's social behavior in school settings. *Journal of Child Psychology and Psychiatry, 29*(1), 91–99.

Sprafkin, J., Watkins, L. T., & Gadow, K. D. (1986). *Curriculum for enhancing social skills through media awarenss.* Unpublished curriculum, Stony Brook: State University of New York at Stony Brook.

Sprafkin, J., Watkins, L.T., & Gadow, K. D. (1990). Efficacy of a television literacy curriculum for emotionally disturbed and learning disabled children. *Journal of Applied Developmental Psychology, 11*(2), 225–244.

Stead, D. (1997, January 5). Corporations, classrooms and commercialism. *The New York Times*, p. 31.

Sternbergh, A. (1996, December 21). Hybrid Web-TVs surf ashore. *The Globe and Mail*, p. C23.

Steuer, J. (1992). Defining virtual reality: Dimensions determining telepresence. *Journal of Communication, 42*(4), 73–93.

St. Peters, M., Fitch, M., Huston, A. C., Wright, J. C., & Eakins, D. J. (1991). Television and families: What do young children watch with their parents? *Child Development, 62*(6), 1409–1423.

Straus, M. (1991). Discipline and deviance: Physical punishment of children and violence and other crime in adulthood. *Social Problems, 38*, 133–154.

Suzuki, D. (1989, April 29). A major in television and a minor in knowledge. *The Globe and Mail*, p. D8.

Tannenbaum, P. H. (1985). "Play it again, Sam": Repeated exposure to television programs. In D. Zillmann & J. Bryant (Eds.), *Selective exposure to communication* (pp. 225–241). Hillsdale, NJ: Lawrence Erlbaum Associates.

Turner, C. W., Hesse, B. W., & Peterson-Lewis, S. (1986). Naturalistic studies of long-term effects of television violence. *Journal of Social Issues, 42*(3), 51-73.

TVO. (1985). *Television and your children.* Ottawa, Ontario: TV Ontario The Ontario Educational Communications Authority.

Valkenburg, P. M., & Van der Voort, T. H. A. (1995). The influence of television on children's daydreaming styles: A 1-year panel study. *Communication Research, 22*(3), 267–287.

Van der Voort, T. H. A. (1986). *Television violence: A child's eye view.* Amsterdam: North-Holland.

Van Dyck, N. B. (1984). Families and television. In J. P. Murray & G. Salomon (Eds.), *The future of children's television* (pp. 87–92). Boys Town, NE: Father Flanagan's Boys Home.

Van Evra, J. (1984). *Developmental trends in the perception of sex-role stereotypy in real life and on television.* Unpublished manuscript. St. Jerome's College, University of Waterloo, Waterloo, Ontario, Canada.

Van Evra, J. (1995). Advertising's impact on children as a function of viewing purpose. *Psychology and Marketing, 12*(5), 423–432.

Viemero, V., & Paajanen, S. (1990). The role of fantasies and dreams in the TV viewing–aggression relationship. *Aggressive Behavior, 18*, 109–116.

Vivian, J. (1997). *The media of mass communication* (4th ed.). Boston: Allyn & Bacon.

Wackman, D. B., Wartella, E., & Ward, S. (1977). Learning to be consumers: The role of the family. *Journal of Communication, 27*(1), 138–151.

Waisglas, E. (1992, February). Listen to the children. *Canadian Living*, p. 59.

Ward, S., & Wackman, D. B. (1973). Children's information processing of television advertising. In P. Clarke (Ed.), *New models for mass communication research* (pp. 119–146). Beverly Hills, CA: Sage.

Wartella, E. (1986). Getting to know you: How children make sense of television. In G. Gumpert & R. Cathcart (Eds.), *Inter/media: Interpersonal communication in a media world* (3rd ed., pp. 537–549). New York: Oxford University Press.

Wartella, E., Heintz, K. E., Aidman, A. J., & Mazzarella, S. R. (1990). Television and beyond: Children's video media in one community. *Communication Research, 17*(1), 45–64.

Watkins, B. (1988). Children's representations of television and real-life stories. *Communication Research, 15*(2), 159–184.

Watkins, B., Calvert, S., Huston-Stein, A., & Wright, J. C. (1980). Children's recall of television material: Effects of presentation mode and adult labeling. *Developmental Psychology, 16*(6), 672–674.

Webster, J. G. (1989a). Assessing exposure to the new media. In J. L. Salvaggio & J. Bryant (Eds.), *Media use in the information age: Emerging patterns of adoption and consumer use* (pp. 3–19). Hillsdale, NJ: Lawrence Erlbaum Associates.

Webster, J. G. (1989b). Television audience behavior: Patterns of exposure in the new media environment. In J. L. Salvaggio & J. Bryant (Eds.), *Media use in the information age: Emerging patterns of adoption and consumer use* (pp. 197–216). Hillsdale, NJ: Lawrence Erlbaum Associates.

Wiegman, O., Kuttschreuter, M., & Baarda, B. (1992). A longitudinal study of the effects of television viewing on aggressive and prosocial behaviors. *British Journal of Social Psychology, 31*, 147–164.

Williams, F., Phillips, A. F., & Lum, P. (1985). Gratifications associated with new consumer technologies. In K. E. Rosengren, L. A. Wenner, & P. Palmgreen (Eds.), *Media gratifications research: Current perspectives* (pp. 241–252). Beverly Hills, CA: Sage.

Williams, P. A., Haertel, E. H., Haertel, G. D., & Walberg, H. J. (1982). The impact of leisure time television on school learning: A research synthesis. *American Educational Research Journal, 19*(1), 19-50.

Williams, T. M. (1986). Summary, conclusions, and implications. In T. M. Williams (Ed.), *The impact of television: A natural experiment in three communities* (pp. 395–430). Orlando, FL: Academic Press.

Wilson, B. J., Hoffner, C., & Cantor, J. (1987). Children's perception of the effectiveness of techniques to reduce fear from mass media. *Journal of Applied Developmental Psychology, 8*, 39–52.

Wilson, B. J., & Weiss, A. J. (1993). The effects of sibling coviewing on preschoolers' reactions to a suspenseful movie scene. *Communication Research, 20*(2), 214–248.

Winett, R. A. (1986). *Information and behavior: Systems of influence.* Hillsdale, NJ: Lawrence Erlbaum Associates.

Winett, R. A., & Kramer, K. D. (1989). A behavioral systems framework for information design and behavior change. In J. L. Salvaggio & J. Bryant (Eds.), *Media use in the information age: Emerging patterns of adoption and consumer use* (pp. 237–257). Hillsdale, NJ: Lawrence Erlbaum Associates.

Winn, M. (1985). *The plug-in drug.* New York: Penguin.

Wober, M. (1978). Televised violence and paranoid perception: The view from Great Britain. *Public Opinion Quarterly, 42*, 315–321.

Wober, M., & Gunter, B. (1988). *Television and social control.* New York: St. Martin's.

Wood, W., Wong, F. Y. & Chacere, J. G. (1991). Effects of media violence on viewers' aggression in unconstrained social interaction. *Psychology Bulletin, 109*(3), 371–383.

Wright, C. R. (1986). *Mass communication: A sociological perspective* (3rd ed.). New York: Random House.

Wright, J. C., & Huston, A. C. (1981). Children's understanding of the forms of television. In H. Kelly & H. Gardner (Eds.), *Viewing children through television* (pp. 73–88). San Francisco: Jossey Bass.

Wright, J. C., Huston, A. C., Ross, R. P., Calvert, S. L., Rolandelli, D., Weeks, L. A., Raeissi, P., & Potts, R. (1984). Pace and continuity of television programs: Effects on children's attention and comprehension. *Developmental Psychology, 20*(4), 653–666.

Wright, J. C., St. Peters, M., & Huston, A. C. (1990). Family television use and its relation to children's cognitive skills and social behavior. In J. Bryant (Ed.), *Television and the American family* (pp. 227–251). Hillsdale, NJ: Lawrence Erlbaum Associates.

Wroblewski, R., & Huston, A. C. (1987) Televised occupational stereotypes and their effects on early adolescents: Are they changing? *Journal of Early Adolescence, 7*(3), 283-297.

Young, B. M. (1990). *Television advertising and children.* Oxford, England: Clarendon.

Zillmann, D. (1985). The experimental exploration of gratifications from media entertainment. In K. E. Rosengren, L. A. Wenner, & P. Palmgreen (Eds.), *Media gratifications research: Current perspectives* (pp. 225–239). Beverly Hills, CA: Sage.

Zillmann, D., & Bryant, J. (1985a). Affect, mood, and emotion as determinants of selective exposure. In D. Zillmann & J. Bryant (Eds.), *Selective exposure to communication* (pp. 157–190). Hillsdale, NJ: Lawrence Erlbaum Associates.

Zillmann, D., & Bryant, J. (1985b). Selective-exposure phenomena. In D. Zillmann & J. Bryant (Eds.), *Selective exposure to communication* (pp. 1–10). Hillsdale, NJ: Lawrence Erlbaum Associates.

Zillmann, D., & Bryant, J. (1986). Exploring the entertainment experience. In J. Bryant & D. Zillmann (Eds.), *Perspectives on media effects* (pp. 303–324). Hillsdale, NJ: Lawrence Erlbaum Associates.

Zohoori, A. R. (1988). A cross-cultural analysis of children's television use. *Journal of Broadcasting and Electronic Media, 32*(1), 105–113.

Zuckerman, D. M., Singer, D. G., & Singer, J. L. (1980). Television viewing, children's reading, and related classroom behavior. *Journal of Communication, 30*(1), 166–174.

Zuckerman, P., Ziegler, M., & Stevenson, H. W. (1978). Children's viewing of television and recognition memory of commercials. *Child Development, 49*, 96–104.

Author Index

Subject Index